ACCOUNTING INFORMATION SYSTEMS

ACCOUNTING INFORMATION SYSTEMS

By

Dr. M. Karthikeyan

Assistant Professor

Department of Cooperatives

Faculty of Business & Economics

Hawassa University

Hawassa

Email: mkeya2003@gmail.com

mkeya2003@yahoo.com

DPH

DISCOVERY PUBLISHING HOUSE PVT. LTD.

NEW DELHI-110 002

Published by:
Tilak Wasan

DISCOVERY PUBLISHING HOUSE PVT. LTD.
4383/4A, Ansari Road, Darya Ganj
New Delhi-110 002 (India)
Phone : +91-11-23279245, 43596064-65
Fax : +91-11-23253475
E-mail : parul.wasan@gmail.com
discoverypublishinghouse@gmail.com
web : www.discoverypublishinggroup.com

First Edition: **2012**
ISBN: 978-93-5056-062-4

Accounting Information Systems

Printed at:
Shree Balaji Art Press
Delhi

Preface

I am very much glad to present a textbook on "Accounting Information Systems", which is unique and rare in the field of accounting and information systems. This work is based on my experience as teacher, trainer and researcher in the field of information systems, management and cooperatives for more than 15 years. The present work is based on under-graduate programme and outcome of my teaching and research experience, and many articles published in reputed journals. This book is very unique in the field of both information systems and accounting. A few attempts have been made in this line of AIS. This book will be very much useful to the student of under-graduate, and also to accounting professionals and managers in companies, and the trainers who are working in various training establishments. I have drawn the inputs from various materials; papers, journals, books and I have consulted several of my friends, colleagues and field experts. I am ever grateful and thankful to them for their immense support and healthy criticism. I hope that the readers of this book will get knowledge on AIS as also the applications. Any useful comments, suggestions to improve the present version are welcome and solicited from the readers. I am thankful and grateful to Parul Wasan, Discovery Publishing House Pvt. Ltd., New Delhi, for publishing the book neatly under his renowned label for the accounting knowledge community.

M. KARTHIKEYAN

Contents

CHAPTER 1 Accounting Basics and Concepts

Accounting — An Overview

The main aim of a business is to earn profit. For earning profit, the businessman will either purchase the goods in one market at certain price and sell it in another market at higher price or will convert the raw materials into finished products and sell it to the different customers at a price, which will give him some percentage of profit on cost of production. But this may not be true in all cases. Sometime it may happen that the goods purchased or produced may go out of fashion and may be unsaleable simply because of depression in the market, or keen competition. He/She may be able to sell the goods either at a loss or at a very small margin. However, he will be anxious at the end of the year to find out whether his goods taken together have been sold at a profit or at a loss and what is financial position on a particular date. Moreover, in big business information is required for planning, control, evaluation of performance and decision-making. This information can be provided only when business transactions are recorded, classified and summarized properly.

In order to achieve the above purpose it would be necessary to record business transactions according to well devised system. Book-keeping (in elementary stage) and Accounting (in advances stage) is the name given to such a system.

Difference between Book-keeping and Accounting

Book-keeping is the art and science of recording, classifying and summarizing transactions in money or money's worth accurately and systematically so that the business person may be able to know his/her profit or loss during a specific period and also his/her financial position on a particular date.

Accounting is a wider term and includes the recording, classifying, and summarizing of business transactions in terms of money, the preparation of financial reports, the analysis and interpretation of these reports for the information and guidance of management.

Table 1.1: Difference between Book-keeping and Accounting

Points of Distinction	Book-keeping	Accounting
1. Object	The object of book-keeping is to prepare original books of accounts, trial balance and final accounts.	The object of accounting is to record, classify, summarize, analyze and interpret the business transactions.
2. Scope	It has limited scope and is concerned with recording, classifying and summarizing of business transactions.	It has a wide scope and covers book-keeping plus analysis and interpretation.
3. Level of work	It is restricted to clerical work and is done by lower levels of management.	It is concerned with all levels of management. Lower level clerks prepare the accounts, medium level report it and top level interpret it.
4. Mutual dependence	It has to depend on accounting for making the accounting records more useful.	It has to depend on book-keeping for getting the required information from accounting records and for making them useful for planning, control and decision-making.
5. Results of the business	It shows the net result and financial position of the business as the scope extends only up to the preparation of final accounts.	It analyzes the operating results and financial position of the business.

Main Objects of Accounting

The main objects of accounting are:

1. *To ascertain whether the business operations have been profitable or not:* Accounting helps you to know whether a business has earned profit or suffered loss during the accounting period. It will give you an idea of efficiency of the business. To determine profit or loss of the accounting period, a Trading and Profit and Loss Account or an Income Statement is prepared by matching revenues and expired costs (i.e., revenue expenditures) incurred for earning the revenues. In the process of determination of profit or loss, its expense or cost that is matched with revenue and not vice versa. Thus, first of all revenues is determined and then expenses incurred for earning the revenue are matched with the revenue for calculating the difference known as net profit or net loss.

2. *To ascertain the financial position of the business:* Balance Sheet or Position Statement is prepared to give an idea of the financial position of the business on a particular date. The financial position of an enterprise is indicated by its assets on a given date and its liabilities on that date. Excess of assets over liabilities represent the capital and is indicative of the financial soundness of an enterprise. A properly drawn up balance sheet gives information relating to:
   (a) the nature and value of assets;
   (b) the nature and extent of liabilities;
   (c) whether the enterprise is solvent;
   (d) whether the business concern is over trading.
3. *To generate information from accounting records:* To generate such information from accounting records which may be helpful to various persons in planning, control, evaluation of performance and decision-making.

Components of Accounting Principles

Generally accepted accounting principles include:

- *Cost principle:* Assets (resources) are recorded at acquisition price (historical cost) and kept at that original price on the balance sheet.
- *Objectivity principle:* Costs used can be verified and are based upon fact.
- *Business entity concept:* Transactions of the business must be kept separate from those of the owner.
- *Going-concern concept:* The entity is assumed to be permanently in business.
- *Money measurement concept:* Money is the only practical unit of measurement that can be employed to achieve homogeneity of financial data. So accounting records only those transactions which can be expressed in terms of money though quantitative records are also kept. Non-monetary transactions or events cannot be recorded in the books of accounts.
- *Dual aspect concept:* According to this concept, every financial transaction involves a two-fold aspect: *(a)* yielding of a benefit; and *(b)* the giving of that benefit. For example, if a business has acquired an asset, it must have given up some other asset such as cash or the obligation to pay for it in the future. Thus a giver necessarily implies a receiver and a receiver necessarily implies a giver. There must be a double entry to have a complete record of each business transaction, an entry being made in the receiving account and an entry of the same amount in the giving account.

Definitions of Accounting Terms

The following are some of the basic accounting terms used in the business:

- *Business transactions:* Any exchange of money or money's worth as goods and services between two parties is called a business transaction.
- *Capital:* This is the owner's financial interest or holding in the business and is represented by the value of net assets (i.e., total assets less liabilities).
- *Goods:* This includes all articles, commodities or merchandise in which the business deals. Thus, cloth would be goods for a dealer in cloth; furniture would be goods for a dealer in furniture and so on.
- *Equity:* A claim which can be enforced against the assets of the firm is called equity. In other words, the rights to properties are called equities. Equities are of two types: the right of creditors and the right of owners. The equities of creditors represent debts of the business and are called liabilities. The equity of the owners is called capital, proprietorship or owner's equity. Thus assets must be the sum of liabilities and capital.
- *Income:* Income represents the inflows for services rendered or products sold during a given period of time. Examples of income are: sales, rental fees, and sales commission earned.
- *Expenditure:* Expenditure takes place when an asset or service is acquired. Expenditure will include both payment of a sum immediately and a promise to pay it at a future date.
- *Expense:* It means an expenditure whose benefit is finished or enjoyed immediately such as salaries, rent, etc. The purchase of goods is expenditure whereas cost of goods sold is an expense. Similarly, if an asset is acquired during the year, it is expenditure, if it is consumed during the same year; it is also an expense of the year.
- *Loss:* A loss is expenditure without any benefit to the concern. On the other hand, expense is incurred to result in some benefit. Thus, amount spent on lighting is an expense but loss due to fire is loss.
- *Voucher:* Any written document in support of a business transaction is called a voucher. It is an objective evidence in support of a transaction.
- *Turnover:* It means total trading income from cash sales and credit sales.
- *Net worth:* It means assets minus outside liabilities. Profits of a business increase net worth whereas losses reduce the net worth of a business.
- *Cash:* Coins, currency, cheques, money orders, certificates of deposit, savings account, and other bank accounts of the entity.

- *Notes receivable:* Contractual agreement whereby the entity has lent money or provided services to someone else (the maker) and the entity has a promise of payment at a specified time from the maker.
- *Accounts receivable:* Agreement from customers of future payment for goods and services provided by the entity. The customers here will also be called as debtors.
- *Inventory:* Goods sold by retail stores, wholesale companies, and manufacturing concerns.
- *Prepaid expenses:* Prepaid economic benefits that will not be used until they contribute to the earnings process. Examples are prepaid rent, prepaid insurance, and prepaid supplies.
- *Land:* Land used by the entity. Land is considered to have an infinite life and therefore is not depreciated.
- *Buildings:* Structures which are used by the entity in its operations. Buildings are depreciated over their useful lives.
- *Depreciation:* Depreciation refers to the process of cost allocation over the useful life of the asset by recognizing as a period expense.
- *Equipment:* Items used in the business with limited useful lives such as office machines, desks, autos, trucks, and cabinets. Depreciation expense is also recognized on equipment.
- *Accumulated depreciation:* A contra-asset account that reflects the cumulative depreciation recognized to date on the building or equipment. Thus, depreciation expense appears on the income statement as the cost allocation for the current period and accumulated depreciation reflects on the balance sheet. The total of all period's depreciation recognized as of a given date for buildings or equipment.
- *Notes payable:* Written agreement whereby the entity borrows money and promise to repay at a specific future date.
- *Accounts payable:* Agreement to pay a vendor for goods or services provided by the vendor. The vendor here is also called as creditor.
- *Salaries payable:* Unpaid salaries due to employees.
- *Unearned revenues:* Obligation to provide goods or services in the future and for which the entity has already received payment.

Summary

- Accounting is a wider term and includes the recording, classifying, and summarizing of business transactions in terms of money, the preparation of financial reports, the analysis and interpretation of these reports for the information and guidance of management.

- There are points of differences between accounting and book-keeping in-terms of object, scope, level of work, etc.

Self-Learning Activity

Try to answer the following questions on your own:

1. Differentiate accounting and book-keeping.
2. What are the objectives of accounting?

CHAPTER 2 Business Information Systems

Evolution of Information Systems

Between 1965 and 1975 organizations concentrated on automating those functions where they could make large efficiency gains. Typical targets were those that processed many routine transactions, such as payrolls, inventory and financial transactions. Department managers often delegated responsibility for information management to their information systems department. These became very skilled at running large, routine and usually centralized systems. The IS function also became influential, and line managers were rarely involved in discussions of IS strategy and development. The technologies had little effect on smaller organizations. The objective of most applications was to process routine transactions more efficiently.

In the following decade automated systems spread widely. Technical developments made smaller systems possible and more attractive to managers in other parts of the organization such as planning, manufacturing and distribution. More departments discovered the possibilities of computer-based information systems and their managers became familiar with issues of budgeting for hardware, requesting support, defining requirements and setting priorities — alongside established IS departments. Suppliers developed systems that were suitable for smaller organizations.

Since the mid-1980s the information systems environment has continued to change significantly. Technical developments have brought information systems to the foreground of corporate policy. Systems that for decades have supported the business functions of finance, manufacture and distribution continue to develop and employ more modern technology. In addition, computer-based systems have extended to serve many other business functions. Software suppliers have expanded product lines to support functions as diverse as production forecasting, supplier rating and project management. Information technology often supports managers and professional staff directly. Non-technical staff or small business owners now depend heavily on computer-based information.

Examples of such new developments are:

- The emergence of fast, relatively cheap and portable computer power.
- The ability to link these into networks (local and in a wider environment).
- The use of the internet to link computer systems with those in other organizations.
- Using information technologies for communication — such as email and video-conferencing.
- Creating integrated database that staff can use in different applications throughout the organization, for example in Customer Relationship Management (CRM).

The rise of the internet since the mid-1990s has further stimulated these developments. It challenges many traditional organizations to innovate their processes and change their operations. But it also enables completely new "dot.com" firms to enter the market place with totally new ways of doing business, and to challenge established players. Figure 2.1 depicts a clear picture on the widening role of information systems for many organizations. The early stages featured single, unconnected systems for separate business functions. In stages 3 and 4 managers are linking systems together and using them to make radical changes to previously separate processes. In stage 5 they are using common information systems based on the internet to move information between organizations and often having direct electronic links with their customers.

Role of Information in Organizations

Data, Information, and Systems

Organizations store and process large amounts of data, which may or may not convert into information. Data refers to recorded descriptions of things, events, activities and transactions. A database consists of stored data items organized for retrieval. Information is data that has been processed so that it has meaning and value for the recipient. This means that information is subjective; what one person perceives as information another may see as data. It depends on their interests and role. People can also use information to create knowledge – the expertise, understanding and experience that comes from learning. Figure 2.2 shows this relation between data, information and the information system that transforms the one to the other.

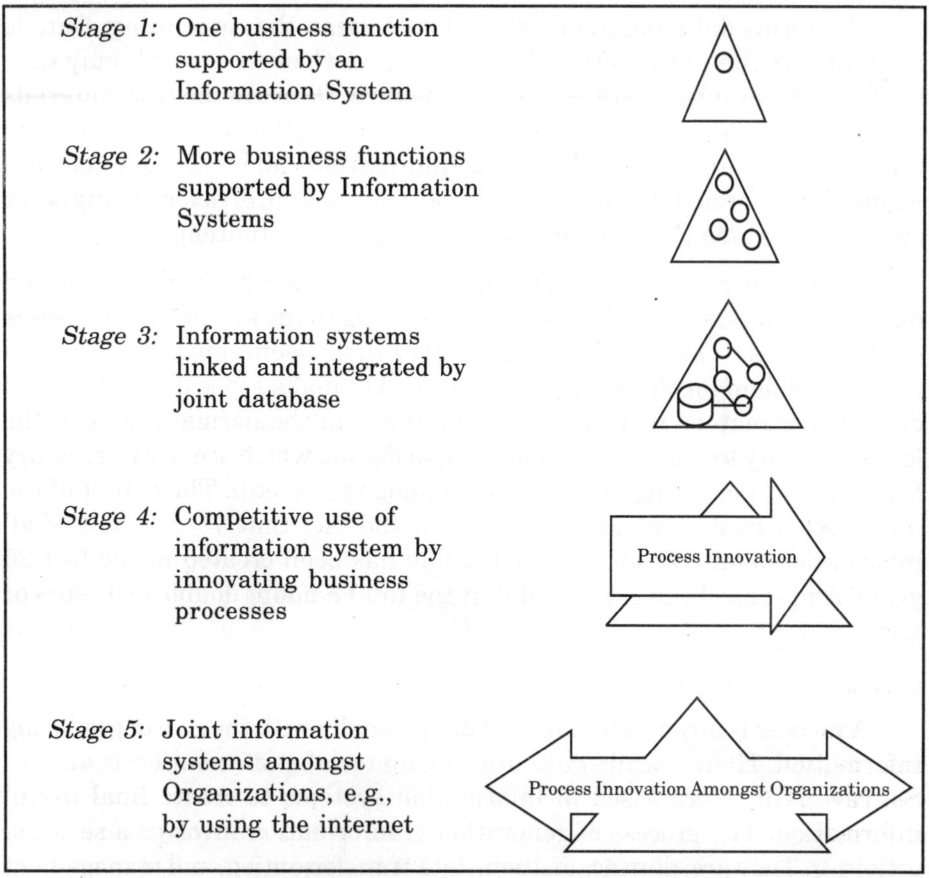

***Fig. 2.1:* The Widening Effects of Information Systems in Organizations**

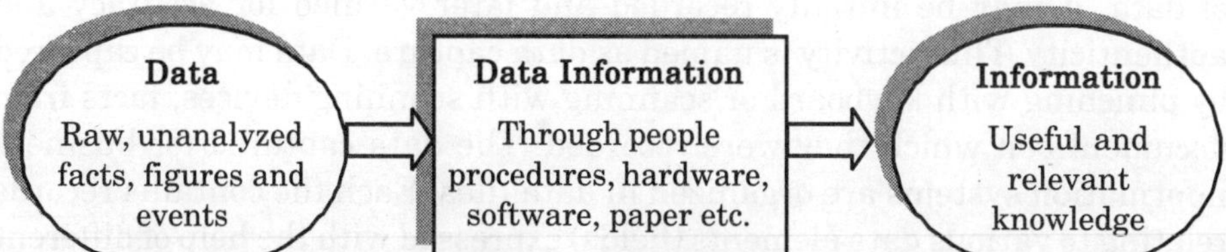

***Fig. 2.2:* Producing information from Data**

Data vs. Information

Any discussion about information systems inevitably involves using the words data and information. But what exactly are these? In normal speech the words are often used interchangeably, but in talking about computer-based information systems it is necessary to make a careful distinction between the two.

The terms data and information do not mean the same thing. Data is the plural of the Latin datum, literally a "given", or fact, which may take the form of a number, a statement, or a picture. Data are the raw materials in the production of information. Information, on the other hand, is data that have meaning within a context. Information can be raw data or data manipulated through tabulation, addition, subtraction, division, or any other operation that leads to greater understanding of a situation.

Data is the raw material of organizational life; it consist of disconnected numbers, words, symbols and syllables relating to the events and processes of the business. Data on its own can serve little useful purpose; in fact, a serious problem for the manager is the need to make sense of the deluge of data that threatens to overwhelm him or her in the normal course of the job. The ability to select those items of information which are truly necessary from the flood of irrelevance is a key management skill. The extent of the information explosion can be seen from the fact that 75 per cent of all information available on the earth today has been created in the last 20 years! And it has been estimated that the total amount doubles 10 years or less!

Generating information

A process is any manipulation of data, usually with the goal of producing information. Hence, while data are raw materials, information is output. So, raw data is processed in information systems to create final useful information. The process of generation of information involves a series of activities. They are: data acquisition, data transformation, and management of information.

Data acquisition means capturing data. Whatever may be the sources of data, it may be initially recorded and later verified for accuracy and authenticity. This activity is named as data capture. Data may be captured by punching with keyboard or scanning with scanning devices, facts from documents on which they were recorded. The data captured for business information systems are organized in data files. Each file contains records relating to various data elements (fields) expressed with the help of different symbols (characters). These files are linked to databases based on the hierarchy of data in business information systems.

Data transformation may be done by performing any of the operations, such as rearranging data in some specified order (sorting of data), classifying the data on the basis of the selected variables/factors, calculating the data by series of calculations, summarizing, which is a process of aggregating various data elements, reducing the bulk of data to a more meaningful form.

Management of information can be performed either by communicating the transformed information or by storing it for future reference. The appropriate channel of communication, the report format and storage medium should be selected and used. Such activities of communicating and/or storing information may be termed as managing information.

Historically people recorded data on paper, transformed it into information and presented it on paper. Now they are more likely to use some form of computer-based information system to record, transform, store and present information. An information system is a set of people, procedures and resources that collects and transforms data into information and disseminates this information. The figure 2.3 presents the elements of a computer-based information system.

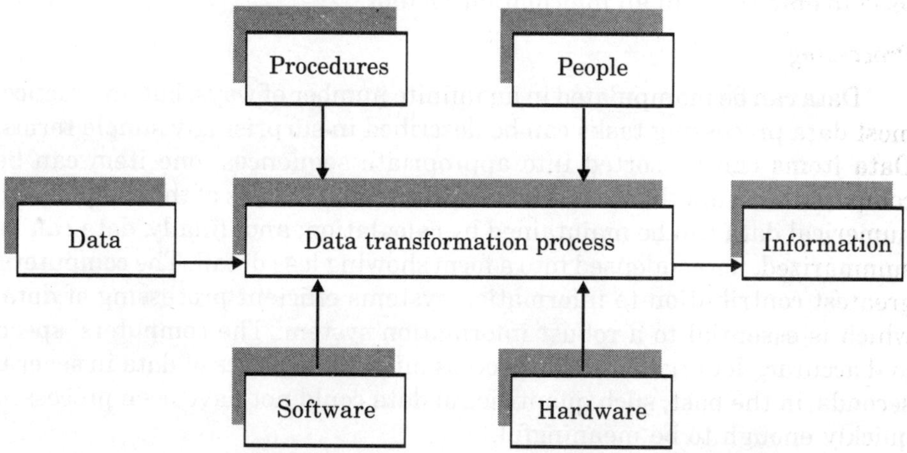

Fig. 2.3: The Elements of a Computer-based Information System

Nature of Data Processing

Information comes from data that has been processed to make it useful in management decision-making. The task of data processing is one which has been performed by people since the earliest days, whether we consider the stone tables of prehistoric man or the quill pens of Dickensian England. Now, increasingly, this task is being undertaken by computes, but the steps are essentially the same whether the process is undertaken manually or electronically.

Stages in Data Processing

Origination

At some point, new data comes into existence. This could be when a customer rings in to a sales department and places an order for a product; at this time new data relating to the customer and his or her needs is identified, where none existed before. From this point on, these data items are processed, partly electronically by formal computer and communication systems and partly by other less formal means such as word of mouth and manipulation in manual records.

Input and Transaction Recording

After origination, the next step in producing information is collecting and introducing data, known as input, into the information system. These data result from transactions undertaken in the course of business. These transactions can be recorded on paper and later entered into a computer system, or they may be directly recorded through terminals of Transaction Processing Systems (TPSs). At this stage input devices like the keyboard, infrared devices that sense bar codes, and voice recognition systems are used to enter data in an information system.

Processing

Data can be manipulated in an infinite number of ways, but, in practice, most data processing tasks can be described in surprisingly simple terms. Data items can be sorted into appropriate sequences; one item can be compared with another and decisions made on the basis of the comparison; numerical data can be maintained by calculation; and, finally, data can be summarized, i.e. condensed into a form showing less detail. The computers' greatest contribution to information systems efficient processing of data, which is essential to a robust information system. The computers' speed and accuracy let organizations process millions of pieces of data in several seconds; in the past, such quantities of data could not have been processed quickly enough to be meaningful.

Storage and Retrieval

A prime need of any business is the storage and retrieval of data. Large organizations can require the filing of staggering amounts of data. We now take for granted that such a mass of records will be stored and retrieved using automatic systems. A major contribution of electronic computer systems in management has been the cost-effective storage and efficient retrieval of data, which electronic storage systems provide. The computer's internal memory stores data and programmes while processing them. For longer storage periods, the computer transmits data to external storage devices such as magnetic and optical discs and tapes, in a form that lets the computer retrieve and process them.

Output

When data has been processed, or retrieved from a storage system, then it will be communicated to data user in some way. This could be achieved by word of mouth, or in the form of a written report or diagram. Computer systems employ a number of methods for outputting data, including display on a VDU screen and printing reports and documents. However, computers can communicate output through speakers in the form of music or speech and can also transmit it to another computer or electronic device in computer-coded form, for later interpretation.

The main (but no means the only) criterion for deciding about information is its usefulness in decision. This point has a number of considerations: firstly, if information is to be useful, then clearly its value depends to a large extent on the recipient and how it is to be used. Information is only useful to somebody and a prime criterion of its value relates to decision. Of course, the decision in question may not be immediate; information can be useful when it informs decisions to be made at some time in the future. In fact, learning is about storing information which may be useful at some time in the future.

All this implies that information which is useful to one person may be quite useless to somebody else, thus we may say that one manager's information may be another manager's data. Consider the staff in a sales office checking sales orders to allocate trade discounts: in this situation, details such as the customer's name and type of business may be items of information used to make a decision about the discount allowable. Now consider the sales manager in the same office as he or she decides whether to allocate more sales people for the amount of business to be achieved that month: in this instance, the total order value achieved so far may be the key piece of information and the details of individual customer names are irrelevant to the decision.

If we were to tell you that, today being Monday, tomorrow is Tuesday, then this piece of information will not be very valuable to you! The information has no surprise value, it tells you nothing you do not already know. Information is of more or less value to the extent to which it reduces our uncertainty about our word. If you were considering placing a bet on the favourite in the 3.30, then the would be uncertainty as to the outcome. If there were not, then you would find it hard to place a bet, because everybody would have knowledge of the result. But there is always uncertainty about the outcome of future events (in management as well as in horse racing). The information you receive about the race and about the horses may act to reduce this uncertainty, and is more or less valuable accordingly. For example, knowing that a horse is favourite tells you something about the possible outcome. Of course, just because the horse is favourite does not mean that it will win; but to a certain degree, your uncertainty about the outcome has been reduced. Knowing the odds, then, on the horses in a race reduces to some extent our uncertainty about the outcome (even if not very much) and hence this information has a certain value.

Essential tools for the input, processing, storage and output of most companies' information systems, computers also introduce another component to information systems: the need to translate instructions from natural — or human — languages into computer languages. Computers understand, give computers directions on how to interpret and manipulate data, and in what form (visual, aural or otherwise) to provide information to the organization. Thousands of programming languages are in use today.

Computer Equipment for Information Systems

The following are the basic components of the computer system within an information system:

- Input devices introduce data into the Information System (IS).
- The computer processes data through the IS.
- Storage devices store data and information.
- Output devices display information.

In addition to communication that takes place between computer components, communication occurs between computers over great distances (call telecommunications). Communications technology lets users not only access multiple input, output and storage devices with a single computer but access data and resources of more than one computer as well. This way, a computer's power may be augmented with the power of an entire computer network.

Desirable Characteristics of Information

In order that it should be valuable to the recipient, information must be of sufficient quality to make it useful in decision. But what is information quality? In practice, there are several rule-of-thumb criteria which help to create better information:

1. *Relevant information:* The need for information to be relevant to the purposes of the recipient in decision-making cannot be overstressed. Irrelevant information constitutes a substantial problem, because it distracts attention from important issues and wastes managers' time. It should be remembered that information which is relevant to one person may well be quite irrelevant to another who has different responsibilities. A further point is that information which is relevant now may become less so over time.
2. *Accurate information:* Information should be accurate enough for the purposes in mine. Clearly, wrong and misleading information can only have harmful consequences, and perhaps is worse than no information at all. However, at the same time, unnecessary numbers of decimal positions which add spurious accuracy will serve no purpose. The level

of accuracy, therefore, should be chosen to suit the circumstances: sterling values to the nearest penny are necessary for personal payslip details; values to the nearest pound may be suitable for supervisors' reports; values accurate to the nearest thousand are usually chosen for the company's published accounts. This point is reinforced in the next paragraph.

3. *Concise information:* The problem of an 'information explosion' for management has already been mentioned. An essential quality of useful information is that it should represent the minimum necessary to convey what is required for the decision in hand. Anything extra beyond what is essential serves only to add to the manager's information overload, and also acts to increase processing costs unnecessarily.
4. *Timely information:* Information which arrives after a decision has been made is clearly of little use, however, accurate and relevant it may have been. Hence the value of most information reduces sharply over time. Computers have often been introduced to lend their very fast processing speed specifically in order to improve the timeliness of information flows.
5. *Well-presented information:* The manner in which information is presented to information has a dramatic effect on its usefulness in decision-making. If key information is hidden in huge volumes of printouts, or if tables of numerical statistics are issued to show trends which might have been better displayed on a graph, then the decision-maker will not have been given the necessary assistance in his or her understanding of the information. Apart from these general points, there is some evidence to show that individuals have certain preferences for information types; for example, some people respond better to information presented visually in the form of pictures or graphs while others are happier if the same information is supplied in a verbal or textual form.
6. *Complete information:* In order to make a decision, the manager need all the information relevant to that task; if key parts of the information set are missing then this will obviously detract from its value.
7. *Up-to-date information:* Information must reflect the current known facts relating to a decision; if it show details relating to the past when more recent information would be of greater use, then, in a sense, it is no longer accurate.
8. *Cost-effective information:* Providing information always costs money (although often the true costs of creating it may be hidden); any decision, however important, can only have a certain value. Information which costs more to provide than the value that can result from a better

decision, is not cost-effective. Often it is just as difficult to ascertain the true benefits from use of information as it is to evaluate the cost of producing it (this point will be taken up in the next chapter.) Nevertheless, the creation and processing of information is a large item of expense for most organizations, and it is necessary to be careful that the benefits derived are not outweighed by the costs of production.

The computer, when employed with care, can assist in the achievement of these desirable characteristics. The successful design and implementation of information systems is rooted in an understanding of how these characteristics can be achieved.

Clearly, the creation and provision of information which has one or more of the above qualities may result in conflict with the other characteristics. For example, to produce information which is complete in all respects may well take too long, so that the information is no longer timely; or to take the extra care required to make sure it is well presented may result in the information no longer being cost-effective. In practice, producing information requires us to select a suitable compromise between the desirable characteristics, which represents the best we can do in a given situation.

Information Value and Costs

Assessing the value of information is not always easy, and there are different views as to how this should be done. Nevertheless, an attempt must be made to consider this point because providing information certainly entails outlay. If you consider the cost of a large computer system and the specialist staff required to run it, then the costs may be very high indeed. How are we to judge whether the costs is worth while without knowing the value of the information provided?

Returning to our racing example, if we could entirely reduce your uncertainty about the outcome of the horse race, then the information would surely have a specific (and possibly very high!) value. The point is that you could calculate quite specifically how much it would be worth paying to have that information. In general, we try to apply the same principles to estimating the value of information in management, i.e. by attempting to assess the value arising from decisions which could be taken more accurately on the basis of the information provided.

In a management setting, information can clearly be seen to have value if it results in somebody taking action which increases profitability. If that extra profit can be measured, then we have a direct assessment of the value of the information which achieved it. For example, if we provide information about optimum stockholding levels and the information can be acted upon so that a direct reduction in stockholding costs of £10,000 per year ensues, then we can claim that the information is worth that much, i.e. it would pay us to spend up to that value to obtain the information.

Unfortunately, the issues are rarely so clear-cut in the management world. The value of information is usually dependent on the recipient's needs and abilities to act in a given situation, and so there is usually no absolute or constant value of any piece of information. This is particularly true for management information systems where information may relate to decisions which in themselves are hard to quantify, or to situations which might arise in the distant future. In practice, then, the costs of information systems are usually justified using qualitative as well as quantitative arguments about the benefits which are to accrue.

Management Use of Information

Of course, individuals differ in the ways in which they respond to information and this inevitably affects the way in which decisions are taken. It has been shown, for example, that people have different cognitive styles, i.e. some people prefer information which is structured and follows a clear path from beginning to end (analytic or systematic style) while others prefer a more intuitive approach and like to see where the information as a whole is going (intuitive or heuristic style).

An oft-quoted example of this style difference is shown in the case of two people who are planning for a car journey. One prefers to drive to the approximate location to see if he can find it—the intuitive/heuristic approach—while the other person prefers to trace a map route from beginning to end—the systematic/analytic approach. Either approach may be more or less effective and successful depending on the circumstances; but the individual's response to information will, of course, be different. Differences such as this call for information systems, which are tailored to the cognitive styles of the people who are to use them. However, this degree of sophistication in business systems design is rather rare.

System

Simply put, a system is an array of components that work together to achieve a common goal, or multiple goals, by accepting input, processing it, and producing output in an organized manner. Needless to say, not every system has a single goal. Often, a system consists of several subsystems — components of a larger system — with subgoals, all contributing to meeting the main goal. Subsystems can receive input from, and transfer output to, other systems or subsystems. Systems are closed or open, depending upon the nature of information that flows within an organization. A closed system stands alone, with no connection to another system: nothing flows from another system; nothing flows out to another system. An open system interfaces and interacts with other systems.

Information and Systems

With an understanding of the words information and system, the definition of an information system is almost intuitive: "an information system (IS) is all components that work together to process data and produce information. Almost all business information systems consist of many subsystems with subgoals, all contributing to the organisation's main goal". An information system is an orderly way of providing information that an organization needs to operate in a successful way and, for a business organization, in a profitable way. Various methods and procedures are combined in numerous means and in various subsystems to make up what may be called an IS. In many companies there may be no formally designated system, but an IS must exist or the company would not continue to operate.

The ways in which similar functions are performed tend to vary from one organisation to another. In some companies many systems functions are performed manually or orally, whereas in other companies the same functions require extensive use of data processing and communications equipment. The basic functions of an IS rarely change, but methods and procedures do change. Thus 'systems work' focuses on indentifying and applying the most effective combination of methods and procedures for a particular organization. Over the years a number of creative people within the business environment have recognized the basic principles required in good business systems. At the same time they have developed the skills and techniques to enable them to design better systems than those in existence.

IS and its components

In an organization, an information system consists of data, hardware, software, telecommunications, people, and procedures as summarized in the Exhibit 2.1. Generally defined, the term information system does not have to include electronic equipment. However, "information system", a system with a computer at its center to which peripheral equipment is connected. That is how we use the term here. In a computer-based information system, computers collect, store, and process data into information, according to instructions people provide via computer programmes.

Exhibit 2.1

Components of an information system

Data	Input that the system takes to produce information.
Hardware	A computer and its peripheral equipment: input, output and storage devices. It also includes data communication equipment.
Software	Sets of instructions that tell the computer how to take data in, how to process it, how to display information, and how to store data and information.
Telecommunication	Hardware and software that facilitate fast transmission and reception of text, pictures, sound, and animation in the form of electronic data.
People	Information systems professionals and users who analyse organizational information needs, design and construct information system, write computer programmes, operate the hardware, and maintain software.
Procedures	Rules for achieving optimal and secure operations in data processing. Procedures include priorities in dispensing software applications and security measures.

Several trends have made the use of information systems very important in business. They are: computers' power has grown tremendously while their prices have dropped; computer programme's variety and ingenuity have increased; quick and reliable communication lines and access to the internet and world wide web have become widely available and affordable; the fast growth of the internet has opened opportunities and encouraged competition in global markets; and an increasing ratio of the workforce is computer literate.

Information Systems and Management

Most organizations, even down to the very smallest, utilize computers in some way or another. The uses to which the computers are put vary enormously, ranging from word processing and elementary accounting systems through to on-line enquiry, sophisticated decision-support systems and mathematical modeling for corporate planning. It is probably true that many of today's businesses simply could not function effectively without automated information processing systems of some form or another. The costs and delays arising from manual processing methods would be truly daunting without automated data processing; consider, for example, the raw data processing involved when next you write a cheque or buy a plane ticket. Increasingly, information systems are seen as a strategic resource within the organization; that is, they have an important impact on key operations which determine the livelihood of the organization.

But it would be wrong to overemphasize the role of computers alone. In practice, most management information systems are an amalgam of human and computer-based activities, where man and machine have different but complementary roles to play in achieving the successful working of the system. The question as to which aspects are best done by machine and which are best done by people is a fascinating one, and, of course, the answer is changing constantly with rapid advances in technology. Table 2.1 compares some of the different capabilities of human and computer as information processors.

Table 2.1: Comparison between Humans and Computers

	Human	Computer
Overhead costs	Expensive	Cheap
Running costs	Expensive	Cheap
Performance over time (stamina)	Deteriorates	Constant
Reliability/consistency	Poor	Excellent
Computation ability	Poor	Excellent
Handling the unexpected	Good	Poor
Commonsense abilities	Excellent	Poor
Language abilities	Good	Poor

Advantages of Computerized Information Systems

There are several distinct advantages, which can accrue from the successful use of computer systems. We use the word can carefully here; it is not certain that any benefits will accrue just because a computer is installed: far from it. In practice it is necessary to plan computer systems with great care and to implement them skillfully in order to realize the full benefits. This book is intended to provide guidance for realizing those benefits and for avoiding some of the pitfalls which may arise.

There are significant advantages to be achieved from the successful implementation of computer-based systems; but these can take several different forms, and it is worth while being quite clear as to which benefit(s) are being sought. Generally, the concrete advantages fall into four categories:

1. Information cost-effectiveness
2. Enhanced business growth potential
3. The automation of decisions
4. Enhancement of decision quality

Information cost-effectiveness

Computers have greatly reduced the need for clerical data processing; at the same time new work roles have arisen, and new information workers have appeared to fill them. In general, computers can process raw data very much more cheaply and accurately than human beings, and this has meant a dramatic reduction in the costs of elementary data processing. Many organizations have justified the introduction of computer systems on the basis that specific cost savings will accrue as result of a direct saving in clerical effort. Most mature organizations will by now have already shed or relocated clerical effort where this can be directly replaced by automated systems and so further cost reductions here are not so easy to achieve. In practice, the direct replacement of human data processing by computers is rarely straightforward and clerical cost reductions must be balanced against a whole host of new costs associated with the new systems.

Enhanced business growth potential

Many organizations find that they are hampered in their search for growth by their administrative paperwork systems, or by the lack of consistent information. The introduction of computer-based systems can overcome these hurdles and allow growth in sales to occur. The costs of manual data processing tend to rise linearly with the volumes of data; i.e. ignoring any learning effects, it costs twice as much to cope with 200 documents as it does to cope with 100. This is usually because the dominant cost element is people. However, this will not be the case with a computer system; once initial installation costs have been overcome it may cost little to expand the system to cope with extra volumes of data.

It can be seen that with small data volumes the computer system initially costs more than an equivalent manual system, because of the capital outlay on equipment and set-up costs. However, as data volumes rise, so the manual system costs rise with them while the computer costs remain roughly constant. This is because more data needs more people, but the computer can take on more work until its capacity is reached. At a certain point, the computer will have reached its limit and will need enhancing or replacing, resulting in a step-change in costs. Thus there is an area of the graph where the computer costs are constant while manual costs are rising. A carefully designed system will exploit the capacity of the computer to soak up increased volumes with little cost increase. (This is of course a simplification of reality, and in reality the people function will be a stepped cost also and there will be a host of other factors to consider).

Automation of decisions

The work of and organization can be seen as being made up of countless elementary individual decisions. Most of these decisions are usually quite straightforward, but the decisions must be taken none the less, and good solutions arrived at or the organization cannot function. Examples of these elementary decisions are legion, but include the allocation of sales discounts to customers depending on pervious sales records, or the calculation of PAYE income tax depending on earnings and tax code. A computer system can handle such decisions accurately and tirelessly, according to a fixed set of rules called an algorithm. A great advantage of the computer is that it can make decisions no matter how complex the decision factors are, always providing that these factors can be defined. This enables consistency and accuracy to be achieved in the organization's work and enables management and staff to concentrate on aspects requiring human judgment and skills.

Enhanced decision-making

Much of the development work in information systems for management is aimed at improving the quality of human decision. This is a different matter altogether from the automation of decisions discussed in the previous section. The intention now is to provide information to enable the manager to make a decision, which, based on more accurate information or assisted by a computer model of the factors involved, will permit him or her to achieve better outcomes than if the decision was made unaided.

Recent developments in decision support systems (DSS) and executive information systems (EIS) have had far-reaching effects on strategic decision-making by senior managers. Decisions, which have crucial long-term effects on the organization can be supported by computer-generated information and decision models so that the long-term effects of different options can be reviewed. Further enhancements to decision quality are possible as a result of developments in the comparatively new field of computer-based artificial intelligence and expert systems. In addition to these cited advantages, information systems are increasingly being considered as strategic; in overall terms they can crucially affect an organization's survival.

Benefits of Human-Computer Synergy

After having understood the advantages of computer-based systems, we should know about the benefits of human-computer synergy also. It is important that computers can only carry out instructions that humans give them. Computers can process data accurately at far greater speeds than people can, yet they are limited in many respects — most importantly they lack common sense. However, combining the strengths of these machines with human strengths creates synergy. Synergy (from the Greek word "work together") occurs when combined resources produce output that exceeds the sum of the outputs of the same resources employed separately. A computer works quickly and accurately; humans work relatively slowly and make mistakes. A computer cannot make independent decisions, however, or formulate steps for solving problems. Thus, human-computer combination allows the results of human thought to be translated into efficient processing of large amounts of data. The Exhibit 2.2 depicts a clear picture on the qualities of human and computers that contribute to synergy.

Exhibit 2.2

Qualities of human and computers that contribute to synergy

Human	Computers
Think	Calculate and perform programmed logical operations extremely rapidly
Have common sense	Store and retrieve data and information extremely rapidly
Can make decisions	Perform complex logical and arithmetical functions accurately
Instruct the computer	Execute long, tedious operations
Learn new methods and techniques	Perform routine tasks less expensively
Accumulate expertise	Adaptable (programmed and re-programmed)

Types of Information System

Formal and Informal Information Systems

Because we concentrate a great deal on formal information systems: accounting reports, computer printouts and so on, we tend to forget that, in fact, managers pay a lot of attention to other, less formal, sources of information. These include managers' own observations of events, and especially the face-to-face and telephone contacts they have with the people around them. In fact, the typical manager spends most of the time gathering information in this way (or being exposed to it) and hence the informal information sources make up a significant part of the manager's world (see Table 2.2).

Table 2.2: Comparison between Formal and informal information systems

Formal	Informal
How communicated Word of mouth, gossip, Printed reports computer terminals	Hearsay
How created MIS, computer-based systems	Personal contacts, 'grapevine'
By whom created Staff specialists IS department Corporate planning department	Managers' interpersonal Networks, including colleagues, subordinates, superiors, friends and allies
Information types Quantitative Financial Economic	Qualitative, personal, non-economic
Information characteristics Regular, scheduled Summarized Aggregated, selected	Unscheduled, chance contacts disaggregated fragments of detail processed

Of course, the informal information is completely different from the sort of thing, which we usually think of as 'management information'. It consists of word-of-mouth, reports about events and people in the organization, usually reported verbally and with little quantitative content. Often the information is inaccurate, it comes form 'the grapevine' and tends to be newsy with snippets of detail about people and events, which are of general personal interest.

The informal information system has obvious drawbacks as regards accuracy, validity and reliability. Nevertheless, managers seem to prefer their informal systems to the formal systems for some aspects of their information needs. The reasons for this are not have to find: the informal information usually has a more immediate character to it, i.e. it relates to the here and now; also, it may be easier to digest and to act upon than a complex report or financial summary. In extreme circumstances informal information may be more trusted than the formal information passed down by senior management.

In fact there are circumstances where informal information is of the utmost importance to managers. Consider the sales director who visits his office in the morning and reads the monthly sales analysis for his division; this report (from the formal information system) tells him which customers have placed orders, and for how much. In the evening he plays a round of golf with a friend from one of his most important client companies; his friend tells him of a rumour (the informal information system) that the client company may be about to place its business elsewhere. This is serious and worrying news (if true) which the sales director acts on the next day by contacting the client directly.

Clearly, the informal information system has a tremendous importance in this instance because it advised the sales director of possible future events. The formal information system would have told him of the problem only after the client company had withdrawn its custom. The issue here is that informal information systems serve a key purpose for most managers, and that formal, computer-based systems have a complementary role. They do not necessarily replace all previous information systems.

The role of computers in management has a broad range of possible applications. Since these different applications often have quite different aims and objectives it is essential to discriminate among the various groups of information systems: data processing, transaction processing systems, management information systems, decision support systems, executive information systems, expert systems, geographical information system, office automation systems, intelligent knowledge-based systems and the personal information systems.

Data Processing

The aims of data processing are to process large amounts of data quickly, cheaply and accurately. Automated data processing (ADP) was the first major application of computers in management, and, indeed, automated data processing of one kind or another had been carried out long before computers became generally available in the 1950s. Herman Hellerith developed the punched card in the late nineteenth century so that machines could process the results of the US population census. The improvements, which these punched-card methods produced, were adopted by many of the larger business organizations, which sought to reduce the costs of their elementary data processing tasks. Payroll and elementary accounting systems were among the first and most popular systems to be automated. The electronic digital computer greatly improved the scope and cost-effectiveness of ADP, and the new technology became known as electronic data processing (EDP). Now it is taken for granted that the elementary data processing tasks of a business will be performed wherever possible by computer; indeed for many firms it is an essential part of their competitive business strategy.

Transaction Processing Systems (TPS)

The earliest electronic information systems in business consisted of computers and programmes used to record and report transactions. Called

TPS they are the most widely used information systems. TPS's predominant function is to record data collected at the boundaries of organization, in other words, at the point where the organization transacts business with other parties. TPSs include cash registers, which record sales; automatic teller machines, which record cash withdrawals, deposits and transfers; and purchase order systems, which record purchases. After data are collected, the information system either automatically processes the data into information or stores it for later processing on demand.

Management Information Systems (MIS)

MIS grew naturally out of the earlier simple data processing systems. While processing data quickly and economically, it was a small extra step to summarize and select information which would help mangers make decisions. For example, while processing the payroll, there is little extra computer processing involved in producing totals of overtime payments, or an analysis of days worked by each department.

In time, it came to be seen that information produced by the computer system could be produced to standards of speed and accuracy which were just not possible before, and that this information could act as a platform achieving a far more efficient business organization. There came to be a special emphasis on the value of management information and this resulted in systems being designed specifically for their information outputs, rather than purely for the data processing benefits. These systems were planned so as to create all (or almost all) the information needed for the monitoring and controlling of an organization's affairs.

Although there is some dispute over the definition of these terms, MIS usually means a system which contains large amounts of information which has been structured to assist management in decision-making. (The relationship between data and information has already been defined in this chapter). Typically, the information is held on some form of database, consisting mainly of financial data from internal company systems, and is used mainly by middle management in monitoring and controlling the organization's business. Management information systems are essentially historic, being concerned with past actions and outcomes.

In recent years there has been a swing away from large-scale MIS systems. It was found that these large, integrated systems were very expensive to build, cumbersome in operation and did not always achieve all the benefits that were expected. Today, it is probably fair to say that there is still an important role for the MIS, but it is no longer seen as the ultimate and final expression of the organization's information needs. Rather, the MIS takes its place among the other types of computer-based information systems, which an organization may utilize.

Decision Support Systems (DSS)

These systems were created, at least in part, as a response to some of the perceived failings of MIS. The MIS, because it was based mainly on internal financial data, did not directly address the needs of top management, or of strategic decision-making. A DSS usually contains specially designed models which provide the user with the means of assessing the consequences of decision. An example of this is known as a "what if?" facility: given the task of deciding between various forms of investment, for instance, the system user can see the consequences of each option when the system evaluates the effect on profitability using a financial model of the organization's finances.

Executive Information Systems (EIS)

Executive information systems or Executive support systems help high-ranking officers direct an organization. Often programmed to integrate thousands of pieces of data and produce summary reports, these systems evolved in the mid-1970's to help executives focus on long range strategic planning within an organization. These information systems generate strategic information and are used by top level managers. They help in identifying options, evaluation of alternative scenarios and making informed choices regarding the business options.

Expert Systems (ES)

Often managers or other workers may need expertise to make certain decisions, not just formulas. In the past, only human experts in a specific line of work could provide advice to decision-makers. Now, information systems can be developed that incorporate human expertise. These systems are called expert systems. These expert systems aim at formalizing expertise and make it available for repetitive type of business decisions. They use artificial intelligence tools to generate knowledge out of the information, existing theories, beliefs, and experiences of managers in various business activities.

Geographical Information Systems (GIS)

In some cases, the information decision-makers' need is related to a map. In such cases, special information systems called 'geographical information systems' can be employed to tie data to physical locations. A GIS application access a database that contains data about part of a city, a city, a county, a state, a country, or even the entire world. By representing data on a map in different graphical forms, a user is able to promptly understand a situation taking place in that part of the world and act upon it.

Office Automation Systems (OAS)

Information technology (IT) is a broad term which has been coined to refer to the range of electronic facilities used in modern management. These facilities include personal computers, word processing and desk-top publishing (DTP), electronic mail, electronic point of sale (EPOS) and electronic funds transfer (EFT). Many of these techniques remove the need for paper-based filing systems of communications, and have given rise to the expression 'the paperless office'. However, most offices are still anything but paperless and the strength of the technology lies primarily in the utilization of computer and communications technology together in information processing and transmission.

Intelligent Knowledge-Based Systems (IKBS)

The search for a means of creating human-like computer systems has been carried out in research departments of universities since the very earliest days of computers. In recent years this has been supplemented by substantial commercial development, particularly in expert systems. The capacity of computers to reproduce human skills and abilities is known as artificial intelligence (AI). A number of special techniques have been developed over the years which enable computers to go some way towards emulating these skills. IKBS utilize AI techniques in order to provide specialist expert systems. It is now possible to store the knowledge of human experts in a computer and to enable the knowledge to be tapped by an enquirer who consults the computer. The system reviews the problem, asks questions if necessary and provides a diagnosis and suggestions for a solution.

Personal Information Systems (PIS)

The personal information systems are used by managers to improve their productivity at work. They help managers perform their jobs more efficiently. The personal information systems involve the use of microcomputers along with softwares for word processing, electronic spreadsheets, personal database management systems, graphics and business presentations and desktop organizing. The PISs are less expensive to install and simple to use as compared to other business information systems. They are more flexible and protected because they are single-hand handled systems. Since they are personal, a manager can use it the way he finds it more productive for him.

Information Systems in Business and Sectors

Without exception, every business function in every business sector employs information systems. Information systems are key tools in transaction processing, decision-making, problem solving, and operations of all business entities. The following section briefly discusses these information systems uses.

Information systems in functional business areas

Different types of information systems serve different purposes of an business organization. Functional areas of business include, but are not limited to, accounting, finance, marketing, production, and human resources; they exist in one form or another.

Accounting: In accounting function, information systems help record business transactions, produce periodic financial statements, and create reports for making business decisions.

Finance: The purpose of financial systems is to facilitate financial planning and financial control. In finance, information systems support prepare budgets, manage cash flows, analyse investments, and make decisions that could reduce interest payments and increase revenues from business financial transactions.

Marketing: Marketing information systems provide information on product, price, physical distribution, promotional activities, and public relations. These information support given by the information systems help the managers to decide the things regarding marketing.

Production: Information systems help production function by providing proper information for production planning and control. The materials information is also provided by the information systems so as to have proper materials system in the business organization.

Human Resources: Human resources management systems encompass the human resource planning, recruitment and selection, training and development, performance appraisal systems. The information systems help to make decisions in all respects of human resources management system.

Information systems in business sectors

Different business sectors use information systems of all types. Also, systems are often adapted for specific needs of the sectors in which they are used. Information systems in different business sectors are discussed hereunder.

Manufacturing: Information systems are used throughout a manufacturing operation, from inventory control to paying supplies. Information systems help allocate resources, such as personnel, raw material, and time, to optimize production and productivity. Manufacturing operations use information systems to process customer orders, prepare production schedules, perform quality assurance, and prepare shipping documents.

Service: Information systems play such a central role in the service sector that they are often the backbone of service organizations. The best example can be the banking sector. Without information systems what banks would do? Bank information systems' input consist the type of account (as well as the dates and quantities of deposits and withdrawals); their output consist of statements on interest paid or owed, balances, etc.

Retail: Because information systems enable a large retail chain to run as a single big store, retail chain gained significant economies of scales using information systems. The major purpose of these information systems is to minimize understocking and overstocking in any of the chain's stores.

Government: In recent years governmental and commercial organizations have installed computer-based information systems to automate the processes and replace the human labour. The business of the government depends heavily on information systems for collecting taxes, paying social security, and purchasing goods and services for various departments.

Enterprise Application Systems are in existence, which are information systems that tie together the different functional areas of a business. Such systems allow business to operate more efficiently by avoiding duplication of information and avoiding rework. The most pervasive type of enterprise applications is Enterprise Resource Planning (ERP) systems, which actually help in more areas than only planning.

At the outset, information systems support all types of organizations in gathering data, processing, storing and dissemination of information with IT infrastructure and resources.

Summary

- Between 1965 and 1975 organizations concentrated on automating those functions where they could make large efficiency gains. During 1980's there was a drastic change in the organizations with information systems.
- Networking concepts are familiar and more developments are coming up with information systems.
- Data, hardware, software, people, telecommunication are the components of an information systems.
- There is a synergy process by integrating manual (human) and computer systems.
- Information systems may be of formal and informal; based on sector, business functions. There are different types of IS.

Self-Learning Activity

Try to answer the following questions on your own:

1. Can you explain about the human computer synergy process?
2. Classify information systems.

CHAPTER 3 Accounting Information System — *Conceptual Framework*

Introduction

Accounting information system (AIS) has three components viz., Accounting, Information and System. Accounting information system can be understood through proper understanding of the three components mentioned above.

ACCOUNTING

American Accounting Association (AAA) defines accounting as "the process of identifying, measuring, and communicating economic information to permit informed judgments and decisions by users of the information".

So accounting is the art of classifying business transactions and summarising the same. Classifying is the process of grouping of transactions or entries of one nature at one place. This done by opening accounts in a book call ledger. Summarising is the art of making the activities of the business and classifies them in the ledger so as to be understandable and useful to management and other interested parties. This involves the preparation of at least two statements viz.

(i) Trading and Profit and loss A/c

(ii) Balance Sheet.

Objectives of Accounting

These include reliable information about:

- changes in financial position resulting from the income-producing efforts of an enterprise;
- earnings of an enterprise, presented in a manner that emphasise the sources and trends of earnings;
- economic resources and obligations of an enterprise;
- changes in net financial resources which result from the financing and investing activities of an enterprise; and

- any additional information, in the form of disclosures, which is relevant statement users in assessing a particular enterprise's prospects.

Functions of Accounting

Moonitz, in his definition of accounting analysed the functions of accounting as:

- to manage the resources held by specific entities;
- to reflect the claims against and the interests in those entities;
- to measure the changes in those resources, claims and interests;
- to assign the changes to specifiable periods of time; and
- to express the above in terms of money as a common denominator.

Characteristics of Accounting

Modern accounting possesses the following basic characteristics:

- Accounting involves recording of economic activities which accompanies the complexity and uncertainty of business. Therefore, while preparing timely accounting statements, estimates and professional judgments must be made.
- Accounting statements are prepared on:
  - *(a)* cash basis of accounting, which recognizes an event as a transaction only when cash is received or paid, or
  - *(b)* accrual basis of accounting, which recognizes revenues earned and expenses incurred as transactions.
- Accounting is historical in nature — it is the recording of past happenings.

Accounting Stages

1. Identifying of business transactions of financial character that had taken place in the past and recorded.
2. Such activity of recording is done in a manner which may be identified by the different classes and types of transactions.
3. The summarizing process is done in such a way that owners or others who have an interest in the business can see the overall efforts of all the business transactions. The statements prepared by such a summarizing will show the profit or loss made by the business over a period of time and total capital employed in the business.
4. Those statements showing the financial position and profit or loss to be used by management and others to make business decision.

INFORMATION

Information and data are interchangeably used by business people. We can define information as data that have been converted into meaningful and useful context for specific end users. In business the information plays a vital role in feeding business information to the decision centres to make decisions. The information refers to the facts or figures that one meaningful to recipients and can thereby be utilized to help them make business decisions. The important function of accounting is to efficiently convert into relevant information to internal and external parties.

SYSTEM

A system is an entity consisting of interacting parts (called sub-systems), which attempt to achieve a multiplicity of goals. In business entity the system have to function effectively and efficiently. For which its sub-systems must interact with each other. This interaction is achieved principally through the effective communication of relevant information among the sub-systems. In any organization, the system of communication follows from the top-level management to lower level management. The top-level management frames the broad goals for the entire system to achieve in the future. The middle level management will execute the operational goals. The lower level management system control and evaluate the operational system of entire organization. This subsystem acquires a large quantity of data from the system's internal and external environment. The data must then be sorted, processed, and communicated through meaningful reports to the other subsystems. Data that are communicated so that they have meaning to the recipient (e.g., a production manager) are called information. In this text the word data will refer to facts or figures with little if any meaning to recipients and therefore not useful to aid their business decision-making activities. On the other hand, the world information will refer to facts or figures that are meaningful to recipients and can thereby be utilized to help them make business decisions. An important function of any modern business system is to efficiently convert the massive amount of available internal and external data into relevant decision-making information. Based upon the types of decision-making information needed by subsystem managers to achieve their operational goals, a communication network of information that flows to the subsystems is thereby established.

Definition of AIS

Each subsystem within the system could be analyzed in considerable depth to understand its contribution to the company's operating-oriented; however, we can now direct our attention to the accounting subsystem's role in a business information system. The accounting subsystem performs a service function for an organization. The service that accounting provides is to transform financial oriented data into useful information that aids management, creditors, current and potential investors and so on, in their decision-making activities. Because accounting's function is to convert data into information for others, the accounting subsystem can often be referred to as the "accounting information system".

We specially define an accounting information system as:

"An organizational component, which accumulates, classifies, processes, analyzes, and communicates, relevant financial-oriented, decision-making information to a company's external parties (such as federal and state tax agencies, current and potential investors, and creditors) and internal parties (principally management)."

From the above definition, it could identify that; it is a major component of a MIS. The Accounting Information System performs the functions of accumulating, classifying processing, analyzing and communicating relevant financial information to top management, middle management and lower management. The lower management identifies to maintain cash balance to meet day-to-day operating expenditures. Hence, the analysis of the communicated accounting information performed to the managers within the specific development at the middle-level management. The AIS provides estimated income and expenditure statement to top management to analysis the financial decision-making.

The accounting information system is actually one major component of a management information system. The difference between the former and the latter is in the scope of coverage. Whereas an accounting information system performs the functions of accumulating, classifying, processing, analyzing, and communication relevant financial information. A management information system performs the above functions for all types of information (financial as well as non-financial) affecting a company's operating activities. Thus, the management information system is concerned with providing relevant decision-making information whether or not this information is accounting-oriented.

AIS studies the structuring and operation of planning and control processes which are aimed at:

- Providing information for decision-making and accountability to internal and external stakeholders that compiles with specified quality criteria.
- Providing the right conditions for sound decision-making; and
- Ensuring that no assets illegitimately exit the organization.

System and AIS

AIS is a subsystem of the total information system. It has its importance and significance in the total system. The figure 3.1 depicts a clear picture of the place of accounting information system.

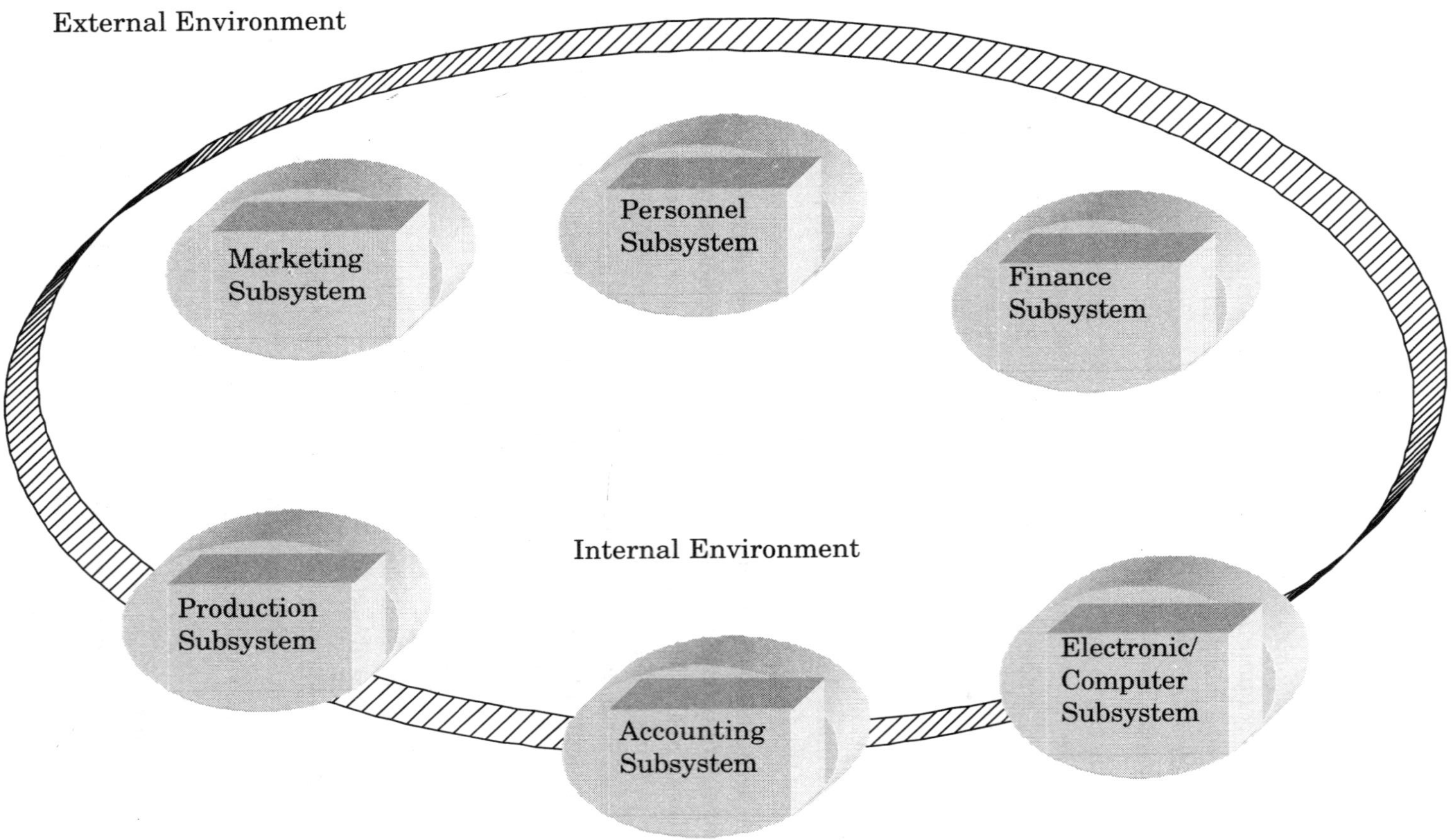
External Environment
Marketing Subsystem
Personnel Subsystem
Finance Subsystem
Internal Environment
Production Subsystem
Accounting Subsystem
Electronic/ Computer Subsystem

Fig. 3.1

Accounting information system as subsystem of the total business system, works for feeding the processed accounting data to the decision centres for taking and making timely valuable business decisions. The very purpose of AIS is to provide financial and managerial information about business enterprise or any other economic entity. In short, anyone who must make decisions regarding a business enterprise has need of accounting information. The workable accounting information system is presented in the following figure 3.2.

Qualitative Characteristics of AIS

The following are the qualitative characteristics of AIS that are used to determine whether an accounting method is acceptable or preferable. In addition these are used by accountants to choose among alternative accounting methods. Therefore, these characteristics of accounting information are those which are of maximum use to the users.

Usefulness: The value of any information lies on its utility. The cost of gathering the information as well as people's appreciation of its use are the two limiting factors of the usefulness of the information.

Comprehensibility: It presupposes the capacity on the part of those who have to make use of the information gathered. It demands a quality, more or less, of the recipient.

Relevance: Relevant accounting information should be capable of making a difference in a decision by helping users (investors, creditors, others) of accounting information to form predictors about the outcomes of past, present and future events.

Reliability: Accounting information is reliable if it is reasonably free from bias and faithfully represents what it purports to present. Reliability is vital to the utility of accounting information.

Timeliness: To be relevant, again, accounting information should be timely. Accounting information which is timely increases ability to influence decisions.

Verifiability: To be reliable, information must be verifiable and must have representational faithfulness validity.

Neutrality: Accounting information should be neutral i.e., it should be compiled and forwarded, as they say, without affection or ill-will.

Comparability: Relativity is the spring-board of all decision-making. Accounting information should, therefore, be characterized by relativity — it must be comparability. It enhances the value of accounting information.

Completeness: Full accounting information should be provided and nothing should be kept hidden.

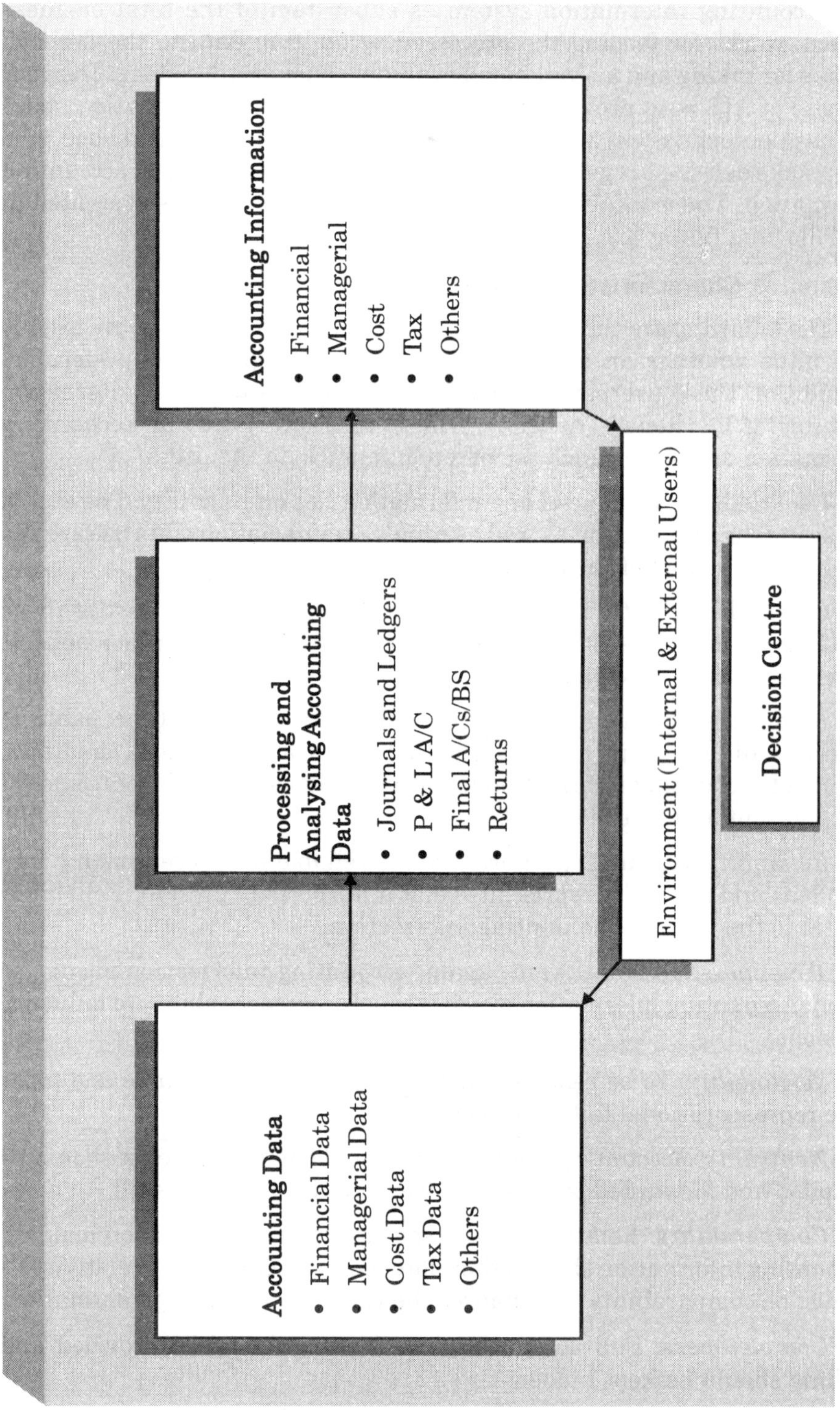

Fig. 3.2: **Accounting Information System**

Users of Accounting Information

Accounting information is needed by two sets of people — internal and external. Internal users (eg. Directors, partners, managers, officers) are those who are associated with management of the concern for which information is sought to be gathered and surveyed. The term managerial accounting relates to internal measurements and reporting; it includes the development of detailed current information helpful to all levels of management in decision-making designed to achieve the goals of the enterprise. The external users consist of several explicit groups: investors, lenders, suppliers, customers, governmental agencies, public and employees. The field of financial accounting is directly related to external reporting because it provides external parties with the financial information they need for decision-making. The Figure 3.3 presents the various users of accounting information.

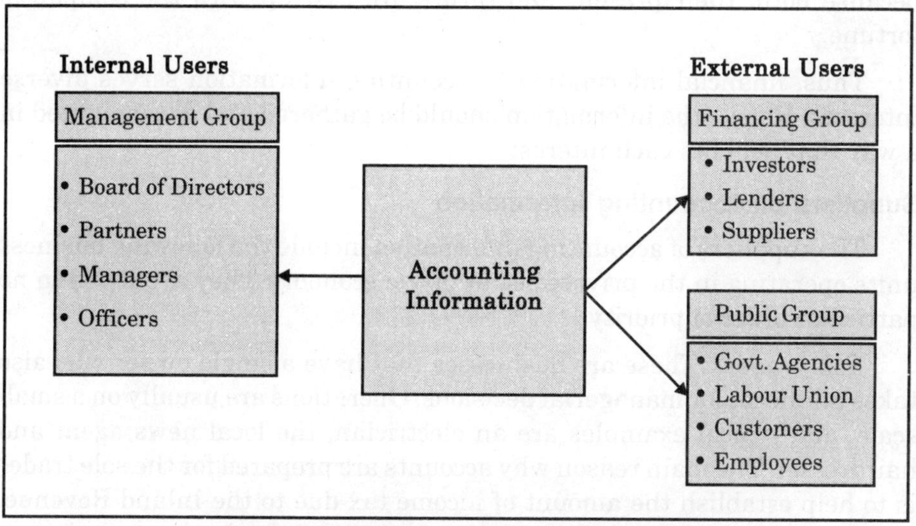

Fig. 3.3: **Users of Accounting Information**

Investors: They supply the risk capital to the business unit. Ownership is separated from management in joint stock companies, and hence, investors need to know their money is being spent by the managers. Financial information helps them to decide about making investments, quantum of investments, and holding on to the equities they own.

Lenders: Accounting information provides lenders with reasonable assurance as to the payment of interest and repayment of the principal.

Suppliers: They normally sell on credit and they must have reasonable assurance that their credit will be honoured. Financial information helps them decide about the credibility of the firm, and whether they should continue supplying on credit.

Customers: Accounting information has a significant role to play in all decisions related to the customers — producers, wholesalers, and the final consumers — so as to retain this composite group.

Governmental agencies: Since the regulation and control of business (economy) is in the hands of the government, the government agencies rely on financial information for permitting expansion or contraction, for import and export of products and / or materials, for allocation of essential resources for regulating labour or taxation, etc.

Public: For members of the public, the financial information is in the nature of a health examination report – it tells them about employment opportunities and general growth in the individual concern and the economy as a whole.

Employees: The employees are interested in the financial information because both, their present and future are tied up with the company's fortune.

Thus, financial information – accounting information serves diverse interests. Hence, the information should be gathered and disseminated in a way that benefits each interest.

Suppliers of Accounting Information

The suppliers of accounting information include the following business units operating in the private sector of the economy. They are listed in no particular order of priority:

Sole traders: These are businesses that have a single owner who also takes all the major managerial decisions. Operations are usually on a small scale, and typical examples are an electrician, the local news agent and hairdresser. The main reason why accounts are prepared for the sole trader is to help establish the amount of income tax due to the Inland Revenue. He/she makes little use of accounting statements for business decisions. Instead these decisions are based on knowledge obtained as a result of direct contact with all aspects of business activity.

Partnerships: These exist where two or more individuals join together to undertake some form of business activity. The partners share between them ownership of the business and the obligation to manage its operations. Professional people, such as accountants, solicitors and doctors, commonly organize their business activities in the form of partnerships. Accounting statements are required as a basis for allocating profits between the partners and, again, for agreeing tax liabilities with the Inland Revenue.

Clubs and societies: There are many thousands of clubs and societies organized for recreational, educational, religious, charitable and other purposes. Members invariably pay an annual subscription and management powers are delegated to a committee elected by the members. The final accounts prepared for (usually large) societies, formed by registering with the Registrar of Societies, are often controlled by statute. Conventional accounting procedures are sometimes ignored in a small organization. Reasons for this are lack of expertise, the meager quantity of assets belonging to the organization and the fact that the accounts are of interest only to the members.

Limited companies: A limited company is formed (registering) under the Companies Act. The directors of all limited companies are under a legal obligation to prepare and publish accounts, at least once in every year, which comply with the requirements of the Companies Act.

Major Classification of AIS

Accounting information system (AIS) within many companies consist of two major components — financial accounting and managerial accounting. Both of these components can be discussed from the viewpoint of their information-providing functions. An important objective of financial accounting is to process efficiently a company's business transactions so that informative financial statements (e.g., the income statement and the balance sheet) can be prepared. Therefore, within our discussion of financial accounting, we can review the accounting cycle activities that enable organizations to process their business transactions. The very purpose of financial accounting information is to provide relevant decision-making information to individuals and groups outside the organization. Financial statements are the major sources of financial accounting information. The field of managerial accounting typically encompasses three major areas:

1. Cost accounting;
2. Budgeting; and
3. Systems study.

It can be depicted as in the Figure 3.4.

The management accounting has as its prime objective providing relevant decision-making information to a company's management, principally the management. The cost information, estimated information and current information can be had from each component of management accounting information system.

Financial Accounting Information

The major objective of financial accounting is to provide relevant decision-making information to individuals and groups outside the organisation's boundaries. Of course, individuals within a company such

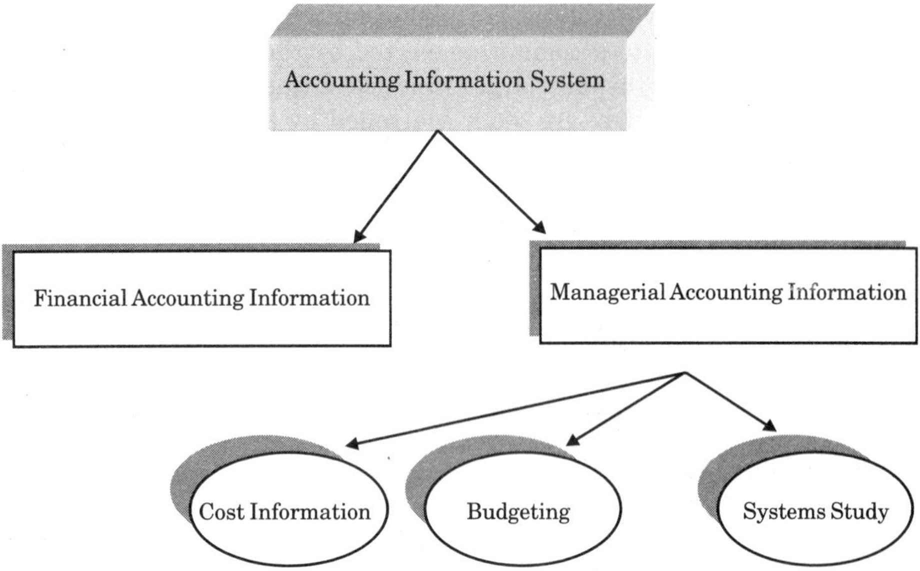

Fig. 3.4: **Classification of AIS**

as the managerial employees also utilize financial accounting information in their decision making endeavours. The external parties include federal and state tax agencies, current and potential investors, and creditors. Financial accounting's objective is achieved principally through the preparation of periodic financial statements like, income statement, balance sheet, retained earnings statement of changes in financial position, etc.

The basic inputs to the financial accounting structure are transactions measured in monetary terms. An audit trail of accounting transactions is maintained within a company's system which enables one to follow the flow of data that moves through the system. A model company's financial accounting audit trail is reflected in Figure 3.5. Upon inputting the relevant data from source documents into the financial accounting structure, these documents are filed for possible later reference and use in preparing financial reports. The processing-of-transactions function encompasses recording journal entries from the source documents, posting these entries to general and subsidiary ledgers, and preparing a trial balance from the general ledger account balances. If a company has an electronic data processing subsystem, this subsystem will handle the processing function. Thus, the journal entries and the ledger account balances information are maintained on computer storage devices (punched cards, magnetic tape, magnetic disk, or some other media). Through computer programmes the company's financial statements are prepared and printed out periodically as are any other desired output reports. A good audit trail within the company's financial accounting information system permits a manager to follow any source document data from the initial input stage to the data's location on an output report. This following of data through a system is possible because an effectively developed audit trail means that people within the system thoroughly understand the methods and procedures for accumulating and processing data. As a result, an individual is able to reconstruct how data were handled by the system.

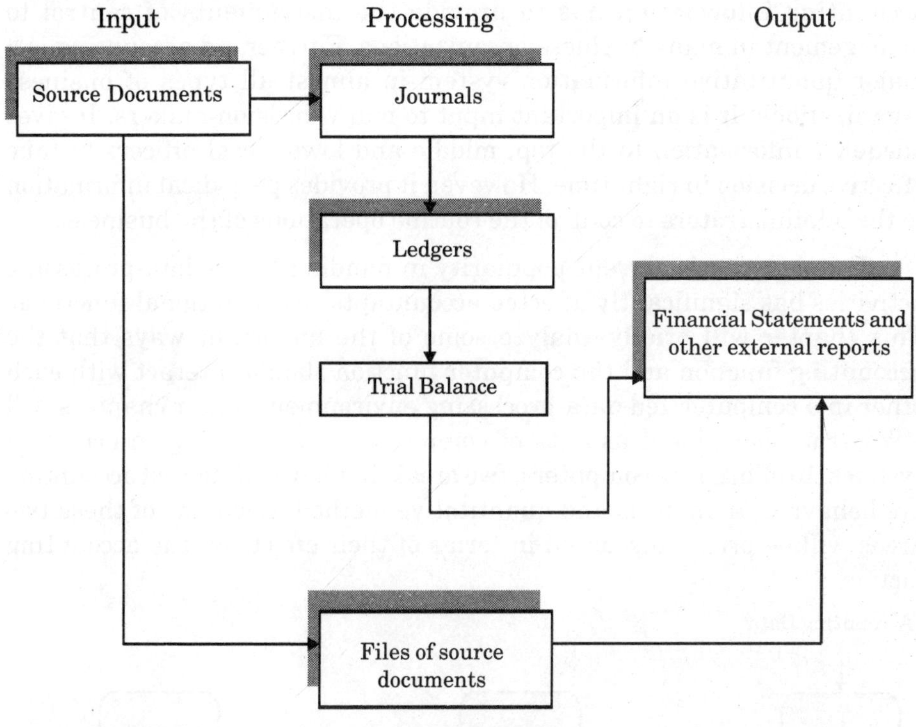

Fig. 3.5: **A Financial Accounting Audit Trail**

Concept and Significance of AIS

The accounting function has an important role in the successful operation of today's business world. This function centers on providing relevant decision-making information to individuals and groups both within and outside of a company's system.

Generally, the functions of accounting have been to record, analyze and to report the result of business organization to the management. The basic accounting system compiles the fundamental data for both financial accounting and management accounting. An effective accounting system provides a large number of tools for analyzing and solving a managerial problem. With accounting information management can plan future operations, control key variables, decide among alternative courses of action and analyze past performance.

Accounting has developed itself into an effective management tool from mere passive record-keeping function. In early days, the accountants were looked upon as mere record keepers or ledger-keepers. With the increasing of volume of business transactions, increasing competition and economic utilization of resources, the accounting information has become necessary to monitor continuously and to control the organization. Therefore, the accounting information has to provide the instruments of control to management in many business organizations. Further, an accounting is a major quantitative information system in almost all types of business organizations. It is an important input to many decision-makers. It gives adequate information to the top, middle and lower level officers to take effective decision in right time. However, it provides periodical information to the administrators to control the routine operations of the business.

The computer's current popularity in handing firms' data-processing activities has significantly affected accountants' organizational functions. This chapter will briefly analyze some of the important ways that the accounting function and the computer function should interact with each other in a computerized data-processing environment. Later chapters will stress the operational aspects of computerized accounting information systems. In addition to computers, two areas that have influenced accounting are behavioural analysis and quantitative method. Each one of these two areas will be briefly discussed in terms of their effects on the accounting faction.

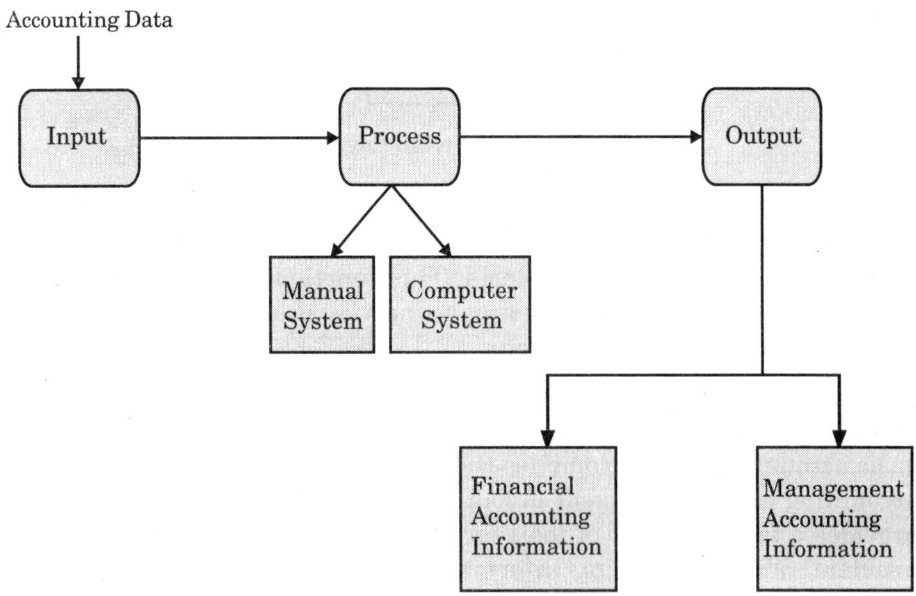

Fig. 3.6: **Accounting data processing system**

For example, the Alan Company's electronic data-processing subsystem may perform an analysis of customer product preferences based upon input data accumulated by the marketing subsystem. The resultant information from this analysis should aid the marketing subsystem in planning the future sales promotion efforts. This market report represents processed information from the Alan Company's management information system, but is beyond the scope of the accounting information system.

The accountants must understand the capabilities and limitations of their company's computer in order to accumulate and classify the accounting data in a suitable form for subsequent computer processing. On the other hand, electronic data-processing employees must understand the processing needs of the accounts so that they can design adequate computer files for storing the accounting data and to enable them to write suitable computer programmes which prepare information reports containing the relevant accounting data for decision-making.

Upon completion of the computerized processing of an accounts receivable aging analysis report, for example, the accountants obtain this report and deliver it to credit and collection department managers for their analysis. Under a manual data-processing system (as discussed above), the accountants normally spend so much of their time in processing accounting data that they often do not participate in the analysis of their communicated report data. With a computerized data-processing system, however, the accountants are relived of many time-consuming processing activities (such as recording and posting journal entries, determining general ledger account balances, and preparing trial balances) and typically become directly involved in the analysis of accounting report data.

Advantages of Accounting Information System (AIS)

The following are advantages of AIS:

- It provides useful information for making decisions.
- It serves primarily those users who have limited authority, ability or resources to obtain information and who rely on financial statements as their principal source of information about an enterprise's economic activities.
- It provides information useful to investors and creditors for predicting, comparing and evaluating potential cash flows in terms of amount, timing and related uncertainties.
- It supplies information useful in judging the management's ability to utilize enterprise resources effectively in achieving primary enterprise goals.

- It provides users with factual and interpretive information about transactions and other events which are useful for predicting, comparing and evaluating the enterprise's earning power.

Managerial Approach to AIS — AIS and Related Disciplines

The discipline of Accounting Information System (AIS) can be studied from a managerial point of view. This view is eclectic, supportive of business administration, and holistic. It combines practice, education, and theory to provide multi-focus insights into the discipline. It also combines business-related issues with information and communication as well as information and communication technology-related (ICT) issues. Moreover, it bridges the gap between strategy formulation and strategy implementation. The context of AIS is depicted in Figure 3.7. There are four main themes: management, internal control, accounting, and information & communication technology.

Management	Internal Control	Accounting	ICT

Fig. 3.7: **Managerial Approach to AIS**

Within the context as sketched, the AIS form a managerial viewpoint includes:

- AIS increasingly provides the information for managerial decision-making;
- An in-depth understanding of how AIS is developed is relevant to managers, so an accountant's or information system developer's approach only causes information overload. Auditors and accountants, in general, must think like managers to be able to add value and, hence, maintain their competitive advantage in an increasingly competitive market.
- Not only general managers but also information managers must understand their role toward AIS.
- Controllers must be able to bridge the gap between workforce and strategic management by entering the data on workforce into AIS.
- Management is responsible for the internal control system, which is an important element of any AIS.

AIS may be considered a discipline as well as a collection of systems. Usually, this distinction is made implicitly and does not lead to confusion between the definition and its context is self-explanatory. However, AIS is collection of systems as well as a discipline. AIS relates to several more elementary disciplines of which accounting and administrative organization (AAO), internal control (IC), managerial information provision (MIP), and information systems (IS) are the main ones (see Figure.3.8).

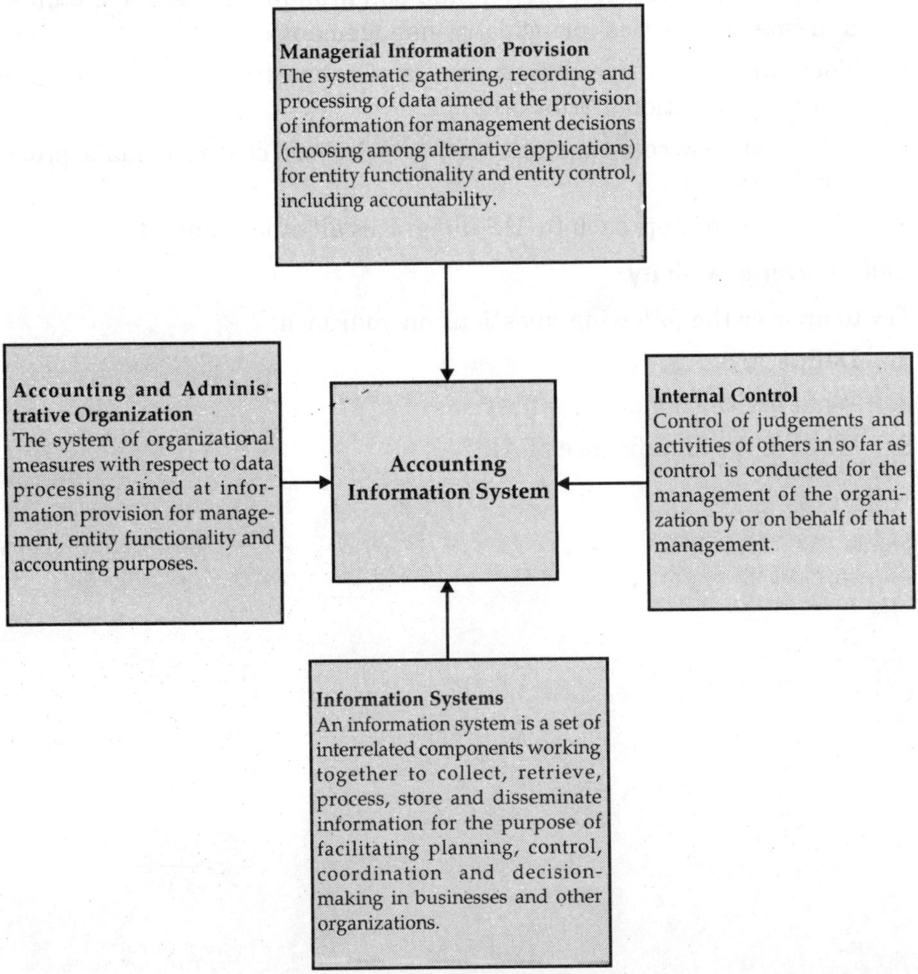

Fig. 3.8: **AIS and Related Disciplines**

There is a strong relationship between accounting and administrative organization, internal control, and managerial information provision. By designing an accounting and administrative organization an adequate information provision can be realized which allows us to improve the quality of decision-making and to get organizations under control. Hence, accounting and administrative organization, internal control and managerial information provision are strongly inter-wined.

Summary

- An organizational component, which accumulates, classifies, processes, analyzes, and communicates, relevant financial-oriented, decision-making information to a company's external parties (such as federal and state tax agencies, current and potential investors, and creditors) and internal parties (principally management).
- There are qualitative characteristics of accounting information based on the information attributes.
- AIS provides accounting information to decision centres to make proper timely decisions.
- Management approach to AIS integrates all other subsystems.

Self-Learning Activity

Try to answer the following questions on your own:

1. Define AIS.
2. What are the major classifications of AIS?
3. What is the significance of AIS?

CHAPTER 4

Accounting Cycle and Accounting Information System

Financial Statements provide useful decision-making information to current and potential investors, creditors management, and so on, regarding the periodic operating success of a company (reflected by the income statement), the financial condition of a company as of a specific date (reflected by the balance sheet), and the periodic sources as well as uses of working capital (reflected by the statement of changes in financial position). In order to obtain the monetary amounts for their financial statements organizations must maintain a record-keeping system on a day-to-day basis. This record-keeping system, in effect, transforms data that are generated by a company's day-to-day business transactions (e.g., selling merchandise, purchasing inventory, and paying liabilities into meaningful information for communication to external parties (as well as the company's management). This record-keeping or data transformation process is called the accounting cycle. Each one of the accounting cycle steps are now examined. The discussions will stress the information providing aspects of these accounting cycle steps.

Step 1

Preparing Transaction Source Documents

An accounting "business transaction" results from any monetary event, which causes a change in an asset, liability, owners' equity, revenue, or expense account. Remember, separate accounts are maintained in an organization for every monetary item so that information is available regarding the money balances of these individual financial items—the balance of cash, the balance of accounts receivable, the balance of notes payable, and so on. Transaction can occur from business activities between a company and either some external party to the company (e.g., when a company sells goods to a customer) or an internal party within the company (e.g., when a company pays its employees their salaries). For a business transaction to enter an organization's accounting information, the transaction must be of a quantitative nature and also be measurable in monetary terms. The source documents like receipts, vouchers, invoice, bill, etc., must be prepared and arranged in a manner to enter or record them in respective records as accounting information.

Step 2

Recording Transactions

Upon collecting accounting data on a source document, the data are then recorded in a company's journal. The purpose of maintaining a journal within an accounting information system is to enable an organization to keep a chronological record of the economic activities (measured in monitory terms) that occur throughout the business life. Many organizations have a large volume of monitory transactions occurring during their accounting periods. Normally, these transactions can be classified within a few broad categories/headings. The classification of transactions by categories permits the firm's accounting information systems to process efficiently the hundreds/ thousands of monitory events that take place during various accounting periods.

Step 3

Posting Journal to the General Ledger

Posting business transactions from the journal to the general ledger can be determined by an individual account balance. Within an accounting system a general ledger is a 'book' containing detailed monitory information about an organization's various assets and liabilities, owners equity, revenues and expenses. Without information available to both external and internal parties regarding money balances of the firms many assets and liabilities and so on, successful business performance would be difficult to achieve the business goals.

Journal provides a chronological record of monitory events acquiring in a company and indicates that the accounts and amounts of the debits and credits for every transactions. This process of transforming individual debits and credits from journal entries to their personal accounts within the general ledger is called "*Posting*".

Step 4

Preparing a Trial Balance

According to the accounting information requirements, company prepares the trial balance and financial statements periodically (i.e., monthly, quarterly, half-yearly, and yearly). Because income taxes, both federal and state, must be paid to the government every year. A firm must prepare financial statements at least once in a year as a basis for computing its tax liability. These account balances are computed as financial schedule called a *Trial Balance.*

A trial balance consist of a list of all general ledger accounts together with their end of period balances of a company. The trail balance facilitates in two ways.

1. The determination of whether the total debit and total credit accounts are equal one.
2. The preparation of company's financial statements periodically.

Step 5

Recording Adjusting Entries in a Journal

After finishing the trial balance of the accounting period some balances represent the accounting balances at the end of the specific period. These adjustment entries will be adjusted while preparing financial statement. They are:

(a) Prepaid expenses, e.g. insurance premium

(b) Income received in advance, e.g. rent received (company building for one year advance)

(c) Advance payment to employees, e.g. salary advance

(d) Depreciation on furniture

Step 6

Posting Adjusting Entries

The adjustment items will be carried out in both statements of final accounts and balance sheet. In the final accounts, the income and expenditure statement, the current year adjustment items will be recorded in the expenses side as well as income side. For example, the depreciation of the buildings and furniture amount of the adjustment will be recorded in the loss side of the income and expenditure statement.

In the balance sheet the adjustment entries will be recorded in both assets and liability sides. If the adjustment entry is a liability one or asset one we have to make the entry according to the headings. For example, the furniture depreciation amount has been recorded in the expenditure/loss side of the income and expenditure statement, the same amount will be deducted from the furniture/buildings in the asset side of the balance sheet. That is the actual furniture or building value as on date.

The next two steps of the accounting cycle will be the internal checking of accounting department with adjustment entries. The last step is post closing trial balance.

The Figures 4.1 and 4.2 present the picture of accounting cycle and the flow of accounting information.

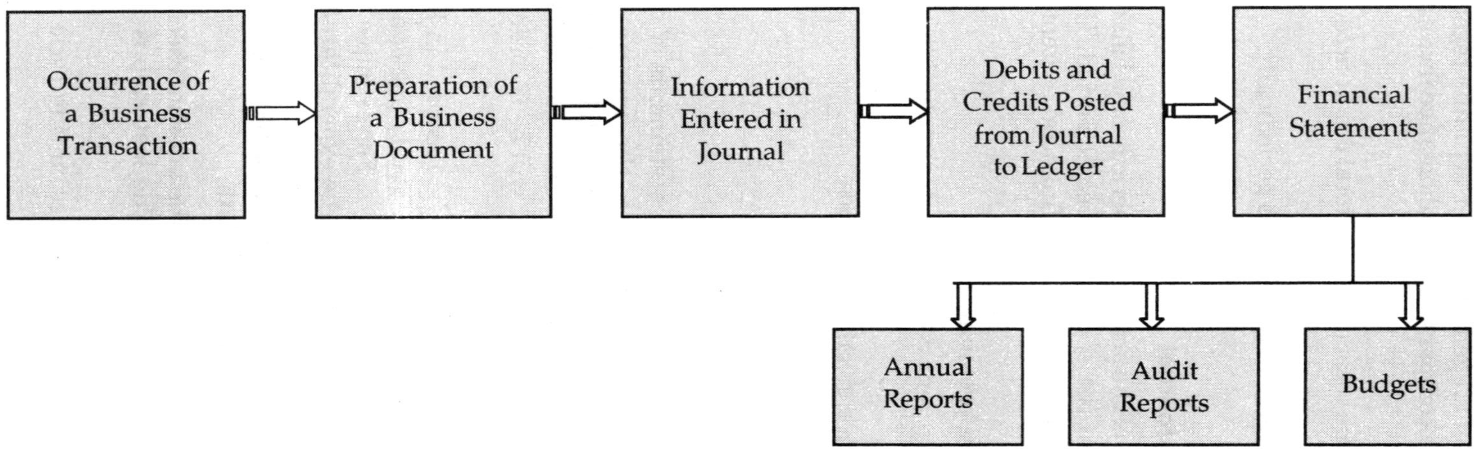

Fig. 4.1: **Accounting Information Flow through Accounting System**

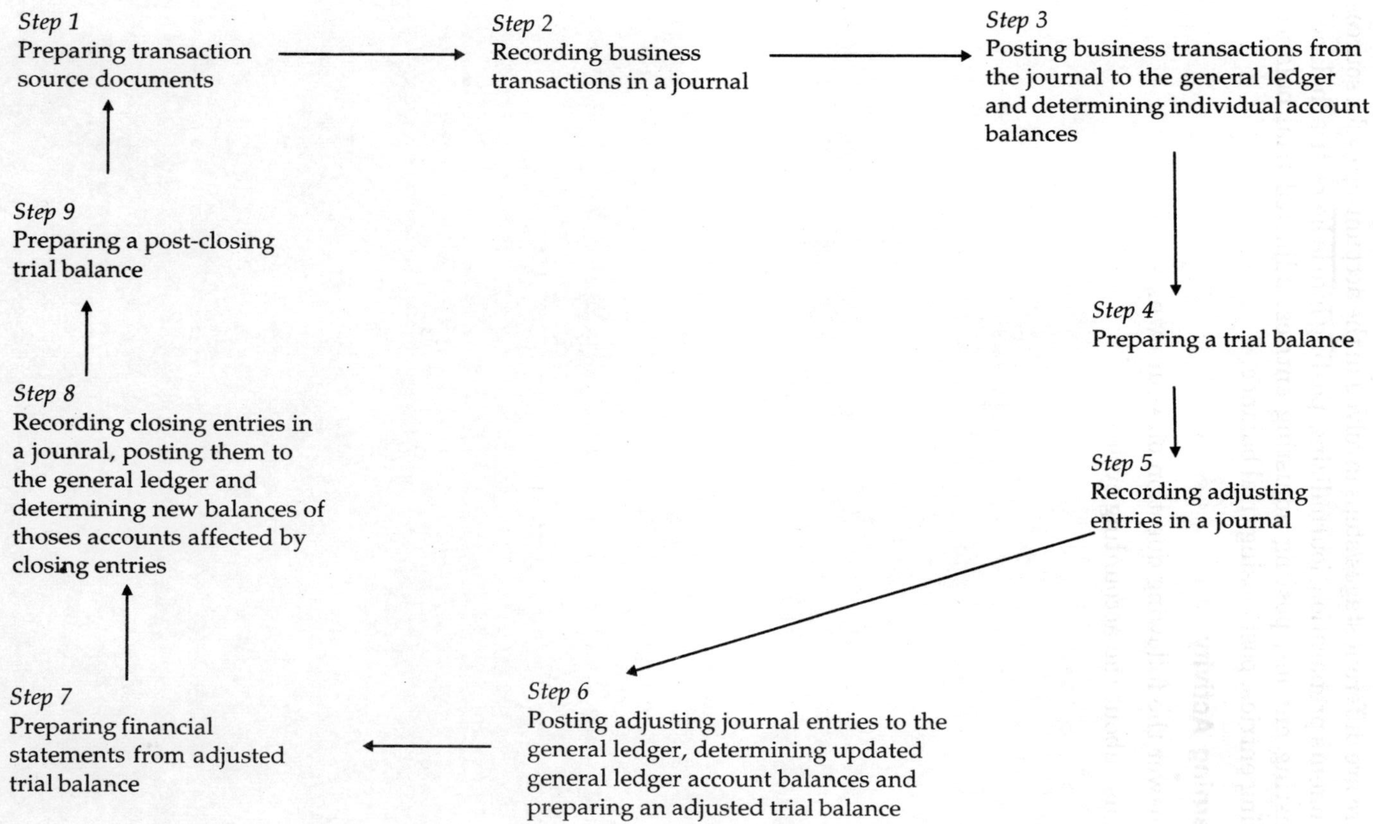

Fig. 4.2: **Steps involved in accounting cycle**

Summary

- There are different stages/steps involved in the accounting cycle: sources documents preparation, journalizing, posting into ledgers, trial balance, adjusting entries, posting adjusting entries, adjusted trial balance, closing entries, post closing trial balance.

Self-Learning Activity

Try to answer the following question on your own:

1. Discuss about the accounting cycle?

CHAPTER 5 Accounting Information System and Accounting Professionals

Accounting information system (AIS) being a separate system in a business organization has its own organization. The accounting professionals (accounting information officers) are performing their duties and responsibilities based on their nature of work to be done in the system of recording, analyzing, processing and reporting the accounting information to the needy persons within and outside the organization. The financial manager (accounting information officer/manager) is generally overall incharge of the finance and accounting activities. Two officers — Treasurer and Controller – work under his direct supervision and control. The functions of treasurer and the controller are discussed below.

Functions of Treasurer

- Managing the firm's funds.
- Forecasting and planning the financial needs.
- Administering the flow of cash, managing credit, raising funds by floating securities and securing loans.
- Maintaining relations with financial institutions and safeguarding securities and funds.

Functions of Controller

Being the chief accounting officer (other titles are: management accountant, chief accountant, head of accounting, chief cost and works accountant) the functions of controller *are:*

- management and control of the firm's resources;
- providing information to formulate business policies and for taking business decisions.

The main functions of an accounting professional (management accountant, financial manager, accountant) is to provide required information to formulate accounting policies and costing policies, preparation of financial reports, direction of internal auditing, budgeting, inventory control, taxes, etc. The accounting professional by supplying accounting information enables the manager in performing the managerial functions of planning and control, and utilizes the accounting information in solving problems that the management frequently confronts in managing the firm's internal operations.

The accounting professionals are responsible for:

- accumulating financial and decision-making information;
- classifying such accumulated information;
- processing accounting information by following certain criteria/norms;
- analyzing economic information; and
- communicating/reporting the processed accounting information to the decision centres to make business decisions on time.

Apart from these, the accounting information professionals are expected to gather, process and communicate the following accounting and decision-making information to the needy personnel in and outside the organization:

- cost information regarding production, human resources, marketing, materials, and other related resources;
- revenue information regarding sales, income from all other sources;
- profit/loss information; and
- all other required accounting and financial information for the internal parties and external parties.

Accountants and Accounting Information System

Financial Management

The financial executive is a relative newcomer to the business scent. While some of the larger companies such as DuPont, General Motors, General Electric, and others may have a history of more than fifty years of financial controls, the area of financial management has substantial programmes in the last few decades.

In the early part of this century, most companies had a treasure and the larger companies may have had a controller, but more than likely a head bookkeeper, chief clerk, or chief accountant. Most of the work at that time consisted of the daily routine of billing, payables, timekeeping, payrolls, and the general ledger. Some companies had cost accounting systems, but not all of these were tied into the books of account and consequently were not as effective as they might have been. Budgetary control and performance reporting were yet to come in most companies.

As the analytical values of accounting techniques came to the more understood and appreciated, many companies hired a controller, often from a public accounting background, to handle the growing amount of information processing and to develop the use of internal management reports and other useful applications such as standard cost accounting and budgetary control. The Controllers Institute of America was established in 1931 with membership limited to those companies of sufficient size that a real controllership function existed rather than in name only. Many years later, the name of this organization was changed to Financial Executives Institute to recognize the changes that were taking place in the finance function.

Finance Function

In the earlier days there was a noticeable amount of confusion between titles and functions. Today it is clearly understood that there are two distance parts to the finance function. One of these parts reports to the treasurer and the other part to the controller. In most large companies, these two individuals would report to a financial management. The financial management functions are viewed by the financial executives institute as illustrated in the Figures 5.1 and 5.2.

TREASURERSHIP

The treasurer, as the name implies, has custody of the liquid assets of the company and the responsibility to see that there are sufficient funds on hand at all times to keep the company in business and operating at a profitable level. In a narrow sense this is a custodianship function, but in actuality there is a much larger function that is performed by a treasurer.

The capital needs of the company have to be met by the treasurer as they develop. Cash forecast and provided for through negotiations with investment bankers or stockholders must foresee long-term financing, either by debt or equity. Working capital requirements would involve arrangements with commercial banks or other lending institutions. To facilitate these arrangements at the proper time requires an extensive programme to see that financial analysts and investment bankers receive the type of information that will enable them to judge the effectiveness of company operations.

The routine daily operations require the treasurer to maintain bank accounts with as many banks as necessary and to oversee cash receipts and cash disbursements. To have the money in the right place at the right time without paying excessive interest charges requires a suitable cash management programme with cash transfers and lockboxes to handle cash collections expeditiously. Cash funds not required immediately can be invested in treasury bills and often can be invested overnight or over weekends in treasury repurchase agreements.

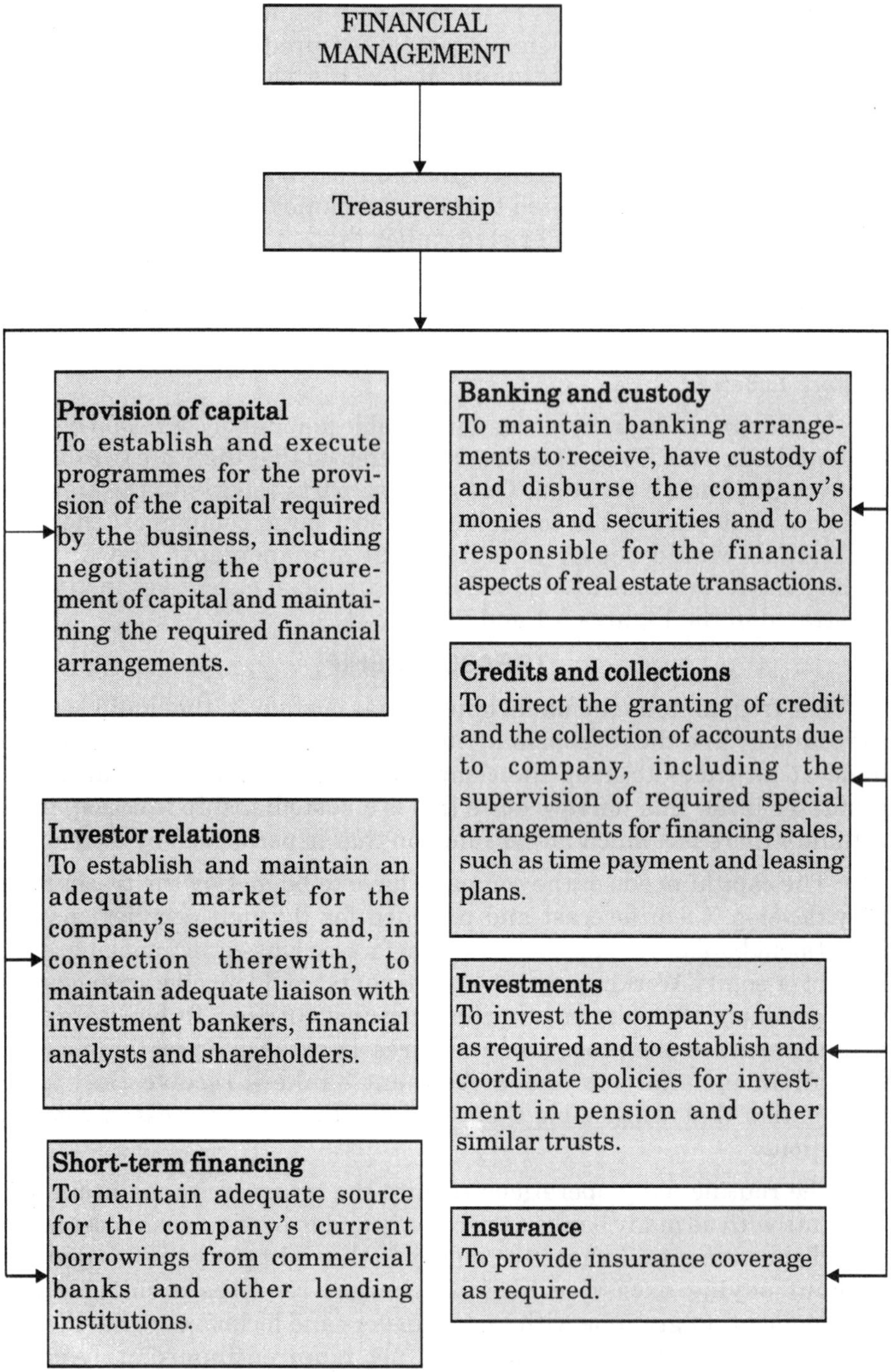

Fig. 5.1: **Financial Management and Treasurership**

The granting of credit to customers on a thirty-day account basis, or for longer periods in the case of installment sales or leases, would normally be supervised by the treasurer who would also have to see that the funds were available or could be obtained for the purpose.

Insurance coverage on the various assets of the company at or near the current replacement cost would also be an important function of the treasurer. This requires accurate property records to provide information not only for the insurance but also in case of claims. In addition, there are various types of liability and risks to be dealt with that can keep an insurance manager quite busy.

CONTROLLERSHIP

The management executive responsible for the accounting records and information is the controller who is vitally concerned with the systems design in the area of responsibility, is the constructive development of a comprehensive financial information system responsibility, for this system is unique in that all of the functions of the business are involved. The out put of the information system is dependent upon data that must be obtained and processed in other functional areas. The information system does not know the organization boundaries of some other areas, for example, the system for processing a sales order usually involves the sales department, inventory control and warehousing, the shipping department, the credit department, the billing department and accounts receivable. The order must be processed through different department before the data necessary for systems design to be implemented throughout the organization not just within the controller own department, is a unique requirement that calls for a depth of understanding and experience on the part of the controller and the systems analyst.

Planning for Control

The controller has the responsibility of profit planning, budgetary control, standard cost accounting performance measurement and other such activities that can aid management in the control of operations. The controller would also be responsible for any forecasts or projections of data in to the future.

The controller has the primary responsibility of reports showing the results of operations and is expected to interpret these results to members of the management team and to the stockholders or owners. This would mean the preparation of reports showing performance against the operating plans and evaluating the results and consulting with the interested parties as to what might be done to improve future results.

The controller is also responsible for filing the tax returns and other necessary reports required by government agencies as well as seeing to it that the assets of the company are responsibly maintained.

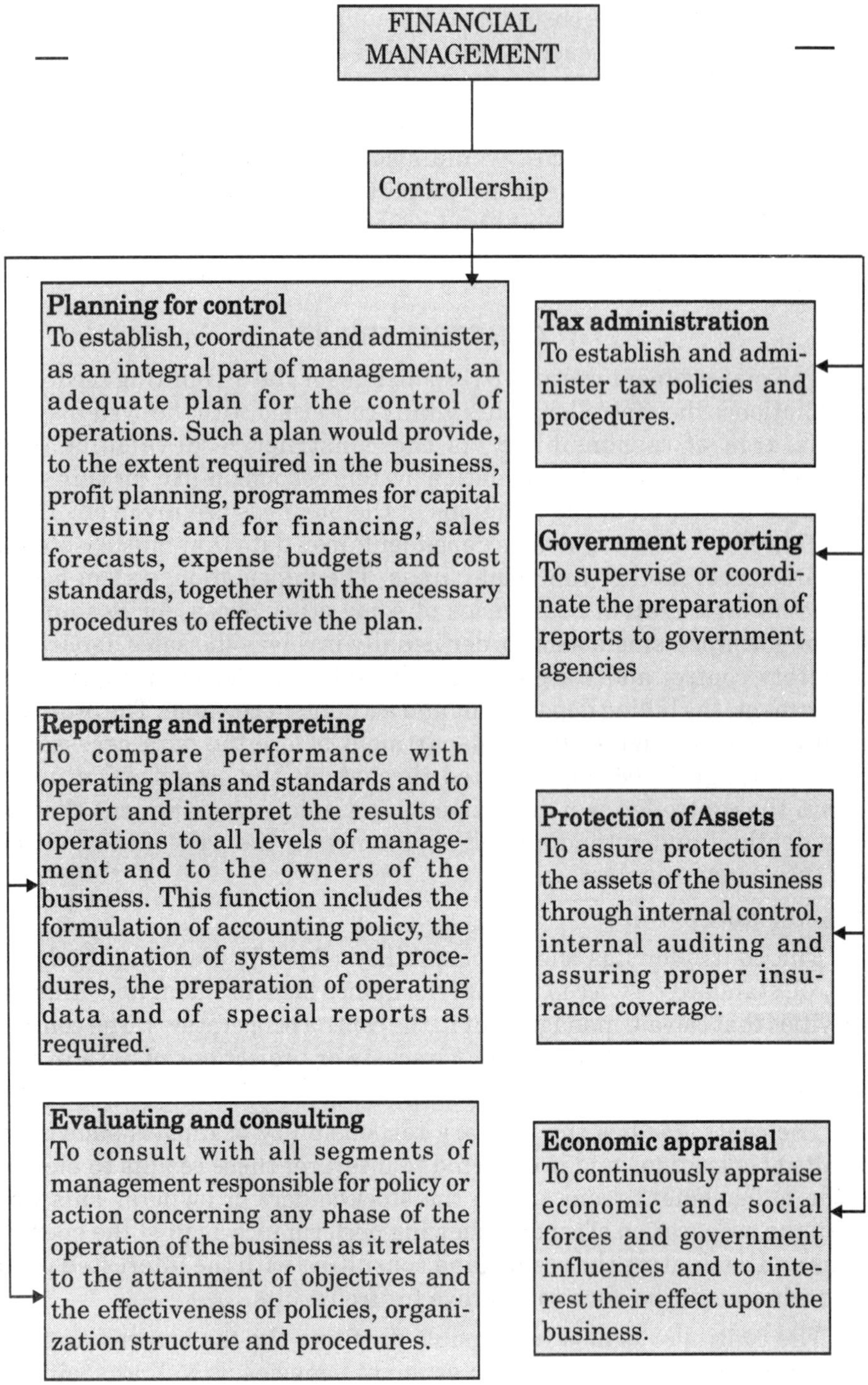

Fig. 5.2: **Financial Management and controllership**

It is clear that the controller has the major responsibility for the information system and while practice varies in different companies more often that not the controller will be in charge of data processing. This usually works out well as the controller is the one who knows just what information is really required to controller activities and is also familiarly with the concept of internal control so as to minimize error and fraud in the company records.

Accounting Information Functional

In a single plant company the activities performed with in the controllers department will generally fall in to the same line and staff relationships as exist for the company as a whole. The complete controller departments are a staff department yet within the department the line and staff activities are apparent. The line activities are those relating to the accomplishment of the major objectives of the department while the staff activities are those that are advisory in nature or that provide generally service as to the controller. In the typical single plant controllers organization the staff functions that exist are dependent upon the needs of the business concerned. An organization chart of a controller department in a single plant concern could be as shown in Figure 5.3.

More staff functions are shown in the illustration than might exist in a single plant concern to show the type of activity that could be accomplished in a given situation. The staff activities that might exist in a specific situation would depend on the needs of the concern.

In multidivisional companies, there will normally be several levels of controllership, for example, in Ford Motor Company there are a number of divisions such as the Ford Division the Tractor division and the Lincoln Mercury division. Within each division there are a number of separate manufacturing and assembly plants, at each level controllership activities are preformed.

The various levels of controllership could be organized according to a number of different patterns. Three such patterns are illustrated in Figure 5.4 and it can be noted that the authority relationships differ in the three illustrates.

Each of the relationship can be fond in actual practice, along with many others. In part (a) of Figure 5.4 each controller is responsible to the line management at each level for workload, salary determination, and promotional opportunities. In part (b) such determinations are made through the controller's department, while part (c) of Figure 5.4 represents a combination of the previous patterns. It seems obvious that the use of staff services by each level of management would be different and that the development of the information system would also be different.

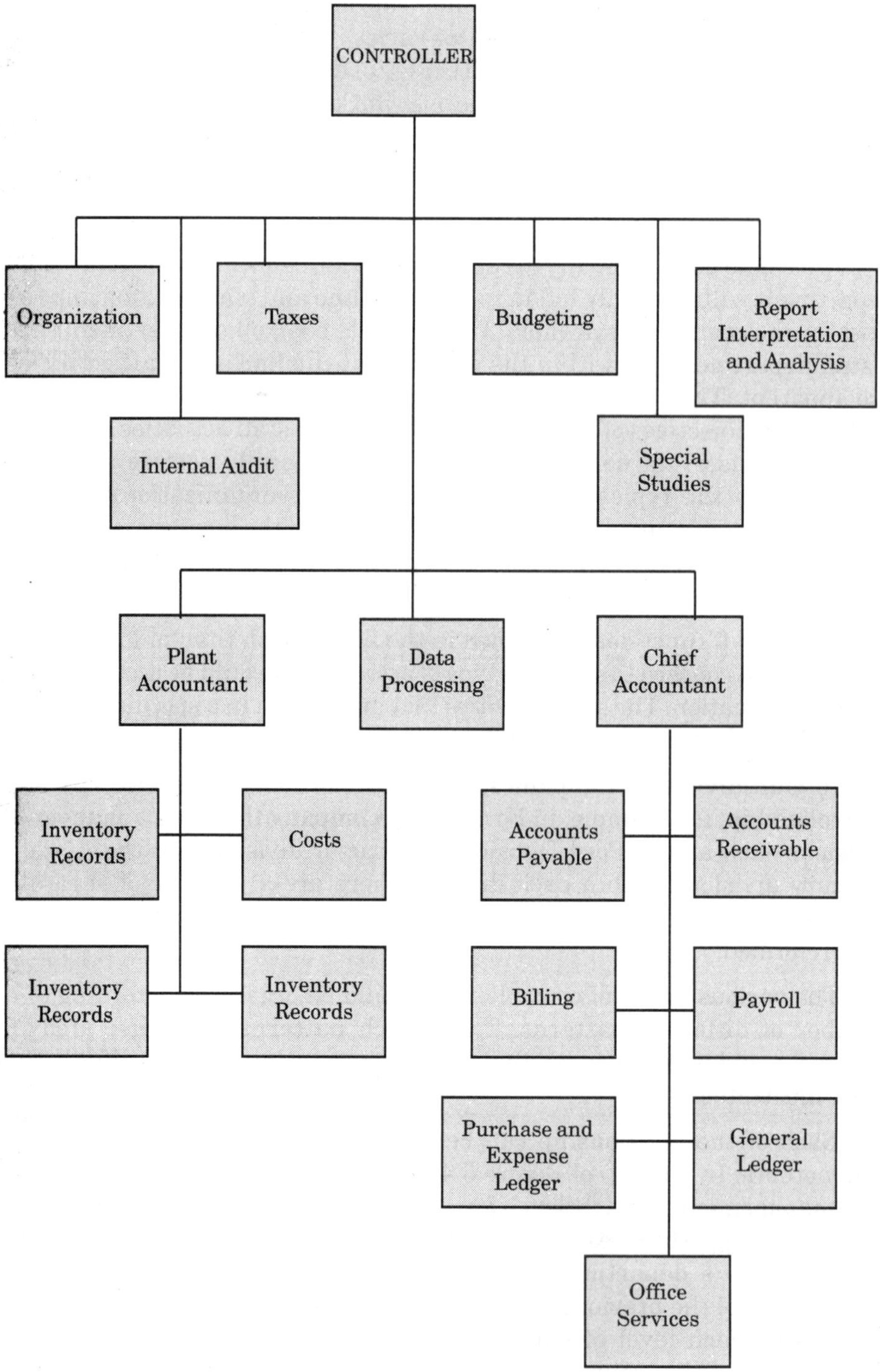

Fig. 5.3: **Single-Plant Controller's Organization**

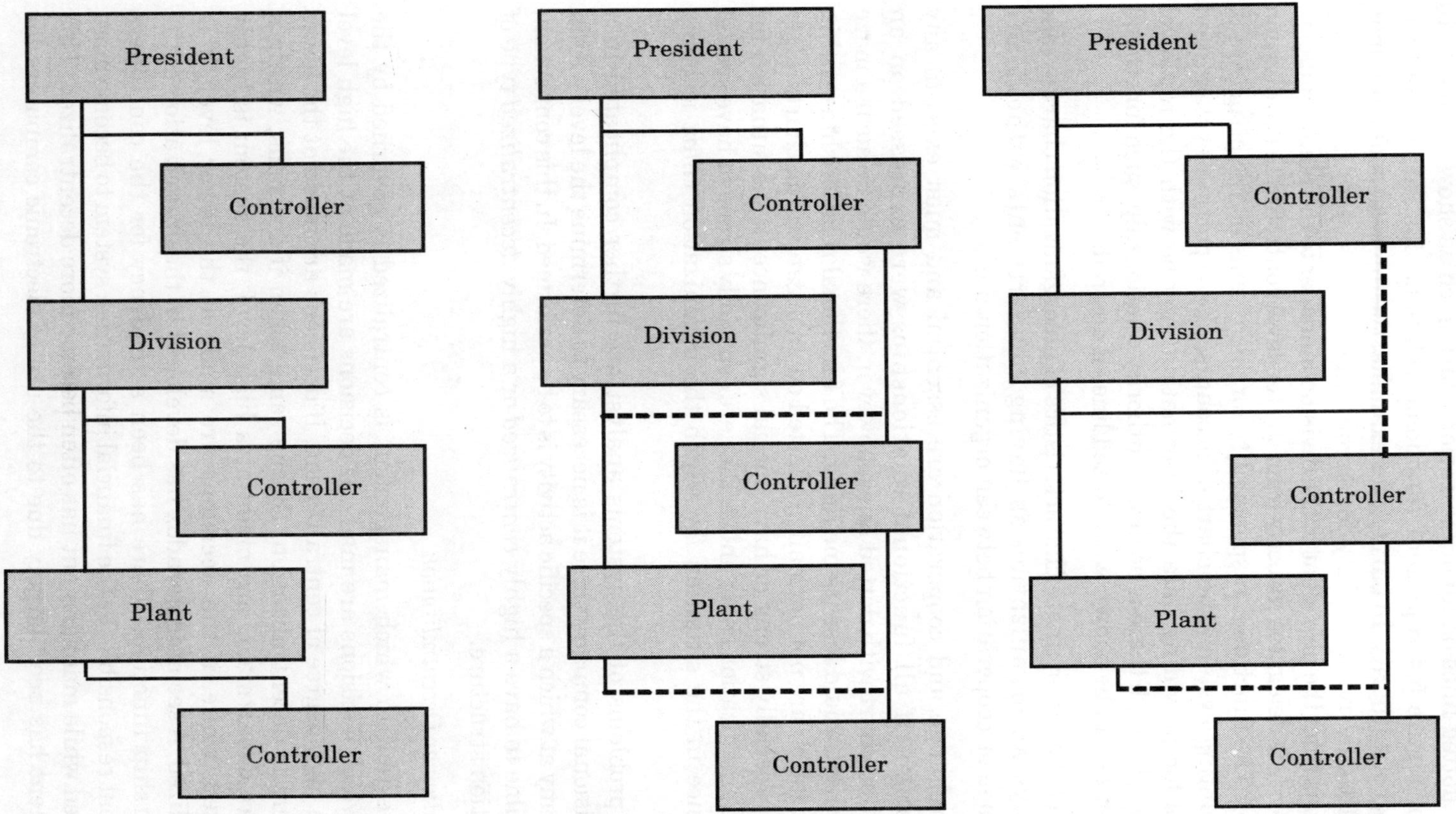

(a) Decentralized *(b) Centralized* *(c) Semi-centralized*

Fig. 5.4: **Controllership Function**

The dotted lines on an organization chart, such as shown in parts (b) and (c) of Figure 5.4 represent functional relationships rather than the delegation of authority. In part (c), for example, the top level controller may have functional responsibility for accounting matters, yet the authority delegated is from the president to the division manager to the plant manager. No authority is delegated directly from the top level controller to the division controller. The functional responsibility for such items as the structure of the accounting system, the chart of accounts, the reporting system, and deadlines for providing data the information may be with the top level controller. Although there is no direct authority relationship; such functional relationships can be shown with dotted lines if desired.

One of the unfortunate characteristics of an organization chart is that it portrays an organization as having compartments without any interchange or cooperation between organization units.

Interchange and cooperation are essential and must exist in any organization. If all functional relationships were expressed on an organization chart with dotted lines, however, there would be such a maze that the chart would lose its meaning. The functional relationships within an organization are not normally reflected on an organization chart unless they are especially strong or have special significance in the situation for which the organization chart unless they are especially strong or have special significance in the situation for which the organization chart is being prepared.

The problems of the systems analyst are further complicated in a multidivisional company since it is necessary to determine the level within the company at which a specific activity is to be performed. In this connection, it is possible to have a highly *centralized* or a highly *decentralized* type of organization structure.

Centralization or Decentralization

The extent to which management is centralized is governed by the level at which decisions are made. If decisions are made at the high level there is a high degree of centralization. If decisions are made at the lower level, there is decentralization. By the same token if decisions, within a controllers department, are made at a high level, the system is highly centralized, while, if the decisions are made at the lower level, it is decentralized. A seeming paradox has developed in the organization of the controllership function. There has been a tendency for the controllers department responsible for the financial information system to become more centralized while management has often become more decentralized. This development has been largely due to the use of electronic computers for major segments of processing and the combining of the facilities in which work is actually performed. Thus the controllership function can be centralized while management is in fact becoming more decentralized.

There is no standard that can be used to determine the level within a multidivisional company at which the various information processing procedures should be accomplished. Generally speaking, however, the major processing installation should be at the lowest level to which authority for profits has been delegated. The managers with profit responsibility must have complete information with which to plan and control. Information must be in the context and of the quality that will suit them. For example, assume that in part (a) of Figure 5.4 the high so that a major processing center could be economically possible, thus the major accounting institution would exist there with data transmission equipment available to obtain the necessary data from the plants each day, such a system could be efficient and the plant level would be that amount necessary to obtain the data to send to the division. The activity at the home office level would be to provide staff coordination, to establish a reporting structure, to enable information consolidation and interpretation and to provide such staff services as might be necessary in the situation to service each division. For example, the tax and internal audit functions may be at the home office level.

Controllership Structure Standards

Standards for the organization of the controllers department provide and excellent basis for measuring the adequacy of its structure. These standards relate to planning interpretation, clerical activities internal auditing and asset custody.

Planning

Planning and improvement activities within the controllers department should be separated from line activities. Such activities as organization planning systems and procedure's special studies and budgeting are for the purpose of establishing and improving systems controls and administrative procedures. Hense responsibilities for these areas are delegated to line activities, almost automatically become secondary duties. The day-to-day operations must be completed before personnel are placed on planning and improvement projects. If planning and improvement activities are to revive the attention necessary they should be divorced from operations.

If the size of the organization does not warrant full time personnel for planning and improvement activities special provision should be made to free a qualities person or persons from their operating duties at specific periods during each year to make certain that the planning and improvement activity receives the proper attention.

Interpretation

The use and interpretation activities should be separated from line activities. Such activities as statically suites report analysis and interpretation are organized to use and interpret records and reports. As in the case of planning and improving activities use and interpretation is of such importance that proper performance cannot be left to the chance that the process of operating activities will preclude the necessary activity. The appropriate use and interpretation of data and information flowing from the system is the difference between an efficient management service and just another overhead cost of management.

The controller is in a key position in the organization and has the choice of limiting service to performing the basic clerical activity of compiling data or of providing a dynamic service in not only compiling but interpreting and presenting findings in non-technical language to other executives with constructive comments and, often, recommendations. The controller must be more than a figure accumulator as no individual is in a more position than the controller to provide an outstanding information service to other members of the management team, including the interpretation of the information that is in the reports that flow from the information system.

The highly mechanical nature of operating activities within parts of the Controller's Department serves to facilitate the application of this standard. Data processing personnel are becoming specialists in their own right, and many of them are technically oriented in the computer applications. Their concern is often more with equipment problems and concepts as compared to the use and interpretation of the data and information that they produce.

Clerical Activities

Major amounts of clerical help are often necessary to process the large volume of media passing through the controller's department. Just a few of the volume jobs that must be handled are accounts receivable, billing, disbursements, accounts payable, and payroll. The control of large volumes of media and posting large numbers of accounts are clerical activities similar in nature. Such activities are usually performed on electronic equipment. The technical aspect of performing the job is relatively simple, but an efficient routine to process and control the large volume must be established. Supervision of the operators who actually perform routine jobs is the major problem in accomplishing the activity once the procedure has been established. Problems of supervision are the same in all of the activities so that grouping the clerical activities together under one operating head can be effective.

In studying the controller's organization structure, it is important for the systems analyst to understand and conceptual differences between different clerical activities such as billing and accounts receivable. In most companies, the billing section is charged with the preparation of the customer's invoice for each sale, for issuing credit sent from the billing section to the accounts receivable section where the customer's account is posted, or where the copy becomes a part of the accounts receivable record, the billing section is responsible for the preparation and the mailing of the invoices and credit memoranda, while the accounts receivable section is responsible for the maintenance of the accounts receivable records and for preparing and sending out periodic statements mats of account.

Internal Auditing

The internal auditing activity should be assigned high enough in the organization structure so that audit recommendations can be implemented. The quality of internal audit work has improved greatly in recent years partly due to the effects of the institute of Internal Auditors to develop professional skills and continuing education for the benefit of their members. It is important for the internal auditors to participate in the systems development work to see that the proper controls are in place. If internal auditing is to be effective within a company, and include special investigations and management (operational) audit type of work, the auditors require professional training and the group should have a separate identity.

Asset Custody

Custodianship activities should not be under the jurisdiction of the controller. Physical control of assets such as cash, inventories, machinery, and equipment should be charged to an activity or function other than controllership. The organizational independence removes the asset being controlled from the function that is charged with the responsibility of providing the information for control.

Summary

- There are accounting professionals like treasurer, controller, or chief accounting officer in the structure. They have their own duties and responsibilities to discharge.

Self-Learning Activity

Try to answer the following questions on your own:

1. Describe the structure of accounting department.
2. What are the duties and responsibilities of accounting professionals?
3. What is the significance of AIS?

CHAPTER 6
Journal Information System

Journal Information—Recording of Accounting Information

The term business transaction means a business event, which can be expressed in money and must be recorded in the accounting records, for example, payment or collection of cash or purchase or sale of goods. A transaction has an accounting value and has an influence on the financial statements. Business transactions are evidenced by source documents such as a cheque, bills (sales and purchase activities). These source documents are the starting point for the flow of accounting information through the accounting system into the financial statements. It has been placed on the analysis of transactions in terms of debts and credits to ledger accounts. Although transactions could be entered directly in ledger accounts, it is much more convenient and efficient in a manual accounting system to record the information shown on business documents, first in a journal and later to transfer the debit and credits to ledger accounts.

Journal

The journal is a book of original entry, recorded in a day-by day activities in a systematic manner. The journal shows all information about a transaction in one place and also provides an explanation of the transactions (debit and credit). Further it provides a chronological record of all the events in the life of a business. The purpose of a journal helps to prevent errors. The process of recording a transaction in a journal is called journalizing the transaction. The accounting records are not an end in themselves. It communicates accounting information to persons who will use this information as basis for business.

The journal or book of original entry is a chronological (day-by-day) record, showing for each transaction the debit and credit changes caused in specific ledger accounts. At convenient intervals, the debit and credit entries recorded in the journal are transferred to the accounts in the ledger. The updated ledger accounts, in turn serve as the basis from which the balance sheet and other financial statements are prepared.

Journal Information

A journal is chronological record of accounting transactions showing the names of accounts that are to be debited or credited, the amounts of debits and credits, and any useful supplementary information about the transaction as given below:

1. The journal shows all information about a transaction in one place and also provides an explanation of the transaction. In a journal entry, the debits and credits for a particular transaction are recorded together, but when the transaction is recorded in the ledger, the debits and credits are entered in different accounts. The journal is the record, which shows the complete story of a transaction in one entry.
2. The journal provides a chronological record of all the events in the life of a business. If we want to look up the facts about a transaction of some myths or years back, all we need is the date of the transaction in order to locate it in the journal.
3. The journal helps to prevent errors. If transactions were recorded directly in the ledger, it would be very easy to make errors such as omitting the debits or credit or entering the debits twice or the credit twice. Such errors are not likely to be made in the journal. "LF" stands for ledger folio, which is the page reference to the ledger accounts where the entry is to be made. It indicates that the entries have been posted to the appropriate ledger accounts. They provide information about an audit trail, a way of tracing the amounts in the ledger back to their sources.

Journal Accounting Records

It is important to keep in mind that accounting records are not an end in themselves. The goal of the accounting is to communicate accounting information to persons who will use this information as a basis for business decisions. These persons include managers, owners, investors, creditors and government agencies looking into the future of a business involves much uncertainty, but the accumulating and interpreting of accounting information are vitally important elements of financial forecasting. The use of journals and ledgers along with the double entry system and the various symbols and technical terms, has developed over a long period of time, because these devices constitute an efficient information system. These information systems absorb each day the economic essence of many business transactions.

Information Available in a Journal

The manager would locate the journal page where the transaction was recorded, compare the transaction with the original source document (e.g., compare the amount of a recorded sales transaction with the field copy of the transaction sales invoices), check for correct posting of the transaction to the general ledger, and also check the mathematical accuracy of those general ledger account balances affected by the transaction. Thus, because all of the accounting work was performed with pencil and paper and could easily be seen by the human eye, the manager would have no difficulties following a transaction's audit trail through the accounting information system. When a company obtained a computer to handle its accounting transaction processing work, however, the processing activities (described above) associated with a business transaction would no longer be visible to the human eye. (The work of recording a journal entry, posting the entry, and determining up-dated general ledger account balances would all be performed internally) within the company's computer. Because the internal processing work performed by a computer cannot be observed visually by an individual, that company's manager would have a more difficult job tracing the audit trail of a specific accounting transaction. Thus a journal contains explicit information/instructions on the revenue and expense items to be recorded in the temporary accounts and the changes to be made to the balances in the permanent accounts. No account balance is ever changed except on the basis of a journal entry. The following journal format presents journal information.

Illustration for Journal Information:

XXX Company

Journal for the period ......

Date/month/year		A/c description	LF	Debit	Credit
Xx	X	Xxxxxxxx	X	Xxx	
		Xxxxx	X		Xxx
		(........................)			

Journal Information Processing and Distribution System

The following figure depicts a clear picture about the accounting information which is processed and distributed through journal system.

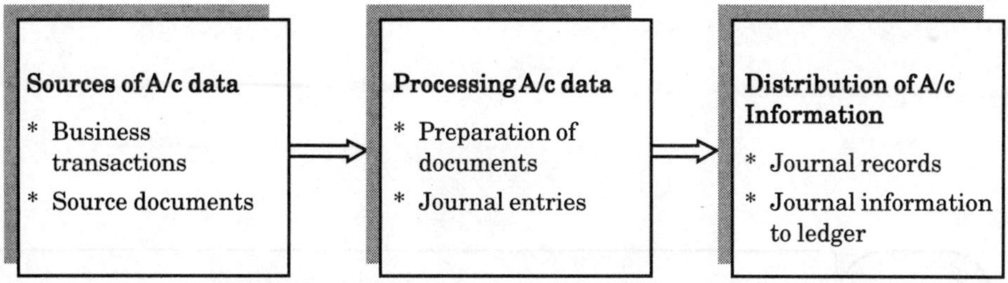

Summary

- The journal is a book of original entry, recorded in a day-by day activities in a systematic manner. The journal shows all information about a transaction in one place and also provides an explanation of the transactions (debit and credit).
- A journal is a chronological record of accounting transactions showing the names of accounts that are to be debited or credited, the amounts of debits and credits, and any useful supplementary information about the transaction.

Self-Learning Activity

Try to answer the following questions on your own:

1. Define a journal accounting information system.
2. What is the information available in a Journal?

CHAPTER 7

Ledger Information System

Ledger Information — Posting and Balancing of Accounting Information

General Ledger

The general ledger is the accounting record that contains information on each of the individual accounts for an entity's assets, liability, owner's equity, revenue and expenses. The general ledger information in the forms of various accounts is the needed information for the preparation of trial balance and general ledger information may expedite the preparation of financial statements.

Posting is the process of transferring the accounting data / information from journal to the appropriate general ledger accounts. Posting can be done daily, weekly, or monthly. In a computerized accounting system, the posting of transaction is often done simultaneously with the journalizing of transactions.

Balancing the accounts is done by the accountants after the posting is over. The balanced information for each account in the general ledger is the base accounting information for the preparation of trial balance at the end of an accounting period. For financial statement purpose, several account balances are often considered into one item. For example, if a company has a dozen cash accounts, the balances in those accounts would be added and the resulting total is listed on the balance sheet line item cash.

General Ledger Information

The following information can be known from the general ledger:

- In the date column of each account, the information about the date of the transaction can be known.
- A brief description of the transaction can be found in the explanation column.

- The amount of the transactions entered affecting each account is found in the initial debit and credit columns.
- Computed new balances of each account and the amount entered in either the debit and credit balance column is found.
- In the post reference column of each account, indicate the journal from which the amount was posted and the page number of that journal. (Post reference makes a transaction easier to trace. With this information available, error in accounting data can be corrected more easily).
- For each account included in the journal entry, information as recording in the post reference column of the general journal, the number of that account is indicated for the appropriate debit or credit amount was posted to that general ledger account.

The following is the format of a general ledger account showing accounting information.

Cash A/c				A/c No.101			
Date		Explanation	Post Reference	Debit	Credit	Balance	
						Debit	Credit
Xx	X	Xxxxxx	Xx	Xxx	Xxx	Xxx	Xxx
							Xxx

Ledger Information Processing and Distribution System

The following figure depicts a clear picture about the accounting information which is processed and distributed through ledger accounting system.

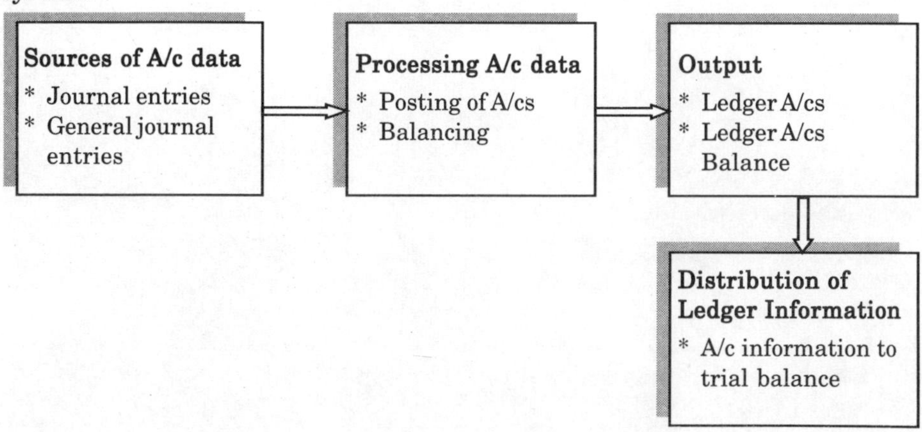

Summary

- The general ledger is the accounting record that contains information on each of the individual accounts for an entity's assets, liability, owner's equity, revenue and expenses.
- Posting is the process of transferring the accounting data / information from journal to the appropriate general ledger accounts.
- Balancing the accounts is done by the accountants after the posting is over. The balanced information for each account in the general ledger is the base accounting information for the preparation of trial balance at the end of an accounting period. For financial statement purpose, several account balances are often considered into one item.

Self-Learning Activity

Try to answer the following questions on your own:

1. Define a ledger accounting information system.
2. Explain a ledger information processing and distribution system.

CHAPTER 8 Trial Balance Information System

Trial Balance Information—Summarizing of Accounting Information

At the end of each accounting period, an entity's accountants must 'close the books' for the purpose of preparing a set of financial statements. One of the initial steps in this process is the preparation of a trial balance.

A Trial Balance is a two-column listing of all account balances, one for accounts with debit balances and another for accounts with credit balances. The balanced accounting information on the total debit and credit in accounts are equal. The item 'trial' balance highlights the fact that this item is a tool for testing whether the accounts are in balance (i.e., whether the total debits equal the total credits). Only the information on accounts with a debit or credit balances at the data of the trial balance are included. Accounts with zero balance are excluded. The account balances in the ledger accounts are the main sources of accounting information for the preparation of trial balance. By having such balanced accounting information the trial balance will give summarized accounting information, which is the base information for the preparation of financial statements. The following format presents the trial balance information.

Format showing trial balance information

XXXX Company

Trial Balance for thc pcriod cnded on ......

Accounts	Debit Balance	Credit Balance
Xxxxxxxxxx	Xxxxx	–
Xxxxxxxxx	–	Xxxxx
Xxxxx	Xx	–
Total	**Xxxxxx**	**Xxxxxx**

Trial Balance Information

From the trial balance we can know the following information:

- Ledger accounts information is available.
- Debit balances of ledger accounts is known.
- Credit balances of ledger accounts is known.
- Information on the total of both debit and credit columns, which are equal is known.

The above process in the accounting information system is regarded as the bookkeeping system that includes journalizing the accounting data, posting and balancing the journal entries in ledger accounts and summarizing of account balances in trial balance. This accounting information in various forms will be the base accounting information for the preparation of final accounts and other financial statements.

Summary

- A Trial Balance is a two-column listing of all account balances, one for accounts with debit balances and another for accounts with credit balances. The balanced accounting information on the total debit and credit in accounts are equal.
- Information available in trial balance: Ledger accounts information is available; Debit balances of ledger accounts are known; Credit balances of ledger accounts are known; Information on the total of both debit and credit columns, which are equal is known.

Self-Learning Activity

Try to answer the following question on your own:

1. Discuss trial balance accounting information system.

CHAPTER 9

Revenue and Cash Collection Processes and Controls

Introduction to Revenue Processes

There are many kinds of companies selling many kinds of products and services. Because there is such a variety of companies and items for sale, and because there are so many methods of conduction of revenue transactions, it is impossible to present an example of revenue and collection business processes that represents all possibilities. For instance, retailers may sell their products to consumers through company-owned department stores, using cash registers with bar coding systems called point of sale (POS) systems. These systems record the sale, collect cash, and update the inventory status all at the time of the sale. On the other hand, a manufacturer may sell products to other companies on 30-day credit terms, deliver the goods and bill the customer at a later date, and collect payment after the 30-day period.

The business processes for a company selling to other companies are likely to be different from a company selling products to consumers. An example of a company that sells to end consumers is Wal-Mart, while an example of company that sells to other companies is Procter & Gamble (P&G). P&G sells consumer products, such as Crest ® toothpaste to companies (like Wal-Mart) who then resell to consumers. Wal-Mart serves as the middleman who buys toothpaste from P&G and resells to consumers. The business processes that Wal-Mart engages in to generate and collect revenue are much different from those of P&G.

This chapter begins by describing a common set of revenue and cash collection processes for companies that sell goods to other companies. Business process maps, document flowcharts, and data follow diagrams are included as visual representations of the business activities. However, the processes illustrated and described in this chapter can focus only on common characteristics of such companies. Not all companies conduct business exactly as presented in this chapter. In a large company there may be thousands or hundreds of thousands of sales transactions occurring each day.

The company must have systems and processes in place to capture, record, summarize, and report the results of these transactions. The processes are the policies and procedures that employees follow in completing the sale, capturing customer data and sales quantities, and routing the resulting sales documents to the right departments within the company. The accounting system uses this flow of sales documents to various departments to record, summarize, and report the results of the sales transactions. For example, when a sale occurs, the information resulting from that sale must flow into the sales recording systems, the accounts receivable and cash collection systems, and the inventory tracking system. In IT accounting systems, these recording and processing systems are called Transaction Processing Systems (TPS). Thus, there is a set of processes within the company to conduct sales and route sales information, and there is a TPS within the IT system to record, summarize, and report sales transactions.

Sales transactions occur daily also generate other related transactions. Those transactions are the movement of inventory to customers, the recording of accounts receivable and the subsequent cash inflow, and sales returns from customers. Processes for each of these types of transactions must be in place for the company to carry out transactions on a daily basis. The business processes that are common in company to company sales transactions are as follows.

- Collect order data from the customer (another company, not end consumer).
- Deliver goods, receivable and bill the customer, handle any product returns from the customer and issue appropriate credit, collect the cash.
- Update the records affected, such as accounts receivable, cash, inventory, revenue, and cost of goods sold.

These types of processes are divided into the following groups:

1. Sales processes, including ordering, delivery, and billing
2. Sales returns processes
3. Cash collection processes

Although different companies conduct business differently, there tend to be similarities in the way they carry out related business processes. For instance, the sales processes generally involve receipt of a customer's order for products or services, delivery of the products or services, and billing the customer for those products or services. Sales processes also need supporting practices such as credit check and stock authorization. Most companies carry out these types of business transactions; however, the ways they do so are likely to differ. For instance, even though most companies collect order data from customers, the manner of receiving order data may vary. Orders may take the form of a mailed purchase order, a website order, or an EDI order.

Sales returns are an exception to the sales process; they are essentially a sale reversal that processes generally involve the receipt of goods and adjustment of customer account, inventory stock records, and other accounting reports.

Cash collections result from completed sales transactions. When cash is received from customers, it must be deposited in the bank. In addition, cash collection processes involve updating and reconciling cash and customer account balances.

The beginning part of this chapter describes transactions within the revenue and cash collection processes.

These descriptions are ordered according to the three categories explained earlier: sales, sales returns, and cash collections. This chapter also considers the following risks that may affect the revenue and cash collection processes:

- Recorded transactions may not be valid or complete; that is, they may involve a fictitious customer, incorrect quantities or terms, or erroneous duplication.
- Transactions may be recorded in the wrong amount.
- Valid transactions may have been omitted from the records.
- Transactions may have been recorded in a timely manner.
- Transactions may not have been accumulated or transferred to the accounting records correctly.
- The internal control procedures and IT controls that help lessen these risks are presented in exhibits following the discussion of each process category.

After describing the business processes for company-to-company transactions, the latter part of this chapter describes alternative business process models to generate and collect revenue. Examples include e-commerce or web-based sales EDI systems, and point of sale systems.

Sales Processes

The business process map in Figure 9.1 depicts the activities related to sales processes. Figure 9.2 shows a document flowchart for the sales process, and Figure 9.3 shows the sales process in a data flow diagram (DFD). The process begins when a buyer, or customer, places an order with the company. The customer and seller refer to the form designating this order differently. From the customer's perspective, this order is called a purchase order (because it is making a purchase), while the seller refers to this same order as a sales order (because it is making a sale).

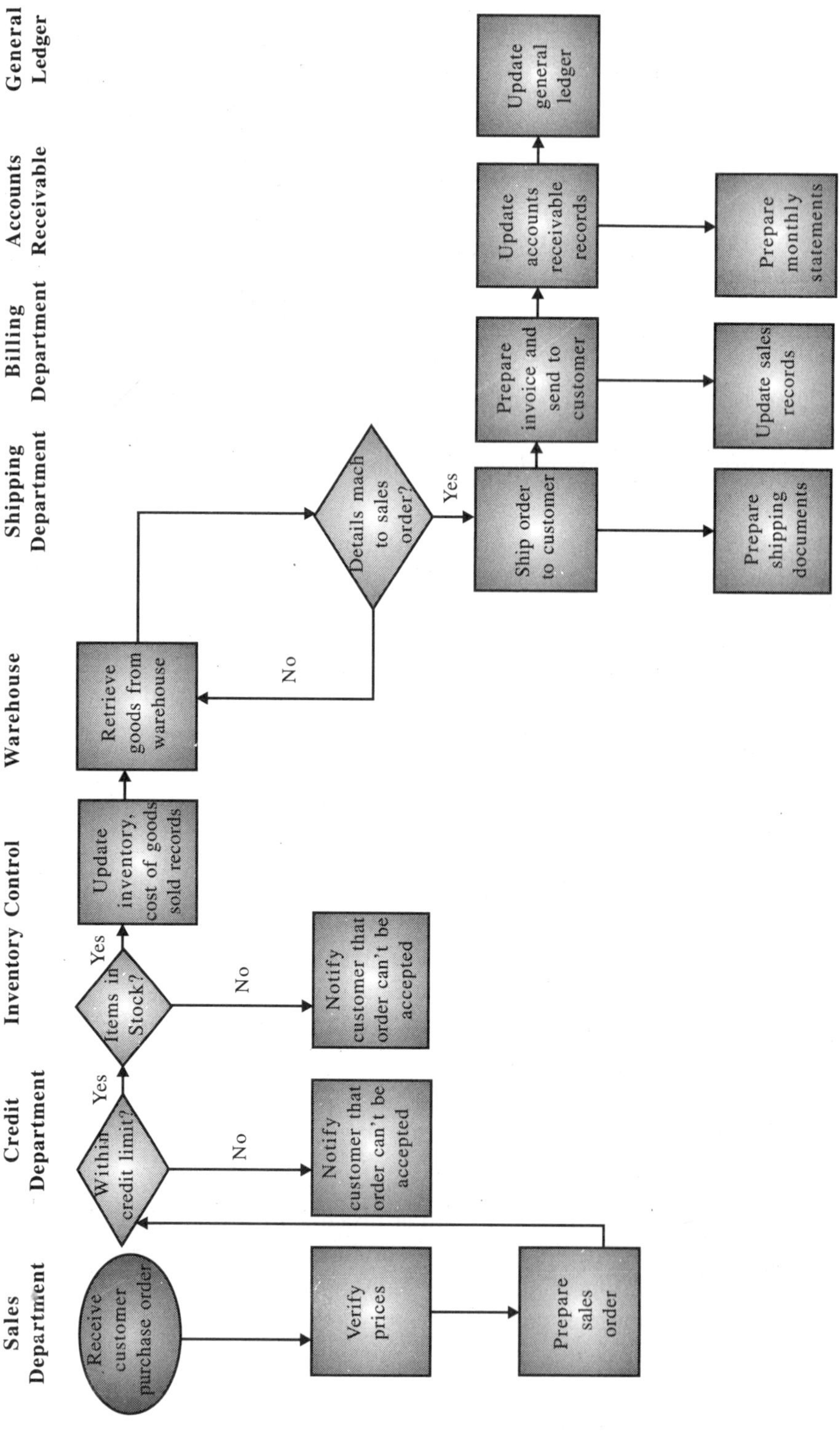

Fig. 9.1: **Sales Process Map**

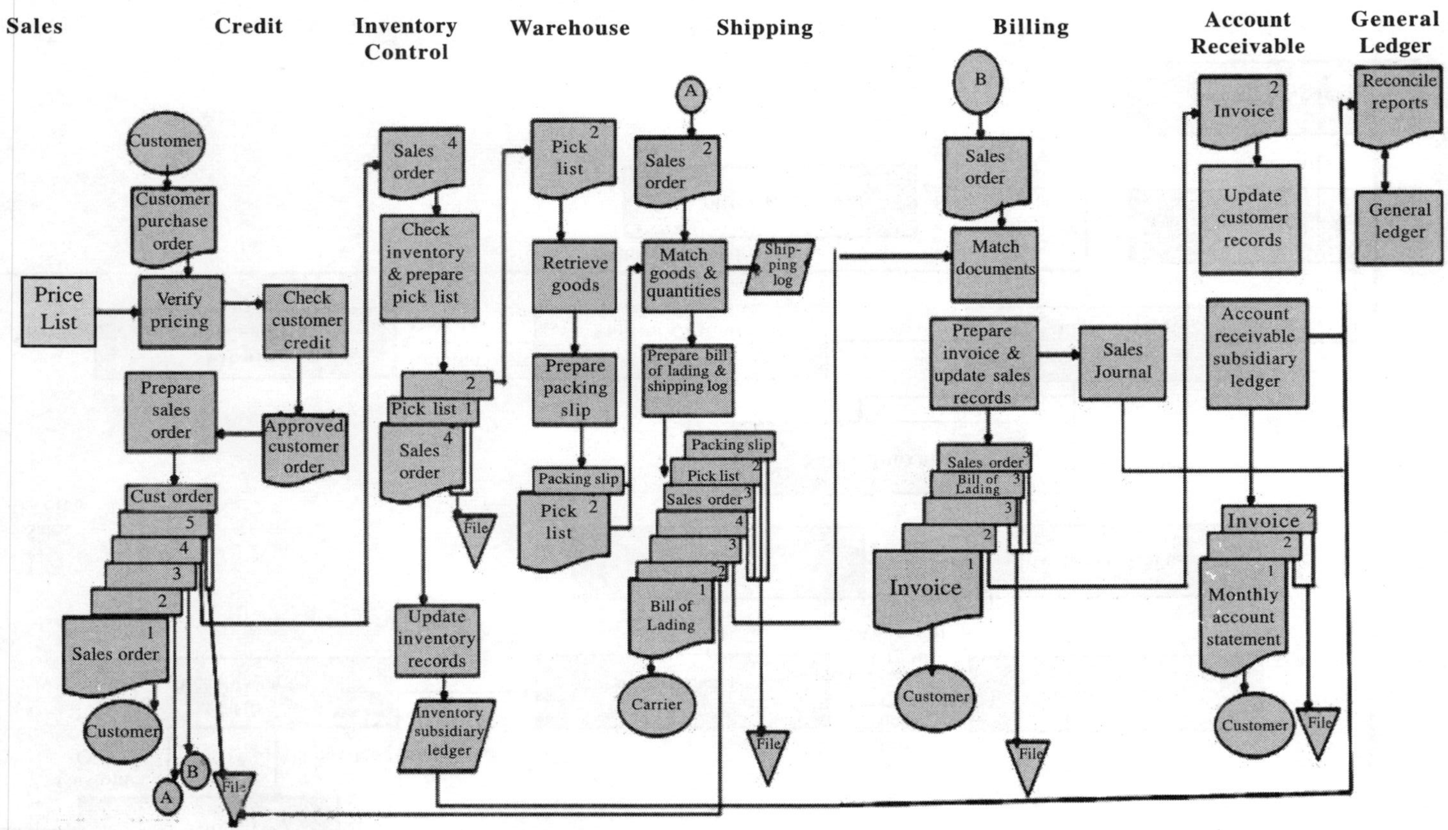

Fig. 9.2: **Document Flow of a Sales Process**

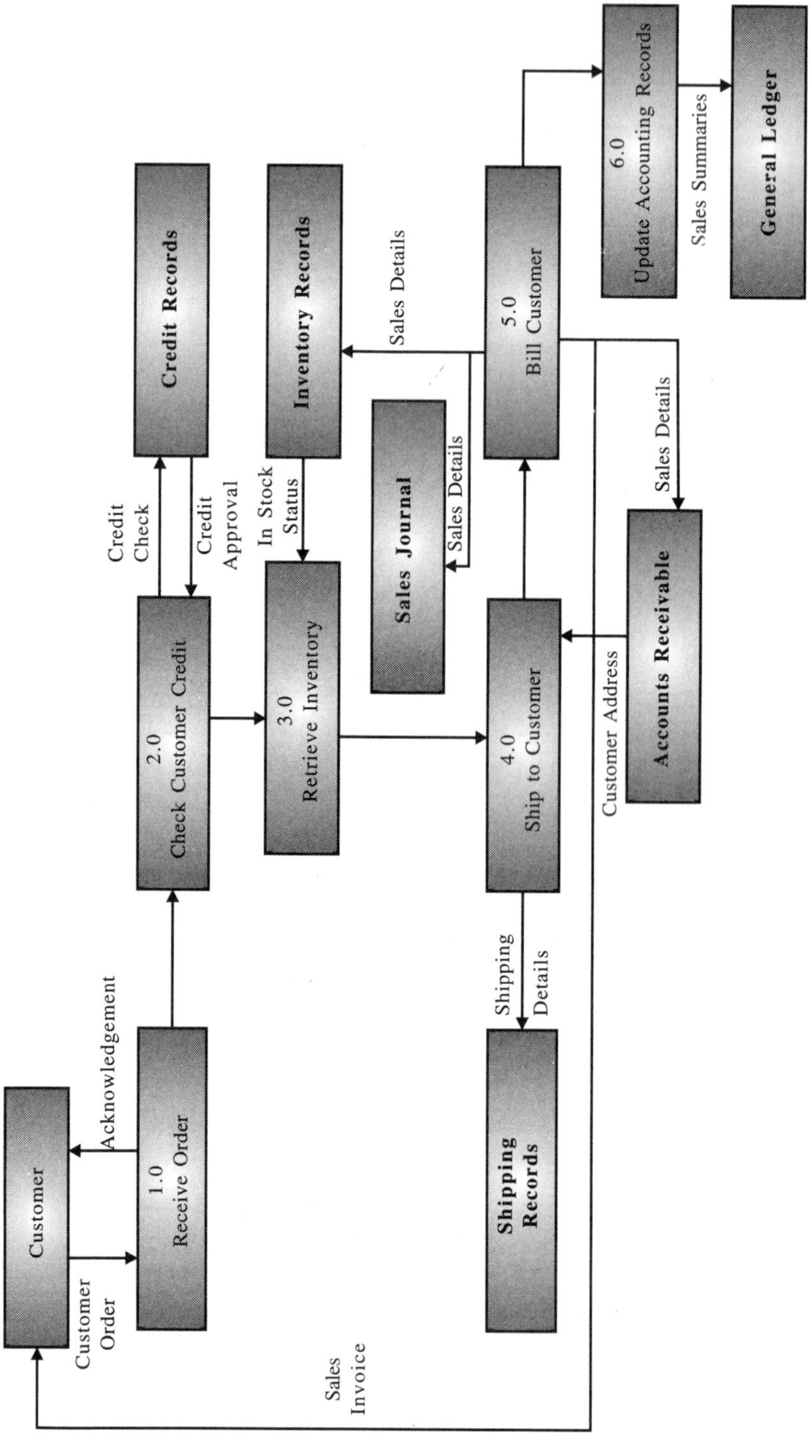

Fig. 9.3: **Sales Processes Data Flow Diagram**

A customer's purchase order is the source document that conveys the details abut the order. When a customer's purchase order is received, it must be entered into the seller's system as a sales order. Depending on the extent of computerization of the seller's system, this could be either manually entered or read automatically by the system. Sales orders are calculated on the basis of current selling prices of the items sold. The source of these prices is the price list. A price list is the entire set of pre-established and approved prices for each product. In most accounting software systems, selling prices are attached to each product in the company's inventory.

If a sales order is for a new customer, the creditworthiness of that customer must be evaluated before the sale is approved. As new customers are entered into the system, a credit limit must be set for them. It is also important to check the inventory to determine whether the items ordered are in stock. If the items are in stock, a pick list is prepared. A pick list documents the quantities and descriptions of items ordered. Items on the pick list should be pulled from the warehouse shelves and packaged for the customer.

A packing slip (or packing list) prepared by warehouse personnel lists all items included in a shipment. For a company sale, the goods are typically shipped by a common carrier such as a trucking company or rail carrier. The terms of the agreement between the company and the carrier are documented in a bill of lading. Finally, inventory records are updated to reflect the decrease in inventory, and a shipping log is prepared. A shipping log is a chronological listing of shipments that allows management to track the status of sales and to answer customer inquiries regarding order status.

Once shipment has occurred, customers should be billed for the sale. A sales invoice is prepared and sent to the customer. The sales invoice (typically referred to as a bill) provides details of the sale and requests payment. The timing of the billing process is important. Since customers will be unhappy if they are billed before they receive the items purchased, billing should not take place prior to shipment. However, it is important to avoid waiting very long after shipping to bill the customer, since that will delay the collection of cash. When customers are billed, accounts receivable records should be updated to reflect the increased amount owed by the customer. Also the sale should be recorded in a sales journal so that the amount will be included in revenue during the current fiscal period. A sales journal is a special journal that records sales transactions. Periodically, the sales amounts in a sales journal are posted to the general ledger. Many companies also prepare customer account statements on a regular basis to accumulate and summarize all the transactions that have taken place between the customer and the company within the period.

Controls Risks and in Sales Processes

Management should strive to achieve a system of internal controls, using both manual and programmed procedures to minimize the chance of error or fraud (Table 9.1). Unfortunately, the existence of good internal controls is not necessarily related to financial success in terms of a company's ability to make money; internal controls do not ensure high sales and profits.

Table 9.1: Sales Processes Risks and Controls

Control	Minimizes the Related Risk of:
Authorization:	
• Approval of sales order prior to shipment, including establishing sales prices, payment terms, and credit limits	• Invalid customers, over-extended customers, unapproved pricing or incorrect amounts
• Approval of shipment for proper customer	• Fictitious customers or wrong customers • Fictitious customers
Segregation of Duties:	
• Separation of responsibility for authorization of new customers from custody of inventory	• Invalid sales or omitted transactions
• Separation of duties related to order entry credit approval, shipping billing information systems, and general accounting	• Invalid transactions, incorrect amounts or accounts, omitted transactions • Omitted transactions
Records and Document:	
• Preparation of packing lists and shipping records on prenumbered forms	• Invalid transactions, omitted transactions, or timing issues
• Preparation of shipping log and packing list only when products have actually been shipped	• Invalid transactions, omitted transactions, or timing issue • Wrong customers or incorrect amounts
• Initiation of the billing function and updating of the sales journal, inventory records, and customer accounts receivable records only when products have actually been shipped	• Invalid transactions incorrect amounts or accounts, timing issues, accumulation issues or duplicate transactions
• Preparation of customer account statements	• Invalid sales or omitted transactions
• Matching of key information of related documents (customers, dates, inventory quantities and descriptions, prices, and account codes) prior to shipment security.	• Invalid sales, omitted transactions incorrect amounts or accounts timing issues accumulation issues or duplicate transactions
• Physical controls in inventory and shipping areas IT controls over computer records and physical controls in records storage areas	
Independent Checks and Reconciliations:	• Omitted transactions, incorrect amounts wrong customers or timing issues
• Comparison of shipping records with sales journal and invoices	• Incorrect amount or timing issues
• Verification of recorded descriptions dates, quantities authorized prices, and mathematical accuracy	• Problems with the accumulation of transactions and transfer to the general ledger and financial statements
• Mathematical variation of sales journal and comparison to accounts receivable subsidiary ledger and general ledger posting	• Invalid customers, wrong customers, omitted
• Review of accounts receivable records and comparison with sales invoices	• Transactions, incorrect amounts, timing issues or problems with the accumulation of transactions.

However, effective and efficient internal controls may relieve managers valuable time that might otherwise be spent on accounting or operational problems, thus making it possible for them to devote more attention to revenue growth and cost reduction. Following are common procedures associated with the sales process:

Authorization of Transactions

Specific individuals within the company should have authoritative responsibility for establishing sales prices, payment terms, credit limits, and guidelines for accepting new customers. Only designated employees should perform these authorization functions. These specific people should have a recognized method of communication when sales transactions have been authorized. For example, a signature or initials on a sales order or shipping document often document approval. Such a signature indicates that a designated employee has verified that the sale is to an accepted customer, the customer's credit has been approved (i.e., it has not exceeded its credit limit), and the price is correct. Once a sales order has been filled, established procedures should be in place for verifying that the shipment represents items ordered. Thus, proper sales authorization control includes obtaining approval prior to processing an order and again before the order is shipped.

Segregation of Duties

Within the sales process, the accounting duties related to order entry, credit approval, shipping, billing, information systems, and general accounting need to be separated in order to meet the objectives of internal controls. Recall that individual with authoritative responsibilities should not also have access to the related records or custody of the related assets. In addition to the authorization responsibilities just described, certain information systems duties are included in the sales process, such as data entry programming, IT operations, and security.

The recording function includes the preparation of sales orders, shipping logs, and sales invoices, as well as that of general accounting reports such as the sales journal, accounts receivable subsidiary records and customer statements, the general ledger, and financial statements.

Finally, the custody function includes product handling and preparing goods for shipment. Ideally, good internal controls within the sales process require that accounting for inventory is completely separate from product handling. Also, any person who maintains detailed accounts receivable records should not also be responsible for maintaining the general ledger for or handling cash.

Adequate Records and Documents

These responsible for recording sales should ensure that supporting documentation is retained and organized. As records are prepared, they should be compared with supporting information to make sure they are accurate and to prevent duplication. Sales orders, shipping loges invoices, customer account statements, and other related documents should be saved and filed. Record files are often organized by customer name or by the numerical sequence of the document. When companies account for the numerical sequence of their documents, it is possible to review the list to determine whether omissions have occurred. In addition, if accounting personnel compare the different documents that make up each transaction, they can find out whether the transaction has been carried out properly. For example, when the customer order, packing list, shipping records, and invoice for a single transaction are properly retained, personnel can verify that the records reflect the correct quantities, prices, customer, timing, etc.

Security of Assets and Documents

A company's inventory of products should be protected by physical controls in the warehouse. Some examples of physical controls are surveillance cameras, security guards, and alarm systems. Likewise, data files, production programmes, and accounting records should each be protected from unauthorized access. Password, backup copies, and physical controls (such as locked file cabinets) can protect a company's records.

Independent Checks and Reconciliation

In order to promote accountability for the sales process, companies should implement procedures where by independent checks and record reconciliations are performed on a regulate basis. These procedures are most effective when someone independent of the related authority, recording, and custody functions conducts them. Within the sales process, the most common types of independent checks include the verification of information in the sales journal and on sales invoices, the reconciliation of accounts receivable detail with invoices and with the general ledger, and the reconciliation of inventory records with actually (counted) quantities of products on hand.

Sales Return Processes

It is nearly always the case that a small portion of sales made to customers will ultimately be returned to the seller. A company must have procedures in place for receiving returned goods crediting the customer's account, and placing the items back in inventory. When customers return goods, the receiving department handles the goods.

Returned goods are typically accompanied by documentation from the customer, such as a bill of lading and packing slip. The goods should be inspected for possible damage, and a copy of the original sales invoice should confirm the historical sale of the goods. A receiving log is prepared that lists the chronological sequence of all returned items, and a receiving report records the quantity received. A receiving report is a source document completed by personnel in the receiving dock that documents the quantity and condition of items received. If the returned goods are accepted, they are placed back in the proper location in the warehouse and the inventory records are updated to reflect the increase in inventory.

A credit memorandum is prepared to document the return and to adjust the amount of the customer's credit status. A journal of credit memos should be maintained in order to provide a complete listing of all credits issued. Reference to the original sales invoice and approved price list will assure that the credit is issued for the correct amount.

Sometimes a refund check may be issued to the customer. In other cases, the customer's accounts receivable balance will be adjusted for the returned items.

Cash Collection Processes

Company-to company sales are typically made on account, and a time span is given for the customer's pay. An example of the credit terms of sale would be net 30. This means the customer has 30 days after the invoice date to pay. Therefore, the timing of a cash collection is such that there will be some number of days between invoice date and collection of the cash. The actual number of days depends on the credit terms of the sale and the diligence of the customer in paying on time.

When the customer sends a check, the company must have processes in place to properly handle the receipt. The appropriate employees should match the check with the related sales invoice; deposit the funds in a timely manner, and update customer and cash records. Figure 9.4 shows cash receipts process map, Figure 9.5 shows a document flowchart of cash collection processes, and Figure 9.6 shows the cash collection process in a data flow diagram (DFD).

Collections from customers typically include a remittance advice, which is the documentation accompanying payment that identifies the customer account number and invoice to which the payment applies. An example of a remittance advice in your personal life is on your credit card statement. Part of your statement is meant to be detached and mailed with your payment account. In the case of company-to-company sales, a remittance advice identifies the invoice and customer account number to which the payment should be applied.

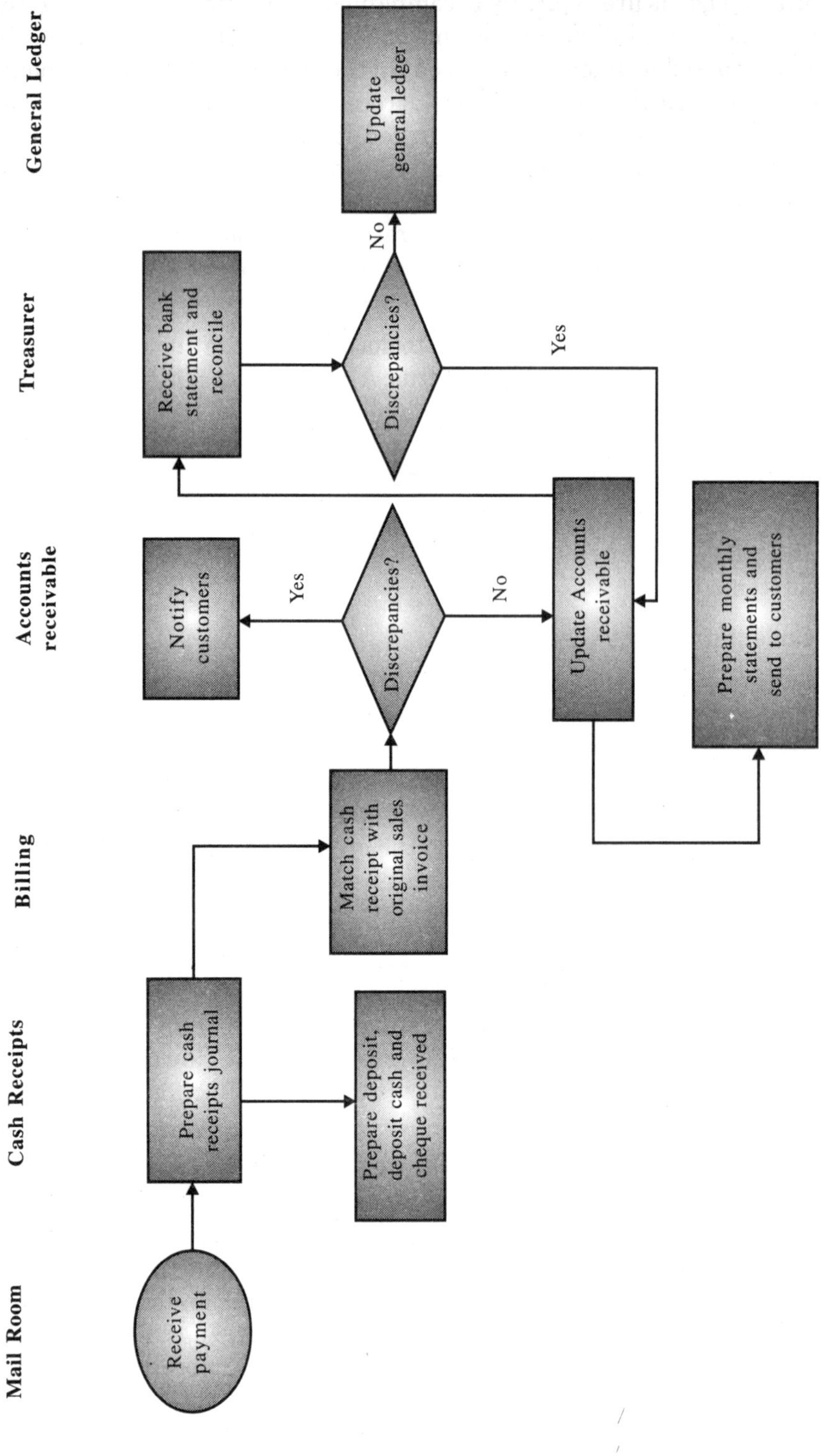

Fig. 9.4: **Cash Receipts Process Map**

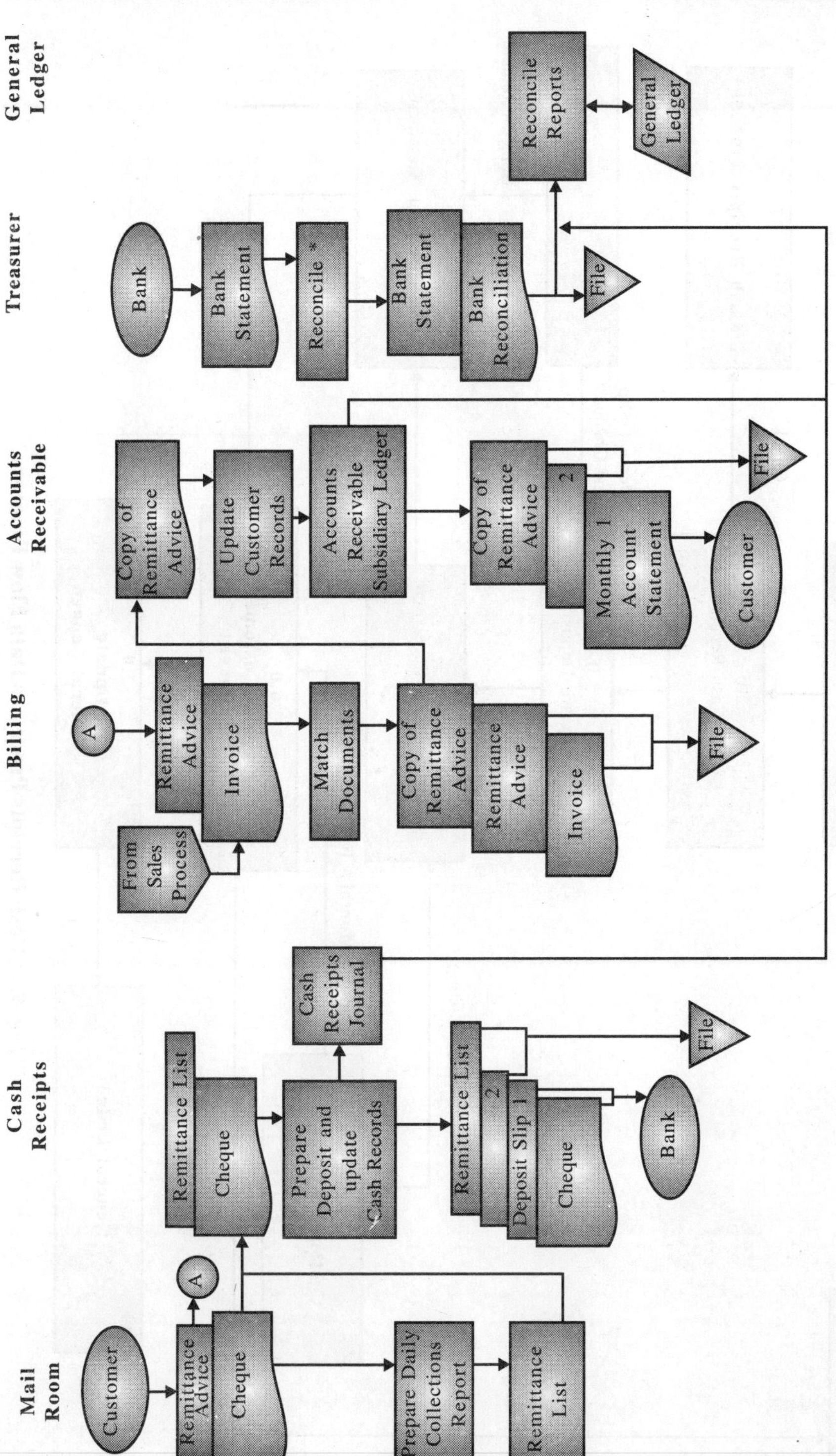

* Involves comparisons of remittance listings, deposit slips and cash receipts journal with information reported on bank statement.

***Fig. 9.5:* Document Flowchart of a Cash Receipts Process**

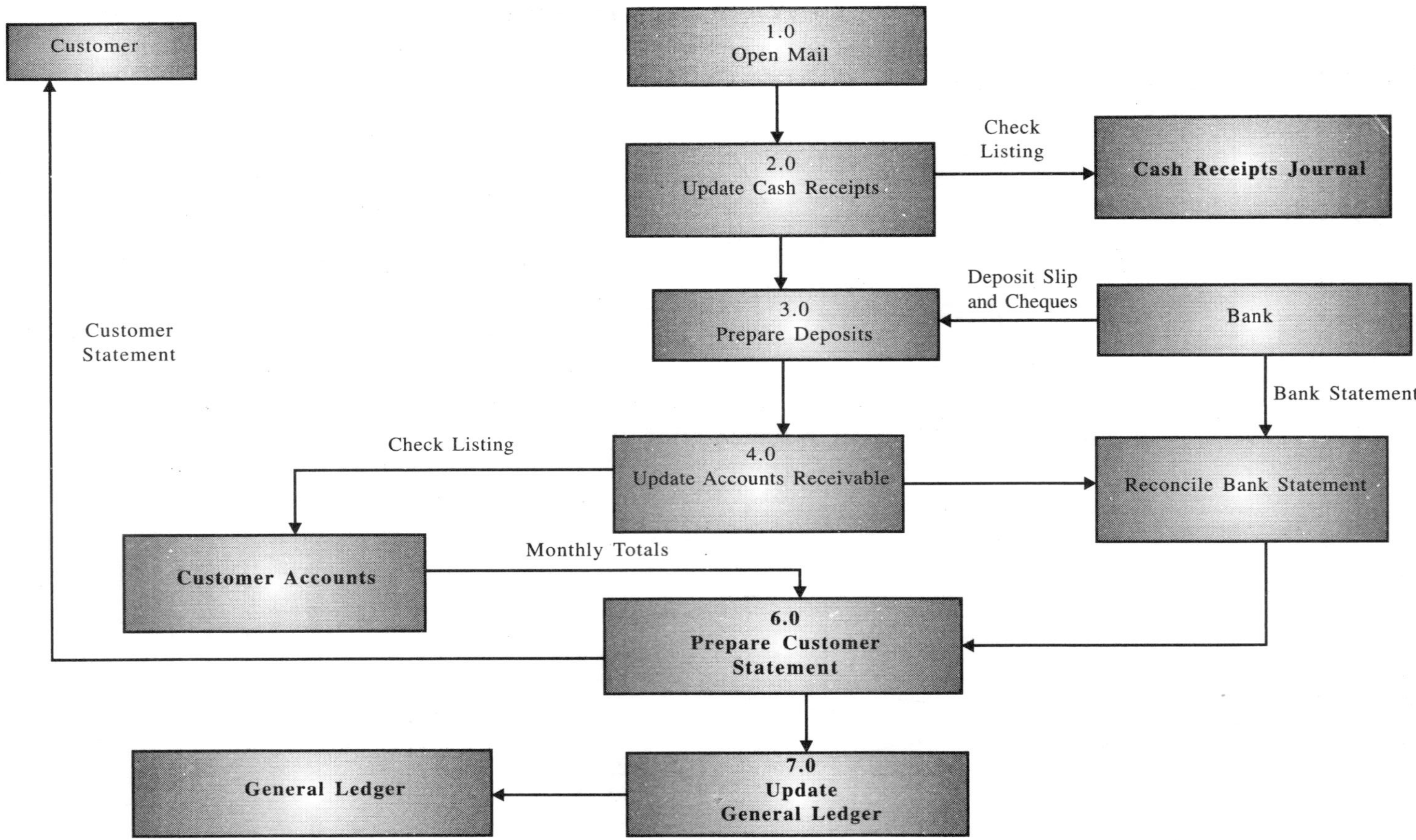

Fig. 9.6: **Cash Receipts Processes Data Flow Diagram**

A cash receipts journal is a special journal that records all cash collections. The listing of collections is to be forwarded along with the payments received, to a cashier who prepares the bank deposit. The payments are deposited in the company account, and customer records and cash records must be updated.

At the end of the month, an updated statement of account will be prepared and sent to the customer. This statement reflects the invoices that have been paid and the decrease in the customer's balance owed as a result of these collections. Also, the bank will send a monthly statement to the company so that the cash records of the company can be reconciled to the bank records.

Risks and Controls in the Cash Collection Processes

We now turn our attention to specific internal controls and related risks associated with cash collections from sales revenues (Table 9.2). Some internal controls present within a cash receipts process are as follows:

Authorization of Transactions

Appropriate individuals should be assigned responsibility for opening and closing all bank accounts and approving bank deposits or electronic transfers of funds. This ensures that records are updated only for author-Data Flow Diagramized transactions.

Segregation of Duties

As you know, authorization duties (described previously) need to be kept separate from recording responsibilities include maintaining a cash receipts journal, updating accounts receivable records for individual customers, and posting subsidiary ledger. Custody responsibilities include opening mail, preparing a list of collections, handling receipts of currency and checks, and preparing bank deposits. At a minimum, those who handle cash should not have the authority to access the company's cash or accounting records or reconcile the bank account. In addition, those with responsibility for information systems programming or control should not also have access to the cash or accounting records.

Furthermore, anyone responsible for maintaining detailed records for daily cash receipts or accounts receivable subsidiary accounts should not also have access to the general ledger.

Adequate Records and Documents

Cash receipts listings should be prepared on a daily basis, so the daily activity of collections should be reconciled to supporting documentation from the bank deposit. Bank deposit receipts should be retained and filed chronologically and regular, timely bank reconciliations should be prepared and retained. Detailed customer accounts should also be maintained and reconciled with customer statements regularly.

Table 9.2: Cash Receipts Controls and Risks

Control	Minimizes the Related Risk of:
Authorization: • Designated person opens/closes bank accounts • Approval of cash receipt prior to bank deposit • Separation of custody of cash from the responsibility for reconciling the bank accounts • Separation of custody of cash from accounts receivable record keeping • Separation of duties related to cash receipts journal preparation, credit approval, inventory handling. • Information systems, and general accounting	 • Invalid bank account or omitted transactions • Invalid bank account or incorrect amounts • Invalid cash receipts, incorrect amounts, omitted transactions • Invalid transactions, incorrect amounts or omitted transactions • Invalid transactions, incorrect amounts or accounts or omitted transactions
Records and Documents: • Preparation of deposit slips on prenumbered forms • Preparation of cash receipts journal and accounts receivable records only when cash has actually been received • Preparation of customer account statements • Matching of key information on related documents (customers, dates, prices, and account codes) prior to reducing customer accounts	 • Omitted transactions • Invalid transactions, omitted transactions, or timing issues • Wrong customers or incorrect amounts • Invalid transaction, wrong customer, incorrect amounts or accounts, timing issues, or duplicate transactions • Lost or stolen cash receipts, invalid receipts or omitted transactions
Security: • Physical controls areas where cash is received • IT controls over computer records and physical controls in records storage areas. • Cash receipts deposited in bank on a daily basis	 • Invalid receipts omitted transactions incorrect omits or accounts timing issues accumulation issues or duplicate transactions • Lost or stolen cash receipts
Independent Checks and Reconciliations: • Cash counts and comparison of daily deposit with cash receipts journal • Preparation of bank reconciliation • Matching of remittance advice with cash receipts journal • Mathematical verification of cash receipts journal and comparison with accounts receivable subsidiary ledger and general ledger posting	 • Invalid receipts lost or stolen cash, omitted transaction incorrect amounts or accounts or timing issues • Invalid receipts omitted transactions, incorrect amounts or accounts, timing issues or lost or stolen cash • Invalid receipts omitted transitions incorrect amounts timing issues or lost or stolen cash • Problems with the accumulation of transaction and transfer to the general ledger and financial statements.

Security of Assets and Documents

Access to cash collections needs to be limited to those who are expressly authorized to handle cash. Controls over cash collections are likely the most important control procedure, because cash is the asset most susceptible to theft or misappropriation. Because of the universal appeal of cash and the difficulty of proving ownership, a company must take extra precautions to protect this asset. Cash collections should be deposited in the bank in a timely manner to prevent the risk of theft. Also related computerized data and programmes must be protected from unauthorized use.

Independent Checks and Reconciliation

A physical count of cash needs to be conduct from time to time in order to compare actual cash on hand with the amounts in the accounting records.

To maximize effectiveness, cash counts should occur on a surprise basis and be conducted by someone not otherwise responsible for any cash receipts functions. Daily bank deposits should also be compared with the detail on the related remittance advice and in the cash receipts journal. In addition, it is important that companies regularly reconcile their cash accounts with the respective bank statements. Like cash counting procedures, someone who has no other responsibility for handling cash or accounting for cash transactions should perform bank reconciliation. The bank statements should be received directly by the person who prepares the reconciliation; to make sure other company personnel do not alter it. Among the bank reconciliation tasks are procedures to ensure that deposits are examined for proper dates and that all reconciling items are reviewed and explained.

IT Enabled Systems of Revenue and Cash Collection Processes

The previous section described the processes related to revenue transactions. In addition to the activities that take place within those processes there must also be accounting systems to record summarize, and report the results of the related transaction. In the majority of organizations, the accounting information system consists of hardware and software within IT systems. However there is such great variety in accounting software systems in terms of their size, complexity, and extent of automation that it is impossible to describe all of the various kinds of systems. In general as complexity and automation increase, there are fewer manual processes and more computerized processes. This is usually true regarding size also. Larger IT systems generally have fewer manual processes and more computerized processes. More computerized processes means there would be a greater need for the type of IT controls and it generally means that there are fewer paper documents within the process. As a simple illustration: Considers two kinds of restaurants you might visit. A small family-owned restaurant might not use computers at all, and the server may simply write your order on a pad. On the other hand, a large restaurant chain might have a system completely based on computers, where servers enter orders on the touch screen of a handheld device that transmits the order to the kitchen.

The family-owned restaurant would have no need for computer controls, while the restaurant chain would need many computer-based controls.

The following section provides a description of a typical revenue processing system and some specialized IT systems:

Figure 9.7 is a system flowchart of a generic version of revenue system with some paper documents. The system flowchart documents a system for company-to-company sales. When the customer's order is received an employee enters it into the IT system by keying the order into an input screen. With online data files, the input data can be edited, the customer's credit status can be reviewed, and inventory levels can be checked. If the order does not exceed the customer's credit limit and the inventory items are available, the order can be processed.

Order processing updates the sales records and the customer's account records. The appropriate documents needed to fill and ship the order are printed. These documents usually include a pick list, a packing slip, an invoice, and a bill of lading. Warehouse personnel to select items from the warehouse shelves use the pick list. Shipping personnel to ensure the correct items are packed uses the packing slip. The bill of lading is the agreement between the common carrier and the company. The invoice is sent to the customer.

Usually at the end of the month, customers are billed and regular monthly reports are printed. Customers are billed according to the customer statement. Regular monthly reports would include sales reports, inventory status reports, and accounts receivable reports.

General controls to prevent network break-ins would be necessary if the system uses any network connections to other systems. The application controls help ensure the accuracy and completeness of processing. Input controls used in this system would be likely to include data preparation and error handling procedures, programmed input validation checks, and control totals. Well-defined procedures for data preparation and error handling can reduce the chance for mistakes in entry into the system. The programmed input checks such as field checks, validity checks, limit checks, and reasonableness checks will help prevent or detect keying errors. If customer orders are entered in batches, control totals can help ensure the accuracy and completeness of input and processing. Output controls help to protect data through proper distribution, storage, and disposal of reports.

The system depicted in Figure 9.7 uses some manual processes, such as keying of data, and some paper forms. More complex IT systems can reduce or eliminate these manual processes and paper forms. For example, orders placed over the Internet would eliminate manual keying by someone within the company.

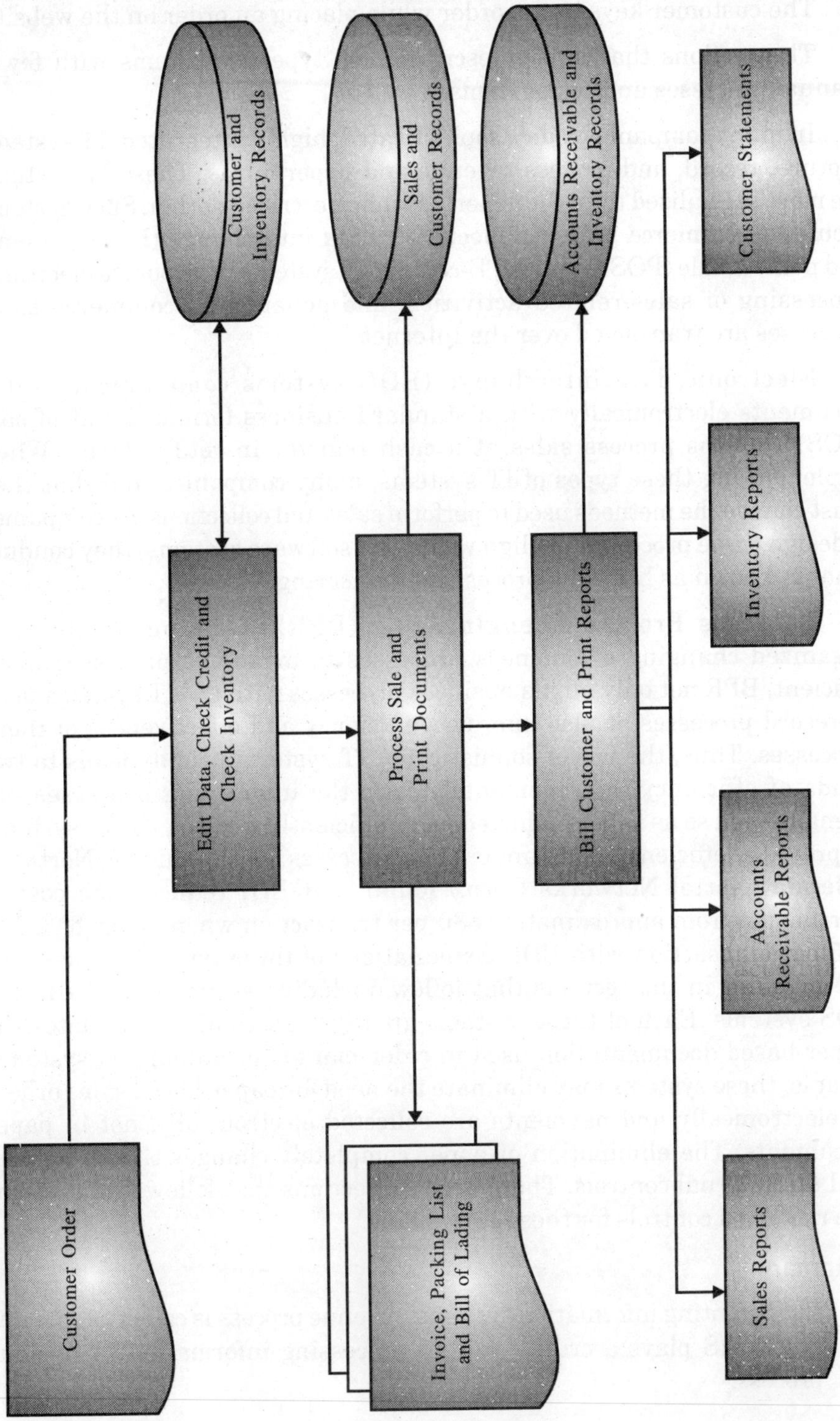

***Fig. 9.7:* Revenue Processes System Flowchart**

The customer keys in the order while placing an order on the website.

The sections that follow describe some types of systems with fewer manual processes and paper forms.

In many companies today, sophisticated, highly integrated, IT systems capture, record, and process revenue and paper forms. These IT systems are more specialized than the generic system described earlier. Such systems include e-commerce systems, electronic data interchange (EDI) systems, and point of sale (POS) systems. E-commerce systems incorporate electronic processing of sales-related activities, and generally, e-commerce sales processes are transacted over the Internet.

Electronic data interchange (EDI) systems communicate sales documents electronically with a standard business format. Point of sale (POS) systems process sales at a cash register in retail stores. When implementing these types of IT systems, many companies find that they must change the methods used to perform sales and collections. As companies redesign these processes to align with their software systems, they conduct what is known as business process reengineering.

Business Process Reengineering (BPR) is the purposeful and organized changing of business processes to make the processes more efficient. BPR not only aligns business processes with the IT systems used to record processes, it also improves efficiency and effectiveness of these processes. Thus, the use of sophisticated IT systems usually leads to two kinds of efficiency improvements. First, the underlying processes are reengineered so as to be conducted more efficiently. Second, the IT systems improve the efficiency of the underlying processes. As an example, Northern Telecom (Nortel Networks Corp.) found that EDI reduced the cost of purchasing from approximately $80 per transaction when paper based to $35 per transaction with EDI. Explanations of three types of IT systems are included in the sections that follow, including e-commerce, EDI, and POS systems. Each of these systems greatly reduces of/or eliminates the paper-based documentation used in older manual or automated systems. That is, these systems may eliminate the need for paper-based sales orders or electronically and payments are collected electronically, not in paper documents. The elimination of paper completely changes the audit trail and the internal controls. Therefore, the sections that follow will describe the risks and controls for these IT systems.

Summary

- In accounting information systems, revenue process is called as revenue cycle. AIS plays a crucial role in processing information in revenue process.

Self-Learning Activity

Try to answer the following questions on your own:

1. Describe revenue process.
2. Give an account of risks that affect revenue and cash collection process.
3. Explain sales return process.
4. What is BPR?

CHAPTER 10

Expenditures Processes and Controls-Purchases

Expenditures Processes

In a large company, there may be thousands of purchasing transactions occurring each day. The company must have systems and processes in place to capture, record, summarize and report these transactions. The processes are the policies and procedures that employees follow in completing the purchase of goods or materials, capturing vendor data and purchase quantities, and routing the resulting purchasing documents to the proper departments within the company. When a purchase occurs, the information resulting from that purchase must flow into the purchase recording systems, the accounts payable and cash disbursement systems, and the inventory tracking systems. In IT accounting systems these recording and processing systems are called Transaction Processing Systems (TPS). Thus, there is a set of processes within the company to company to conduct purchases and route purchasing information, and there is a TPS within the IT system to record, summarize, and report these purchasing transactions.

Every company acquires materials or goods and must therefore have expenditures. It is a fundamental process of all businesses as they buy the resources needed to conduct operations, record the resulting liability, and eventually pay cash to the vendor. This process is somewhat similar to the revenue processes, except that goods and cash flow in opposite directions. Accordingly, the company is a vendor from the customer's perspective. Accountants must always be mindful of the processing flow of the transaction in order to properly recognize it.

There are many different kinds of resources that may be needed to run a business, such as materials, supplies, equipment facilities, and a skilled workforce, to name a few readily observable examples. Because of the large volume of expenditures transactions the most companies process and the differing nature of these transactions; this text will divide the expenditures process into two parts. Part 1 addresses purchases of materials and supplies and the related cash disbursements, sometimes known as the procurement or purchasing process.

Much like the methods of earning revenue presented at the beginning of Chapter 9 there is great variety in the purchasing activities of businesses. A merchandising company, such as Banana Republic, will purchase finished merchandise that it will sell to its retile customers, whereas a manufacturing company, such as General Electric, will purchase raw materials that will be transformed into new products. Even companies in the same line of business are likely to have differences in their purchasing habits, as they may have unique characteristics in terms of product features, business practices, storage capacities, and vendor relationships.

Most companies acquire their resources on credit terms and pay for them at a later date. This chapter concentrates on purchasing and cash disbursement transactions common to a wide range of companies acquire an inventory of goods or materials from other companies on account and sell goods or products to other companies. Not every company will carry out its expenditures processes exactly as depicted here, but this chapter provides a practical presentation of a typical approach.

The most common expenditures processes include the following:

- Prepare a purchase requisition and/or purchase order for goods or services needed.
- Notify the vendor (supplier) of goods or services needed.
- Receive goods or services, often via common carries.
- A common carrier is a trucking, rail, or airfreight company.
- Record the payable.
- Pay the resulting invoice.
- Update the records affected, such as accounts payable, cash, inventory and expenses.

The first part of this chapter describes a typical purchasing system, which includes three primary categories of processing processes, purchase return processes, and cash disbursement processes (or payments). In addition, controls and risks related to these processes are presented. For each category, the goal of the system's internal controls in to reduce the following types of business risks:

1. Invalid (fictitious or duplicate) transactions may have been recorded.
2. Transactions may have been recorded in the wrong amounts.

3. Actual transactions may have been omitted from the accounting records.
4. Transactions may have been recorded to the wrong vendor or wrong account number.
5. Transactions may not have been recorded in a timely manner.
6. Transaction may have been accumulated or transferred to the accounting records incorrectly.

This chapter also examines computer-based purchasing and cash disbursement systems. Finally, some prevalent business ethics and corporate governance topics related to the expenditures processes are presented in the latter part of the chapter.

Purchasing Processes

The business process map in Figure 10.1 illustrates the flow of activities in a typical purchasing system. Figure 10.2 is a document flowchart depicting the related records used in a purchasing system. Figure 10.3 is a data flow diagram of the purchasing processes. This process begins when an employee of the company recognizes the need to make a purchase, typically as a result of observing low inventory levels or unfilled sales orders.

Purchasing needs may change daily with the occurrence of shipping and receiving transactions, production transfers, and new sales orders. It may be that a warehouse attendant notices a particularly low stock level, and accountant detects potential shortages in documented inventory quantities, and operations manager becomes aware of additional quantities that will be needed to produce upcoming sales orders or an IT system determines an order is necessary. Regardless of the manner in which the purchase is initiated, the appropriate purchase requisition form should be prepared to document the need and request that the specific items and quantities be purchased. A designated member of management must then authorize a purchase requisition. The purchase requisition triggers the next steps in the purchase process.

Once a purchase requisition has been approved, it will be forwarded to the purchasing department within the company, where a purchase order form is prepared. A purchase order (PO) is a document issued to a seller by a buyer that indicates the details-products, quantities, and agreed upon prices—for products or services that the seller will provide to the buyer.

When goods are received from the vendor they generally are delivered via common carrier, such as a trucking or rail company. Company personnel in the receiving area should inspect all goods received. The quantity should be counted, and the useable condition of the goods should be assessed to determine any damage or substitutions.

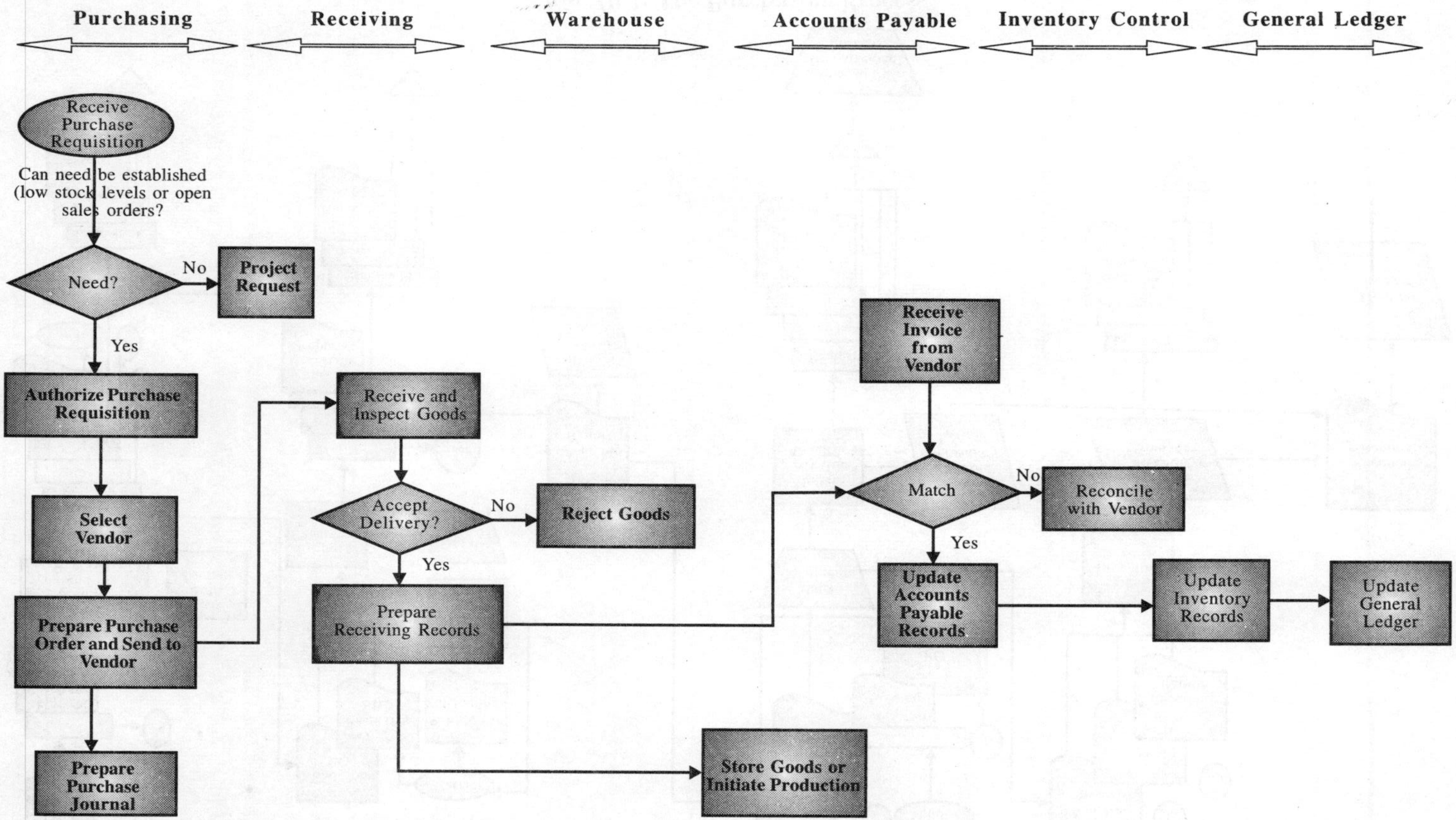

Fig. 10.1: **Purchasing Process Map**

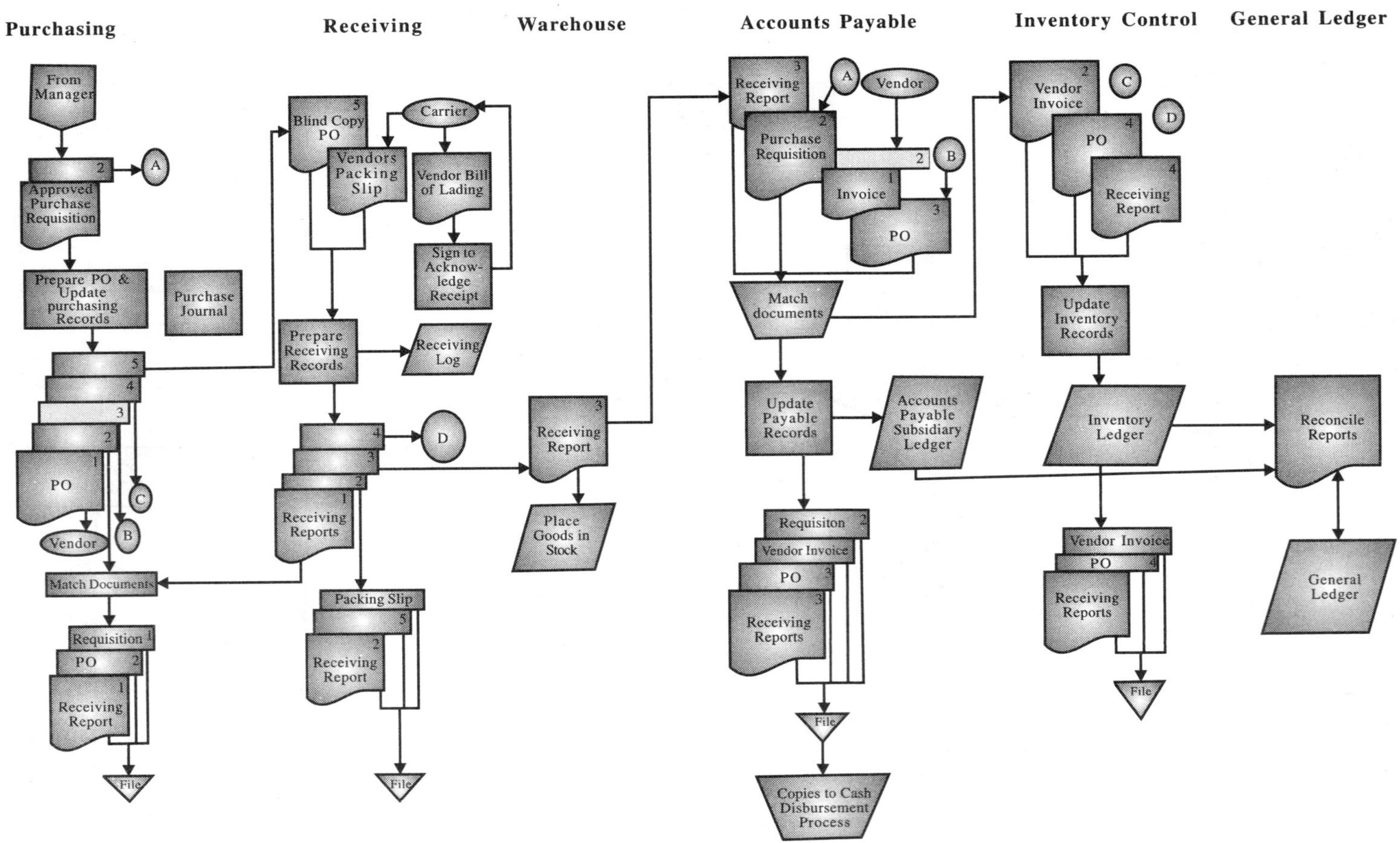

Fig. 10.2: **The Purchasing Process**

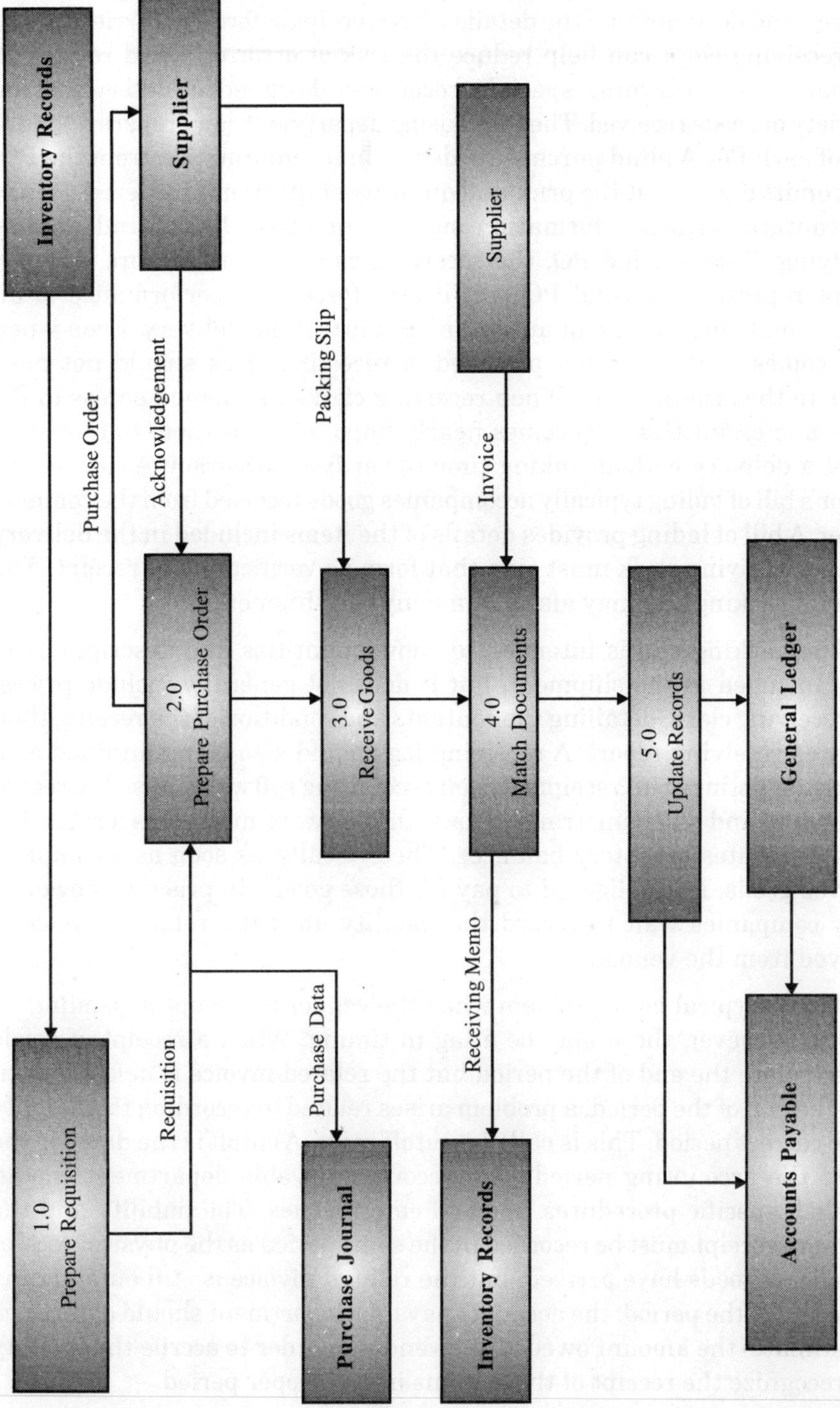

Fig. 10.3: **Purchasing Process Data Flow Diagram**

The receiving clerk is responsible for counting for inspecting all items received and documenting the details of the receipt before the carrier leaves. The receiving clerk can help reduce the risk of error or fraud related to purchases by performing special procedures designed to determine the propriety of goods received. The purchasing department can prepare a "blind" copy of each PO. A blind purchase order includes information from the PO, but it omits data about the price and quantity of the item(s) ordered. It may also contain critical information such as quantity limits and quality specifying. With a blind PO, the receiving clerk can make sure that the receipt represents a valid PO, yet it still forces the performance of an independent check of the quantity and quality of the delivery. Even when blind copies of POs are not provided, a receiving clerk should not have access to the original POs. When receiving clerks are denied access to PO prices and quantities, it becomes nearly impossible for them to hurriedly accept a delivery without taking time to verify its accuracy. A copy of the vendor's bill of lading typically accompanies goods received from the common carrier. A bill of lading provides details of the items included in the delivery and the receiving clerk must sign that form as verification of receipt. The vendor's packing slip may also accompany the shipment.

The packing slip is intended to show quantities and descriptions of items included in the shipment, but it does not generally include prices. The receiving clerk, detailing the contents and condition of the receipt, then prepares receiving report. A receiving log should also be maintained as a sequential listing of all receipts. When accounting software is used to record purchasing and receiving transactions, the software maintains a receiving log and updates inventory balances. Theoretically, as soon as a company receives goods, it is obligated to pay for those goods. In practice, however, many companies wait to record the liability until the related invoice is received from the vendor.

This is typical not a problem when the vendor is prompt in sending its invoice. However, there may be a lag in timing. When a receipt of goods occurs before the end of the period but the related invoice is delayed until after the end of the period, a problem arises related to recording the liability in the correct period. This is called a cutoff issue. A cutoff is the date for the end of the accounting period. The accounts payable department should establish specific procedures to avoid cutoff issues. The liability and the inventory receipt must be recorded in the same period as the physical receipt of goods. If goods have arrived, but the related invoice is still outstanding at the end of the period, the accounts payable department should determine (or estimate) the amount owed to the vendor in order to accrue the liability and recognize the receipt of these items in the proper period.

The accounts payable department is responsible for recording the liabilities for goods received in the accounting records. Caution must be exercised to be certain that vendor invoices represent goods that were actually ordered and received. The accounts payable department maintains copies of purchase orders and receiving reports so that the documents can be compared before the accounting records are updated.

This comparison helps ensure that invoices represent goods actually ordered and received. Also, the accounts payable department will ensure that the correct vendor account is immediately adjusted for each purchase transaction so that the company will know the correct amount owed to the vendor. An accounts payable subsidiary ledger includes the detail of amounts owed to each vendor. Finally, the accounts payable department maintains a file of outstanding invoices awaiting payment.

This file is usually organized in alphabetical order by vendor name. A copy of the invoice is also given to the cash disbursements department, where it is filed by due date or by the discount date, such as ten days after invoice is also given to the cash disbursements department, where it is filed by due date or by the discount date, such as ten days after invoicing for 2/10, n/30 terms. Many of the goods received are likely to be inventory items. Therefore, the inventory control department is part of the purchasing process. The inventory control department maintains inventory records, which must be increased for the proper item, quantity and dollar amount each time a purchase occurs.

To complete the purchasing process, the general ledger function is designed for posting and reconciling transactions from the respective accounts payable and inventory subsidiary ledgers.

Risks and Controls in the Purshasing Process

Management is responsible for implementing internal controls over each business process. Accordingly, the purchasing process needs special attention to reduce the risk of fraud or errors specific to these types of transactions. The next section identifies common procedures, organized according to the five internal control activities (Table 10.1).

Authorization of Transactions

Specific individuals within the company should be given authoritative responsibility for the preparation of purchase requisitions and purchase orders, including approval of the specific items to purchase, order quantities, and vendor selection. Only those designated individuals should have the opportunity to carry out these tasks. The company should establish specific procedures to ensure that POs have been properly authorized before the order is officially placed with a vendor.

Table 10.1: Purchasing Controls and Risks

Control	Minimizes the Related Risk of:
Authorization: • Approval of purchase transaction prior to placing an order *Segregation:* • Separation of authorization of purchases and new vendors from custody of inventory in the receiving area • Separation of inventory custody from the account payable record keeping • Segregation of the ordering receiving inventory control amounts, accounts payable information systems and general accounting functions *Records it Document:* • Timely updating of the purchases journal for all purchase transactions • Preparation of receiving reports on pre-numbered forms so that the sequence of receipts can be reviewed for proper recording • Immediate preparation of receiving reports for all actual related goods prior to recording matching of vendor invoices with related PO and receiving report for verification of vendors, authorized prices mathematical accuracy account coding quantities and descriptions of goods • Monthly review and reconciliation of vendor statements with accounts payable records • Requirement for accounts payable records to be updated only when receiving report verifies actual receipt of goods • Performance of end of period review to determine whether purchases are recorded in the proper period *Security:* • Physical controls in the warehouse, receiving and areas access to inventory items • Physical and electronic controls covering to the purchases and accounts payable records *Independent checks:* • Comparison of receiving reports with the purchases journal • Matching of purchase records and verification for item descriptions quantities dates authorized prices, and mathematical accuracy • Review of purchases journal for mathematical accuracy reconciliation to the accounts payable records and correct posting to the general ledger • Requirement for receipts to be inspected counted and compared with "blind" copy POs • Performance of physical inventory counts and reconciliation with the inventory records • Verification of accounts payable subsidiary ledger for mathematical accuracy and proper posting to the general ledger	• Invalid vendors over-extended credit limits unapproved pricing or quantities • Fictitious purchases • Fictitious purchases • Fictitious purchases, omitted purchases wrong vendor, timing issues • Fictitious purchases, omitted purchases omitted purchases • Timing issues, omitted transaction, invalid purchases • Fictitious purchases, duplicate purchases, incorrect amounts or accounts, wrong vendor, timing issues • Omitted purchases, fictitious purchases incorrect amounts, wrong vendor, timing issues • Fictitious purchases, duplicate purchases, incorrect amounts, wrong vendor, timing issues • Timing issues, duplicate purchases, omitted purchases • Stolen goods Fictitious purchases, duplicate purchases, incorrect amounts, omitted transition, wrong vendor, timing issues, accumulation problems • Omitted purchases, duplicate purchases, incorrect amounts, omitted transactions, wrong account number, timing issues • Incorrect amounts, invalid purchases, timing issues • Incorrect amounts, incorrect accumulation or posting, omitted purchases, wrong account numbers, duplicate purchases • Fictitious purchases, duplicate purchase, incorrect quantities • Stolen goods, omitted purchases, fictitious purchases, wrong amounts, duplicate purchases, timing issues. • Incorrect amounts, incorrect accumulation or posting, omitted purchases, wrong account numbers, duplicate purchases.

The authorized individual typically includes his or her signature or initials on a purchase requisition to indicate proper authorization. In an automated system, limiting access to the authorizations function can control specific authorization for purchase transactions. This is a critical control in that no purchasing events should begin until the initial authorization occurs. In most organizations, the approval of a purchase requisition is the initial approval that triggers the remaining purchasing processes. A company should have established guidelines for managing vendor relationships, including securing competitive bids for purchase requisitions, negotiating payment terms, and maintaining current price lists. These functions should be limited to designated individual within the company.

Segregation of Duties

Within the purchasing process, the accounting duties related to requisitioning, ordering, purchase approval, receiving, inventory control accounts payable, information systems, and general accounting should be segregated in order to meet the objectives of internal controls. In general, responsibilities for authorization, custody, and record-keeping functions should each be separated in order to prevent the possibility of error or fraud. The authority function includes approval of purchasing transactions and certain information systems tasks such as data entry, programming, IT operations, and security. The custody function includes inventory handling and receiving, as well as the related cash disbursement duties.

The record-keeping function includes preparation of POs, as well as the general accounting reports such as the purchases journals, the accounts payable subsidiary ledger, the inventory ledger, general ledger, and financial statements. Ideal internal controls involve complete separation of inventory custody from inventory accounting. With respect to the purchasing process, this control is especially important in reducing instances of fraud. If, on the other hand, individuals have an opportunity to both handle inventory and access the related records, theft could occur and be concealed by altering the records. If custody and record keeping are segregated, the person having access to the goods may have an opportunity to conduct the theft, nut will not have the capability to alter records.

Adequate Records and Documents

Accounting personnel should ensure that adequate supporting documentation is maintained for purchasing transactions. Files should be maintained for purchase requisitions, POs, receiving reports, invoices, etc. These files should be organized either in chronological order by due date in numerical sequence by form number or inventory item number, or in alphabetical order by vendor name. When documentation is well organized, a company can establish the validity of its transactions and determine whether omissions have occurred. For instance, if the purchase requisition, PO, receiving report, and invoice are each retained and matched, accounting personnel can determine that each purchasing transaction is carried out properly with respect to quantity, quality, price, vendor, timing etc. Proper documentation also establishes an audit trail and facilitates the performance of independent checks and reconciliation.

Security of Assets and Documents

Purchasing records and programmes must be protected from unauthorized access through the use of electronic controls, such as passwords, and physical controls such as locked storage cabinets. Physical controls should also be used in the company's storage warehouse and receiving area, in order to protect purchased items from theft.

Independent Checks and Reconciliation

Some specific internal control procedures to be performed to achieve accountability for this process are presented next. The performance of these functions by some one, independent of the related authority, custody, and record-keeping functions for the purchasing process will enhance their effectiveness. For example, periodic physical inventory counts should be reconciled with the inventory ledger and general ledger control account to make sure inventory is being properly accounted for.

Significant differences may indicate that purchases have been omitted or theft may have occurred. Independent reconciliation of the accounts payable subsidiary ledger to the general ledger control account also helps ensure that transactions have been properly posted.

Purchase Return Process

Occasionally, the company may reject goods received and initiate the purchase return process. This may occur for a variety of reasons including the following:

1. Goods received are unacceptable due to these situations: quantity or quality discrepancies:
   - Damage or defects
   - Errors in the type of goods delivered or ordered
   - Discrepancies in the terms of the purchase
   - Timing issues
2. Changes in the company's needs regarding future sales or production. The unacceptable-goods circumstance noted in the first item listed are typically detected immediately, since goods are inspected upon receipt.

Sometimes, however, unacceptable goods may be discovered at a later date especially in the case of defective goods quality discrepancies, and purchase terms discrepancies. Changes in company needs, the second item, may occur at any time, as the company may have unforeseen changes in its business activities. Regardless of the reason for rejecting a purchase or the timing of the return, a company must have specific procedures in place for handling its returns to a vendor. These exhibits depict a return process whereby the items being returned had been received and accepted at an earlier time rather than being rejected immediately upon receipt.

Once rejected goods are identified, management approval must be obtained in order to formally make the decision to return the purchase. A debit memo should then be prepared. A debit memo is the document that identifies the items being returned, along with relevant information regarding vendor, quantity, and price. This form should be prepared by the accounts payable department on the basis of information from the related purchasing records such as the PO receiving report, and/or invoice after the debit memo is prepared, the goods can be physically returned to the vendor. At that point, the company should prepare a record of the return shipment similar to the procedures described in Chapter 8 for shipments related to the sales process. It is a good practice to keep a record of all shipping activity whether it is related to sales or purchase return transactions. It is also necessary to update inventory records so that the returned goods are no longer recorded as company assets. (Note that the accounts affected will depend on the type of inventory system used by the company, either perpetual or periodic).

Occasionally communications with the vendor regarding purchase returns indicate that there is no need to physically return the goods. In the case of defective goods for example, a vendor may wish to avoid the costs of shipping the items and may therefore instruct the company to dispose of the goods rather than return them. When this happens the company may need to implement additional controls to be sure that the disposal is not overlooked in the accounting records. Because there will be no shipping report for this item, company personnel may need to make an extra effort to be sure that the debit memo is properly prepared and recorded. Finally, the company will receive a refund or credit from the vendor for the returned (or disposed) goods.

Cash Disbursement Processes

The processing flow related to procurement activities require that payments be made for purchase obligations that have been incurred. The cash disbursements process must be designed to ensure that the company appropriately processes payments to satisfy its accounts payable when they are due. Cash disbursements may include payments made by cheque or with currency. Most companies conduct business transactions with cheques so that a written record is established of the cash disbursement. Because the practice of writing cheques enhances internal control. Here we will describe cash disbursements made by cheque. Figure 10.4 presents a business process map of a typical cash disbursement system, while Figure 10.5 shows the document flow chart for that process. Figure 10.6 is a data flow diagram of cash disbursements.

The accounts payable department is generally responsible for notification of the need to make cash disbursements and the maintenance of vendor accounts. Before payment is made to a vendor, specific steps should be taken to enhance the effectiveness and efficiency of the process.

These steps include vendor account reconciliation, cash management techniques, and payment authorization. Cash management is the careful oversight of cash balances, forecasted cash payments, and forecasted cash receipts to insure that adequate cash balances exist to meet obligations. An important aspect of this cash disbursements document flowchart is that the documentation must support or agree with the invoice before payment is approved and a check is prepared. The purchases order receiving report, and invoice must be matched to make sure that a valid order was placed, the goods were received in good condition, and that the vendor billed the correct quantities and prices. The process of matching these documents is extremely important in cash disbursements. No payments should be made until the documents are properly matched.

Accounts payable records need to be reviewed for accuracy on a regular basis. Many vendors send account statements to their customers each month to provide detail of amounts owed and paid. Accounts payable personnel should reconcile these statements with the company's accounts payable records. Accounts should be reviewed for agreement of amount and due date for each transaction. Any discrepancies should be resolved as soon as possible. Even if a vendor statement is not received, the company should have records of its obligations to each vendor (established during the purchasing process upon receipt of goods and the related purchase invoice). Some companies streamline the process by using a voucher system, where by multiple transactions involving the same vendor may be combined into a single cash disbursement.

Copies of invoices should be filed in the accounts payable department in chronological order by due date. Accounts payable personnel should review this file regularly so that disbursements can be initiated in a timely manner. This provides for efficient cash management. A company typically desires to keep its cash for as long as possible. However, it must also be mindful of paying by the due date in order to avoid late payment fees, to establish trust, and to stay on good terms with its vendors.

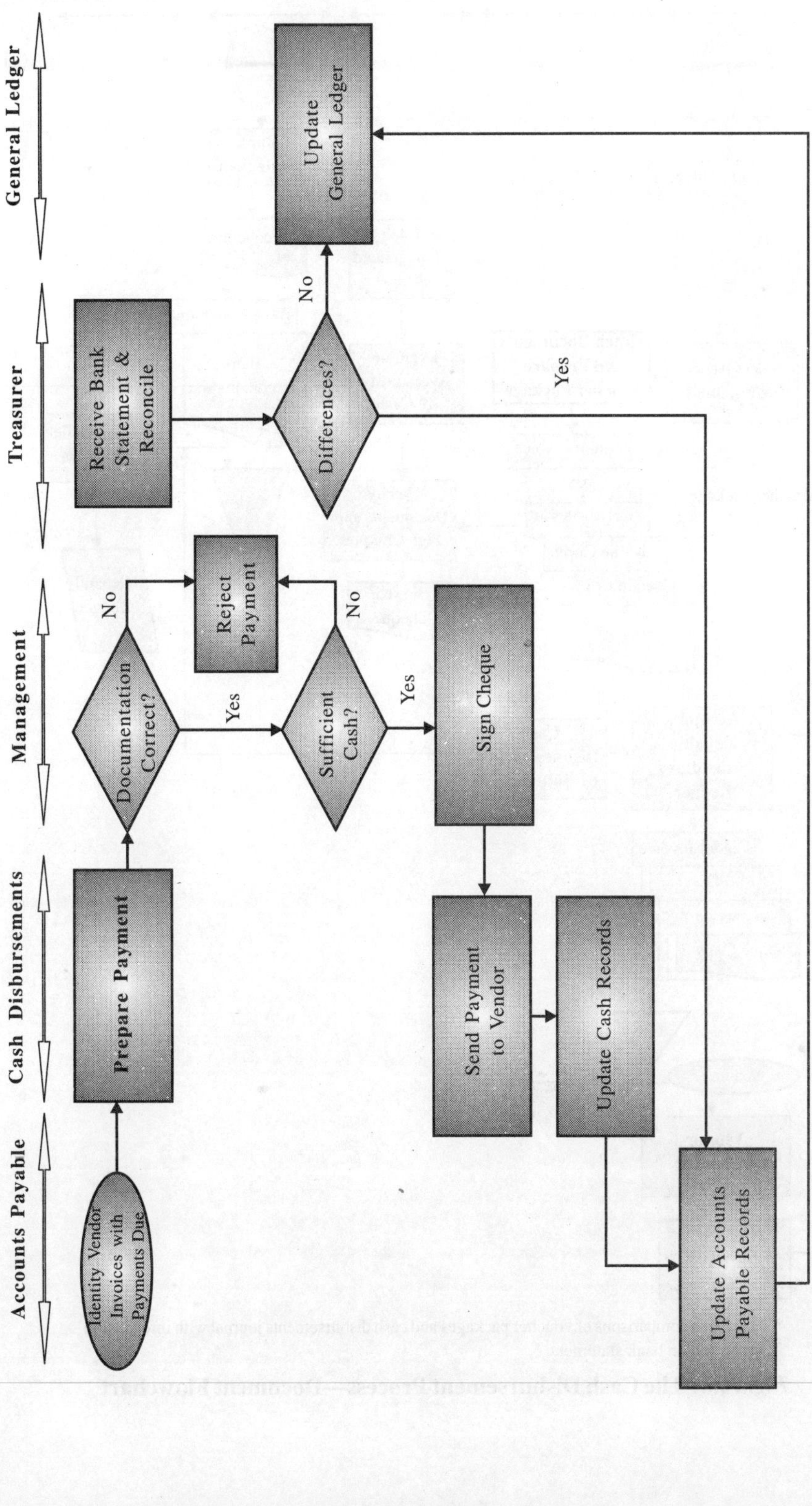

Fig. 10.4: **The Cash Disbursement Process**

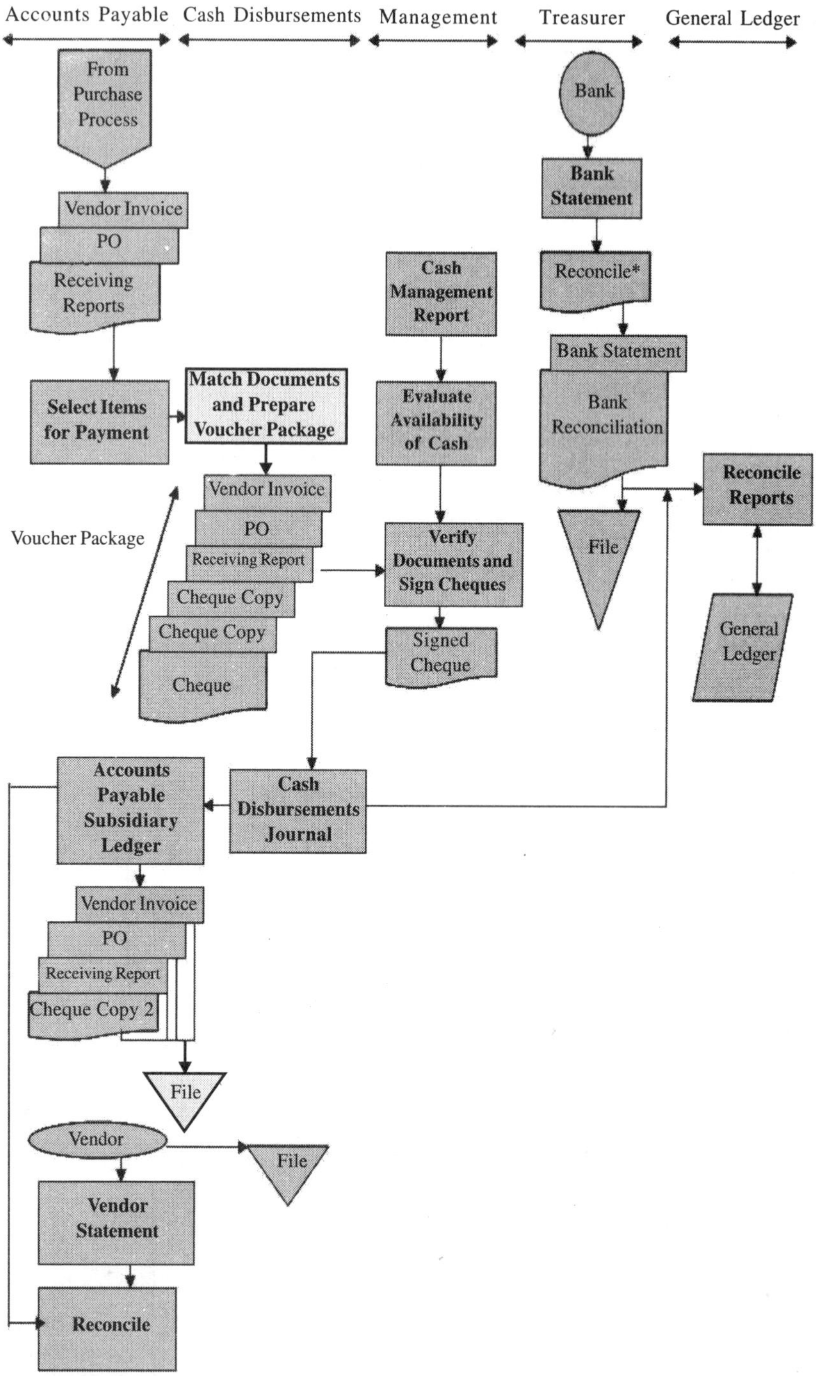

* Involves comparisons of voucher packages and cash disbursements journal with information reported on bank statement

Fig. 10.5: **The Cash Disbursement Process—Document Flowchart**

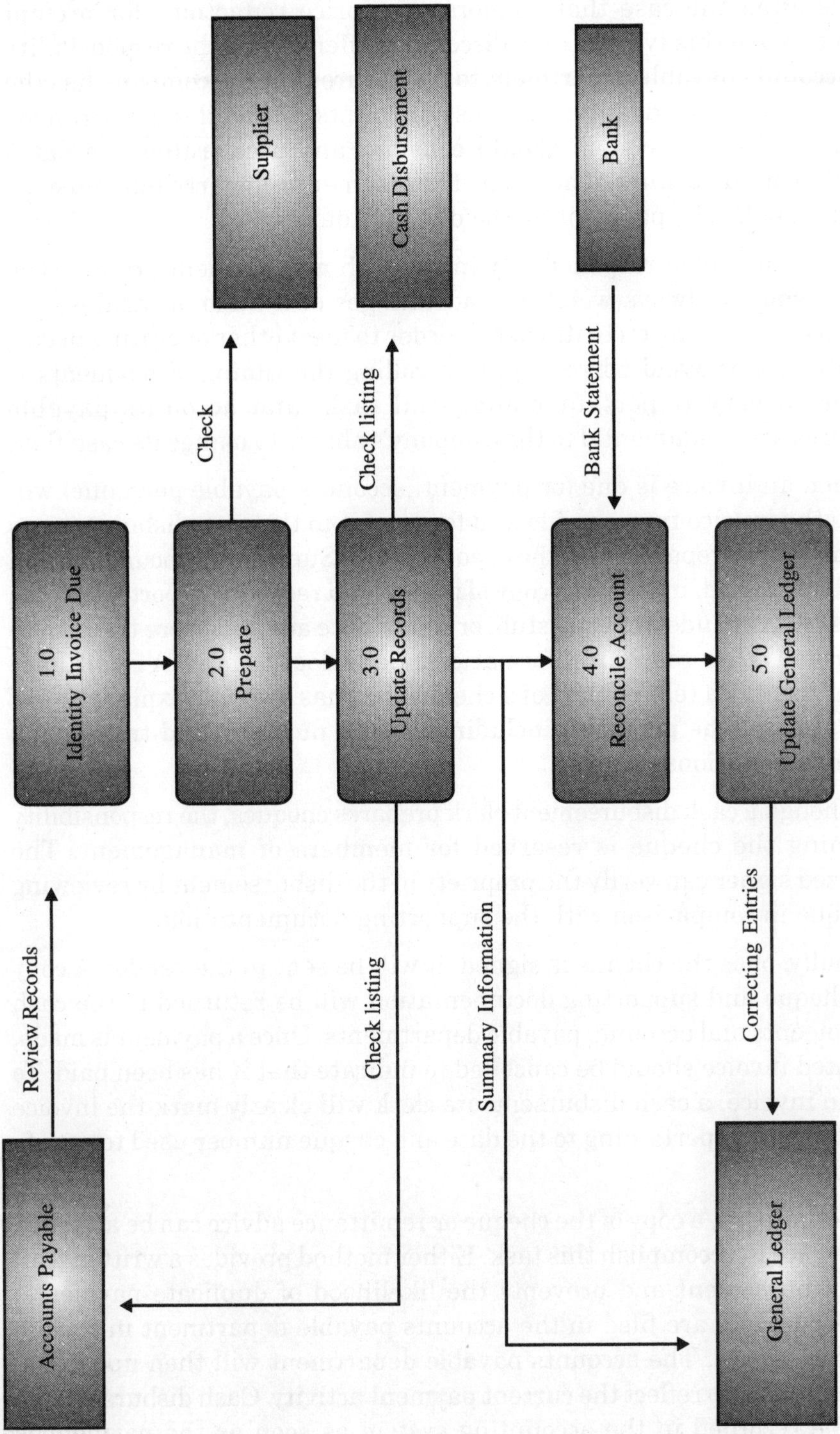

***Fig. 10.6:* Cash Disbursement Process Data Flow Diagram**

It is often the case that vendors offer price reductions for prompt payment. When this type of trade discount is offered, it is the responsibility of the accounts payable department to make sure that the company has the opportunity to take advantage of these discounts. If the files are arranged chronologically, the system should consider any accelerated due dates warranted by discounts. The cash disbursements department must be notified to make the payment by the discount date.

This is an added responsibility in the cash management process. The company should always weigh the advantages of a discount against the advantages of holding on to its cash in order to meet other operating needs, earn interest, or avoid borrowing. Controlling the timing of payments is therefore a very important managerial task, and accounts payable procedures are fundamental to the company's ability to mange its cash flow.

When an invoice is due for payment, accounts payable personnel will retrieve the invoice from the file and forward it to the cash disbursements department for preparation of the cheque detail. Supporting documentation should be attached, including a copy of the PO and receiving report. Business cheques often include a cheque stub, or remittance advice, where the invoice number and other relevant information can be documented. A remittance advice is usually a tear off part of a cheque that has a simple explanation of the reasons for the payment, including invoice numbers and transaction line-item descriptions.

Although a cash disbursement clerk prepares cheques, the responsibility for signing the cheque is reserved for members of management. The authorized signer can verify the propriety of the disbursement by reviewing the cheque in comparison with the supporting documentation.

Finally, once the cheque is signed, it will be sent to the vendor. A copy of the cheque and supporting documentation will be returned to the cash disbursements and accounts payable departments. Once a payment is made, the related invoice should be cancelled to indicate that it has been paid. To cancel in invoice, a cash disbursements clerk will clearly mark the invoice with information pertaining to the date and cheque number used to satisfy this obligation.

Alternatively, a copy of the cheque or remittance advice can be attached to the invoice to accomplish this task. Either method provides a written trail of the disbursement and prevents the likelihood of duplicate payments. These documents are filed in the accounts payable department in cheque number sequence. The accounts payable department will then update its vendor accounts to reflect the current payment activity. Cash disbursements should be recorded in the accounting system as soon as the payment is made. A cash disbursement clerk will prepare a cash disbursements journal, which is a chronological listing of all payments. This listing is sometimes called a cheque register and is similar to the record kept for a personal checking account.

The cash disbursements journal is used to prepare a daily journal entry, where by the cash and accounts payable accounts are updated to reflect the day's payments.

Risks and Controls in the Cash Disbursement Processes

Authorization of Transactions

Only the accounts payable department should authorize the processing of a cash disbursement transaction, according to the need to satisfy a vendor obligation. The authorization occurs when the accounts payable department matches the purchase order, receiving report, and invoice, and then forwards these matched documents to the cash disbursement department. In addition, designated members of management should be given responsibility for authorizing the actual payments by their signatures on the face of the cheque. This means that only one or a few people should have cheque-signing authority. The bank will keep records of the signatures of those authorized cheque signers and should not pay a cheque unless it bears the signature of an authorized party. Finally, the board of directors should authorize all bank accounts that are established in the company's name.

Many companies establish special cash disbursement authorization policies and procedures applicable to large cheques whereby a dual signature requirement is in palace for cheques over a specified dollar amount. Dual signature means that two people sign the cheque. This additional control requires the approval and signature of two authorized persons, thus reducing the risk of a significant fraud or error. The company's bank plays a crucial role in enforcing this policy, as it must not pay cheques over the threshold amount unless two authorized signatures are included.

Segregation of Duties

Effective segregation of duties reduces the likelihood of undetected errors or fraud by providing accounting control over the cash disbursement processes. If the purchasing, receiving, accounts payable, and cash disbursement functions are segregated, then the opportunity for theft or error within the processes should be minimized. No person should have the ability to initiate a false purchase transaction and simultaneously pay for it and account for it. Ideally, individuals within the cash disbursements department should not have cheque-signing authority and should not have access to the cash account or to the company's accounts payable records. In addition, information systems operations and programming related to the cash disbursements and accounts payable departments should be separated from those having responsibility for custody, authorization, or record keeping within those functions.

Adequate Records and Documents

An account payable subsidiary ledger and a cash disbursements journal are fundamental records in the cash disbursement process. Also, the practice of issuing checks on pre-numbered forms created a record of sequence of transaction. And the orderly maintenance of accounts payable records facilitates effective cash management techniques.

Security of Assets and Documents

Access to cash should be limited to the authorized cheque signers.

Physical controls should be in placing the areas where cash is retained and disbursed. Similarly, the company's stock of unused cheques should be protected and controlled. Access to the records should be limited to designated persons within the accounts payable and cash disbursements functions.

Independent Checks and Reconciliation

The cash disbursements journal and accounts payable subsidiary ledger should be reconciled to the general ledger control accounts on a regular basis. Also someone separate from the cash disbursements and accounts payable functions should be responsible for reconciliation of the bank statement on a monthly basis. Procedures for adequate reconciliation of the bank account include the direct receipt of the bank statement by the designated employee so that no others may have an opportunity to alter the document. If copies of cheques are returned with the bank statement, these cheques should be completely reviewed for dates, payees, and signatures.

Information Technology Systems of Expenditures and Cash Disbursement Processes

Even in computerized accounting systems, there can be many manual tasks. This is usually true for small or midsize companies with small scale Information Technology (IT) systems.

A three-way match is the matching of a purchase order to the related receiving report and invoice. The person operating the computer software must still physically match the purchase order to a receiving report and invoice, deciding which invoices match which purchase orders and receiving reports. Employees must complete the following tasks:

Table 10.2: Cash Disbursement Controls and Risks

Control	Minimizes the Related Risk of:
Authorization:	
• Board of Directors, authorization for all company bank accounts • Approval of cash disbursement transaction prior to preparation of a cheque • Dual signature requirement for disbursement of large sums of cash	• Invalid payments, stolen cash • Invalid payments, incorrect amounts • Invalid payments, incorrect amounts
Segregation:	
• Separation of cheque-signing authority from accounts payable and cash disbursements record keeping and custody of cash • Separation of the ordering, shipping and receiving, inventory control, accounts payable, cash disbursements, information systems, and general accounting functions	• Invalid payments, incorrect amounts, stolen cash • Fictitious payments, omitted payments, wrong amounts wrong vendor, timing issues. • Omitted payments • Fictitious payments, duplicate payments, incorrect amounts or accounts, wrong vendor, timing issues
Records it Documents:	
• Preparation of cheques on prenumbered forms prior to preparation of a cheque, matching of supporting documents (vendor invoices, authorized prices, mathematical accuracy, account coding quantities, and descriptions of goods • Updating of the cash disbursements journal and accounts payable records as soon as cheques have actually been disbursed cancellation of supporting documentation once payment has been made • Monthly review and reconciliation of vendor statements with accounts payable records	• Invalid payments, duplicate payments incorrect amounts, timing issues • Duplicate payments • Omitted payments, fictitious payments, incorrect amount, wrong vendors, timing issues • Stolen Cash • Fictitious payment, duplicate payments, incorrect amounts, omitted transactions, wrong vendor, timing issues, accumulation problems
Security:	
• Physical controls covering cash and the company's • Supply of cheques • Physical and electronic controls over access to the cash disbursement and accounts payable records	• Invalid payments, incorrect amounts, omitted payments, issues timing • Incorrect amounts, invalid payments, timing issues
Independent Cheques:	
• Monthly performance of bank reconciliation • Matching of cheques with original purchase documentation and verification for item descriptions, quantities, dates, authorized prices, and mathematical accuracy and proper posting to the general ledger • Verification of accounts payable subsidiary ledger for mathematical accuracy and proper posting to the general ledger	• Incorrect amounts, incorrect accumulation or posting, omitted payments, wrong account numbers, duplicate payments • Incorrect amounts, incorrect accumulation or posting, omitted payments, wrong account numbers, duplicate payments.

1. The purchasing department orders items from a vendor, and an employee must enter a purchase order into the accounting software by keying data into the fields of a purchase order form on the screen.
2. The receiving department receives the goods and compares the packing slip with the purchase order to confirm part numbers and quantities.
3. A receiving report is prepared by an employee filling in the appropriate fields in a receiving screen in the software. The person completing this screen must choose the purchase order that matches this receiving report. When the vendor name or ID number is entered, the system will list open purchase orders with that vendor.
4. After the vendor has provided an invoice must also be entered into an invoice entry screen in the accounting software. Again the proper purchase order must be chosen from a list of open purchase orders.
5. If the purchase order, receiving report and invoice match as to part numbers, quantities and prices the liability is approved for payment.
6. At the discount date or due date of the invoice, a designated person must date of the invoice, a designated person must select certain invoices to pay and have the system generate a batch of cheques.

This manual entry and matching system is extremely time consuming and expensive. It is time consuming due to the complexities of purchases. Purchasing and payments can become complex because a vendor may occasionally substitute items ship a different quantity (under ship or over ship) notifies the buyer of back orders, or fill a partial order. Thus, matching takes a large amount of human time to reconcile and approve for payment. This is true even if the accounting system is maintaining records and generating checks electronically.

The problems with this system are as follows:

1. The total salaries or wages paid to employees who match these three documents can be very expensive.
2. Mismatches as to part numbers, quantities or prices can take much time to investigate and reconcile, which causes the cost of this manual processing to be even higher.
3. Employees must manually key into the software the details of purchasing, receiving, and invoicing. This also is expensive and time consuming. In addition, keying errors can be made.

Many organizations are using advances in IT systems to reduce the time and expense of purchase and payment processing. With technology, processes can be changed to lessen or eliminate the aforementioned problems. The process undertaken to change processes to enhance efficiency is called business process reengineering. Recall that business process reengineering (BPR) is an organized change in business processes for the purpose of improving efficiency and effectiveness. BPR aligns business processes with the IT systems in order to accomplish these improvements. In the case of purchasing and paying for purchases, BPR facilitates reductions in paperwork annual processing, and processing costs. In many cases, IT systems are used to enhance the efficiency of purchasing and payment processes. Implementing these IT systems usually entails BPR to make the processes fit the IT system. Examples of IT system that usually involve BPR in purchasing and payments include the following:

- Computer-based matching and checking of purchasing documents
- Evaluated receipt settlement (ERS) an invoice-less processing technique
- Electronic forms of purchase and payment such as e-business, e-payables, and EDI

For example, EDI reduces or eliminates the manual keying of invoices because the invoice is communicated electronically between the buyer and the vendor. This section describes these IT systems that allow organizations to reduce the time and cost of processing purchases and payments.

Conversion Cycle

Accounting transactions recorded when converting purchased inventory into salable finished products. This cycle has only one main event: materials, labor and overhead are consumed in the conversion process. The conversion cycle is different from the revenue and expenditure cycle in that it has more than one component. The *payroll* component is present in every type of organization so we will consider it in detail; the *Inventory and Cost Accounting* components vary by the kind of company—manufacturing, merchandising or service. Obviously, the conversion cycle of a manufacturing firm will be more complex than the conversion cycle of a service company. We will not be covering Inventory and Cost Accounting in this class; many of the issues associated with those cycles were covered in Cost Accounting.

Internal controls (information) frequently missing for payroll.

Segregate personnel, timekeeping, payroll preparation, and paycheque distributions.

Time clocks used where possible. Job time tickets reconciled to the time clock cards.

Time clock cards approved by supervisors (overtime and regular hours). Treasurer signs paycheques.

Summary

- Like revenue cycle, we have expenditure cycle also. AIS plays an important role in processing accounting information related to expenditure cycle regarding risks and controls.

Self-Learning Activity

Try to answer the following questions on your own:

1. Expenditure processes include what?
2. What are the risks and controls in purchase process?
3. Discuss about cash disbursement process?
4. Write short notes on conversion cycle?

CHAPTER 11

Trading/Manufacturing Information System

Trading Account Information

Trading account gives the overall results of trading i.e., purchasing and selling of goods. In other words, it explains whether purchasing of goods and selling them has proved to be profitable for the business or not. It takes into account, on the one hand the cost of goods sold, on the other the value for which they have been sold away. In case the sales value if higher than the cost of goods sold, there will be a profit, which a reverse case, there will be a loss. The profit disclosed by the trading account is termed as 'Gross Profit'. Similarly, the loss disclosed by the trading account is termed as 'Gross Loss'.

Equation for preparing trading account information

1. *Gross Profit* = *Sales – Cost of goods sold*
2. *Cost of goods sold* = *Opening stock + Purchase + Direct expenses – Closing Stock*
3. *Gross Profit* = *Sales – (Opening Stock +Purchase + Direct expenses – Closing Stock)*

Important Information Regarding Trading Account

1. *Stock Information*

The term 'stock' includes goods lying unsold on a particular date. The stock may be of two types: they are opening stock and closing stock. The term opening stock means goods lying unsold with the businessman in the beginning of the accounting year. This is shown on the debits side of the trading account. The term closing stock includes goods lying unsold with the businessman at the end of the accounting year. It should be noted that stock at the end of the accounting year is taken after the books of accounts have been closed. The amount of closing stock is shown on the credit side of the trading account. The closing stock at the end of the accounting period will become the opening stock for the next year.

2. *Purchase Information*

The term purchase includes both cash and credit purchase of goods. Assets purchased for permanent use in the business such as purchase of plant furniture, etc. is not included in the purchase of goods. Similarly, purchase of articles such as stationary and other items meant for using in the business.

3. *Expenses on Purchases*

A trader has to incur various types of expenses for purchasing of goods as well as for bringing them to his shop for sale. Such expenses such as, commission paid to agents for purchase of goods, carriage charges for bringing the goods to the trader's shop, wages paid to coolies for transportation of goods, etc.

4. *Sales Information*

The term 'sales' includes both cash and credit sales. Gross sales will be shown in the inner column of the trading account out of which "sales returns" will be deducted. The net sales will then be shown in the outer column of the trading account. Proper care should be taken in recording sale of those goods which have been sold at the end of the financial year. The trading account information can be in a systematic format as follows:

Trading account

Dr			*Cr*		
Particulars	Amount		Particulars	Amount	
To opening stock		xxxx	By sales	xxxx	
To purchase	xxxx		Less sales returns	xxxx	xxxx
Less returns (purchase)	xxxx	xxxx	By closing stock		xxxx
To direct expenses		xxx	Total		
Total					
Gross Profit			Gross Loss		

Trading Account Information Processing and Distribution System

The following figure depicts a clear picture about the accounting information which is processed and distributed through trading account.

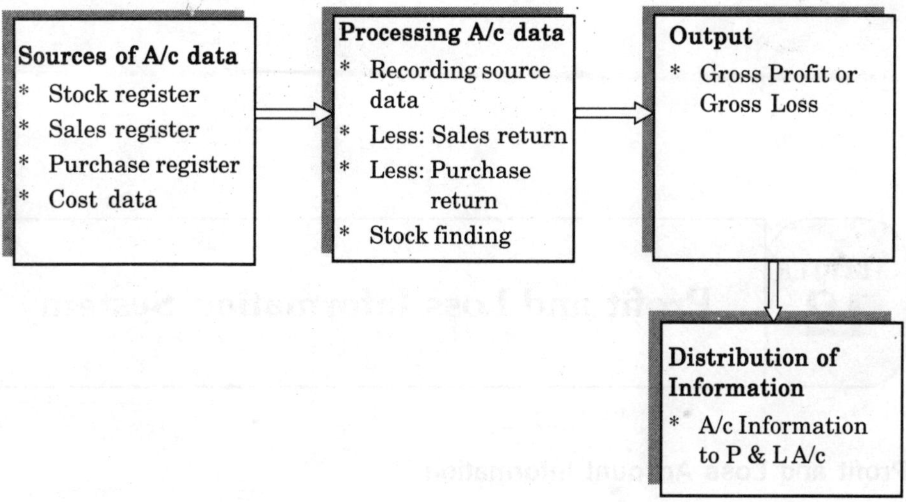

Summary

- Trading account information processing and distribution system deals with information on stock, sales, sales return, purchase, purchase returns, direct expenses on purchase. It receives data trading activities, processes and disseminate to the next system.

Self-Learning Activity

Try to answer the following questions on your own:

1. What is stock information?
2. Discuss about trading account information processing and distribution system.

CHAPTER 12

Profit and Loss Information System

Profit and Loss Account Information

In order to ascertain the true profit or loss, which the business has made during a particular period, it is necessary that all such expenses and incomes should be considered. Profit and loss account considers all such expenses and incomes and gives the net profit made or loss suffered by business during a particular period.

The profit and loss account provides information regarding the following details:

- It provides information about the net profit or net loss earned or suffered by the business during a particular period. Thus, it is an index of the profitability or otherwise of the business.
- The profit figure disclosed by the profit and loss account for a particular period can be compared with that of the other period. It helps in ascertaining whether the business is being run efficiently or not.
- An analysis of various expenses included in the profit and loss account and their comparison with the expenses of the previous period or periods helps in taking steps for effective control of the various expenses.
- Allocation of profit among the different periods or setting aside a part of the profit for future contingencies can be done. Moreover, on the basis of profit figures of the current and the previous period estimates about the profit in the year can be made.

A profit and loss account has got two sides. One is losses/expenses side and another one is profit/income side. The information on expenditures is listed on the left side. They are:

(i) Salaries

(ii) Rent and taxes

(iii) Printing and stationary
(iv) Advertising
(v) Insurance
(vi) Discount paid
(vii) Interest paid
(viii) Commission paid
(ix) Traveling expenses/allowances
(x) Legal charges
(xi) Repairs
(xii) Office expenses
(xiii) Other nominal expenses
(xiv) If gross loss any

Profit and Loss Account Format

Dr		*Cr*	
Particulars	**Amount**	**Particulars**	**Amount**
To gross loss b/d	xxx	By gross profit b/d	xxxx
To salaries	xxx	By discount received	xxx
To rent	xxx	By commission earned	xxx
To discount paid	xxx		
To advertisement	xxx		
Net Profit	xxx		
	xxx		xxx

On the other hand, in the right hand side the information on incomes is listed out. They are:

(i) Gross profit transferred from the trading account
(ii) Discount received
(iii) Interest earned
(iv) Commission earned
(v) Bad debts recovered
(vi) Profit on sale of investments
(vii) Other nominal incomes

Profit and Loss Account Information Processing & Distribution System

The following figure depicts a clear picture about the accounting information which is processed and distributed through profit and loss account.

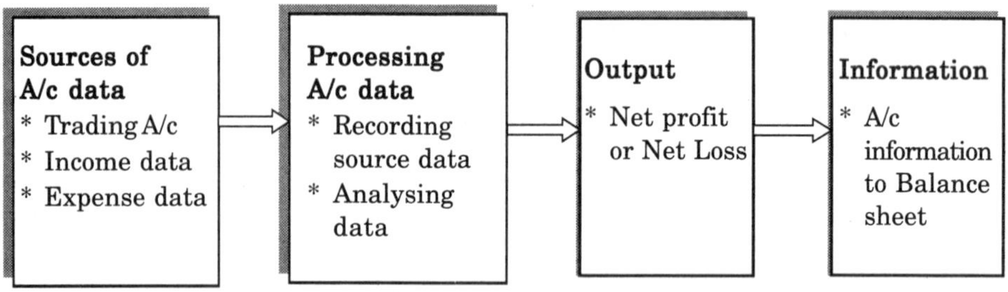

Summary

- Profit and loss account information processing and distribution system deals with information on income and expenses given in the text. It is a system which provides accounting information to the next i.e., balance sheet information system.

Self-Learning Activity

Try to answer the following questions on your own:

1. What is the information in profit and loss accounting system?
2. Discuss about profit and loss account information processing and distribution system.

CHAPTER 13

Balance Sheet Information System

Financial Statement Information (Balance Sheet Information)

The Balance Sheet is an all-important statement, but easy to be misunderstood. It is not an account like the Profit and Loss Account. But it is simply a 'sheet' of balances. It shows in a classified form, all the balances remaining in the books, after the nominal accounts have been closed. It is generally thought that the Balance Sheet is a statement of Liabilities and Assets. All items of assets and other debit balances left open are shown on the right-hand side and the liabilities and other credit balances left unclosed are set out on the left-hand side of the sheet. In short, a Balance Sheet is a statement of affairs prepared with a view to ascertaining the exact financial position of the business on a particular date.

Information Available in a Balance Sheet

The following information can be seen in a balance sheet:

- *Fixed Assets:* Land, building, machinery, furniture, etc.
- *Current Assets:* cash and bank balances, stock of raw materials, work-in-progress, finished goods, debtors, bills receivables, short-term investments, pre-paid expenses.
- *Intangible Assets:* Goodwill, patents, trade marks, etc.
- *Fictitious Assets:* Formation expenses (registration fee, etc.), discount on shares.
- *Fixed Liabilities:* Capital, long-term loans.
- *Current Liabilities:* Accounts payable, outstanding expenses, bank overdraft, short-term loans, advance payments received for future supply.

Balance Sheet Information Processing and Distribution System

The following figure depicts a clear picture about the accounting information, which is processed and distributed through balance sheet.

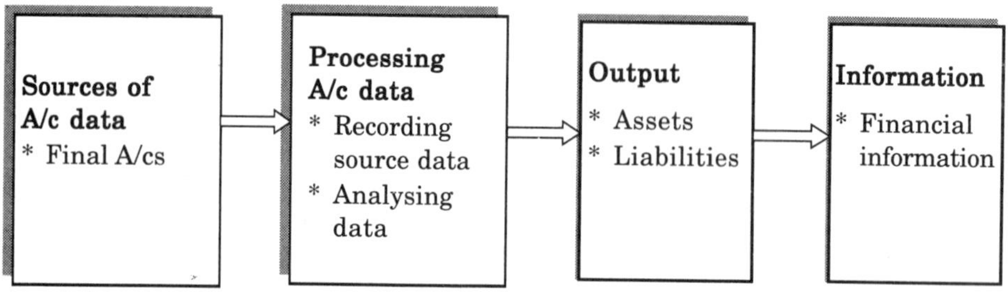

Summary

- Balance sheet information processing and distribution system deals with information on assets and liabilities given in the text. It is a system which provides financial information.

Self-Learning Activity

Try to answer the following questions on your own:

1. What information can be had from balance sheet information system?
2. Discuss about balance sheet information processing and distribution system.

CHAPTER 14 Resource Management and Major Classification of Accounting Information System

Resource Management and Sources of Accounting Information

Accounting information system (AIS) plays an important role in the operation of today's success. It provides service by supplying information to the needy personnel in the organization. For which the resources of the organization should be managed properly.

Resources

The basic resources known as five M's — are: Money, Manpower, Materials, Machine, and Methods. The management authorities have added one more M called Management of Information. These resources are to be maintained and managed in a right manner to have a well-defined and well-designed accounting information system. In order to manage the resources of the organization effectively and efficiently, the managers incharge of these resources must take effective steps to gather required information on each resource. The role of accounting information system in this respect is very significant.

Sources

The data or information which flow through an AIS come from three sources:

Business activities with individuals or organizations external to the business, such as sales, purchases, payment of cash or receipt of cash, etc;

Internal business activities, such as placing raw materials into process using direct labour, and transfers; and

Feedback resulting from output information and managerial decisions, such as need to place orders for materials when the inventory reaches the order point, the need for or use of equipment, authorization for overtime work, or the decision to write off an account receivable or obsolete inventory.

The AIS managers must make sure that the resources of the organisation, sources of information, and the factors influence the AIS are managed properly. The Figure 14.1 presents the idea about the consideration of the above.

Sources of Information	Resources	Factors Influence AIS
Internal	Money	Behavioural Analysis
	Manpower	
	Materials	Quantitative Methods
External	Machines	
	Methods	
	Management of Information	Computers

Fig. 14.1: **Relationship between and among Sources, Resources and factors**

The Figure 14.1 depicts that there is relationship between and among the sources of information, resources and factors influencing AIS. There should be coordination between these three elements. The internal sources of information may be the journal information processing system, ledger information processing system, trial balance system, final accounts information system and financial statements information systems. The external sources may be the government, creditors, suppliers, public, etc. Modern organizations caused accountants' information providing function to become more difficult. To meet the challenges of complex systems accountants have expanded their knowledge beyond traditional accounting subject matter.

The resources or factors that affect AIS are:

Behavioural Analysis — Accountant must recognize that people work in the system. The people must be given consideration when designing the system. They are the basic resources. Accountants understand how people are motivated toward positive organizational performance. Communicating accounting information is a job of accountant and relationship must be maintained with the people working in the organization;

Quantitative Methods — As a resource, quantitative methods include statistical analysis, linear programming, PERT, waiting line theory, simulation, regression analysis, decision-making techniques;

Computers — This includes the EDP accounting. The accounting system must continually interact with the EDP sub-system. Accountants should understand the capabilities and limitations of a computer so that they can perform their job efficiently.

AIS and Sub-systems

Information may be of quantitative information and non-quantitative information. Again the quantitative information can be divided into accounting information and non-accounting information. Accounting information (AI) can be divided into several sub-systems. Many authors classified AI into major classifications in their own view. For our purpose, we may classify broadly the AI sub-systems into four categories. They are: Cost accounting information, management accounting information, financial accounting information, and tax information. These classifications of sub-systems of AIS are discussed hereunder.

Cost Accounting Information System

Cost Accounting Information

The cost accounting is primarily concerned with the ascertainment of cost and profitability and with the control of costs through budgetary control, standard costing, etc. It evolved out of financial accounting. It provides information, largely in the area of costs, which will be useful in controlling the business operations. Cost accounting provides just cost information for managerial purpose. The cost accountant suggests to the management the best of the alternatives by use of different cost methods. The main components of cost accounting information system are: cost information ascertainment, cost information presentation and cost information for control. The following are the purposes of cost accounting information system:

- Cost information enables the management to ascertain the cost of product, job, contract, service or unit of production so as to develop cost standards.
- Cost information may be ascertained, under different circumstances, using standard costing, managerial costing, uniform costing methods.
- Cost information leads to cost control — minimizing the cost of manufacturing and comparison of actual cost with standards.
- Matching the costs with revenues is possible.
- Special cost studies and investigations are the basis for the management in decision-making process.
- Cost information helps for the preparation of financial statements and final accounts.
- Cost information records provide the information relating to each department.
- It aims to guide the management for proper planning, control and decision-making.
- Cost information is the base for analyzing product-wise profitability of the organization.

- It supports to have an effective inventory control system.
- It helps to minimize the wastage, shortage, loss, etc.
- Cost accounting information prevents frauds and manipulation.
- Cost estimation is possible.

Cost Classification and Cost Accounting Information

The cost accounting information helps to identify the cost classifications. The cost classifications are: cost behaviour by volume of activity, sunk costs, relevant and non-relevant costs, avoidable and unavoidable costs, opportunity costs, and marginal costs or incremental costs. These cost classifications can be identified and proper decision can be made through cost information that is gathered through cost accounting system.

Cost Information and Parties

The following exhibit reveals the cost information required by the parties both within and outside the organization and information support of cost accounting system.

Management:	* Reveals unprofitable activities (waste, shortage also) * Decision making information * Efficiency improvement * Fixing price * Inventory control * Standard fixing * Tool for management control * Furutre prospects (cost estimation also)
Employees:	* Sound wage policy * Higher bonus plans * Distinct efficient and inefficient workers * Security of job
Creditors:	* Cost information through statements
Government:	* Great use of national plans * Policies on tax, import and export.
Public:	* Get better quality goods * Pay fair price * Employment opportunity.

Cost Information

Cost information can be: direct materials, direct labour, direct expenses/ overheads, production overheads, department/general, which is the composite of production cost. Along with these, administrative cost, selling/ distribution expenses leads to total cost.

Management Accounting Information System

Management Accounting Information

The accounting information specially prepared to aid the managers is called management accounting information. This information is used in three management functions (see Figure 14.2). They are: Planning, implementation, and control functions.

Management Accounting Information in Planning: performed by managers at all levels, planning is the process of deciding what actions should be taken in the future. Decisions are arrived at by different stages. Accounting information is useful especially in the analysis step of the decision making process.

Management Accounting Information in Implementation: managers must make more detailed implementation plans and take necessary actions. It requires supervision on the part of the managers. Accounting information system provides required information regarding this aspect to make the implementation stage effective.

Management Accounting Information in Control: Accounting information is used in the control process as a means of communication, motivation, attention getting, and appraisal. As a means of communication, accounting reports can assist in informing employees about manager's plans and in general about the types of action management wishes to take. As a means of motivation, accounting reports can include members of the organization to act in a way that is consistent with the organisation's overall goals and objectives. As a means of attention getting, accounting reports signals that problems may exist that require investigation and possibly action. This is called as feedback. As a means of appraisal, accounting information helps show how well managers has performed.

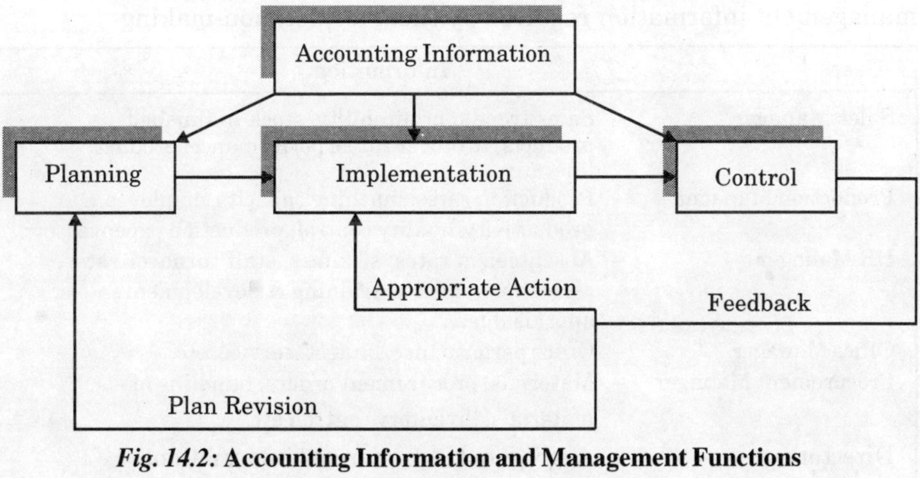

Fig. 14.2: **Accounting Information and Management Functions**

Thus, management accounting information system is a systematic approach to planning, implementing and control functions of management. It generates information for establishing plans and controls. It provides for a system of setting standards, plans or targets, and reporting variances between planned and actual performances for corrective actions. In management decision-making process, management accounting information system provides selective and pertinent information out of mass of data gathered. Management accounting information system is the process of:

- identification of economic events;
- measuring the economic events;
- accumulation of economic events;
- analysis of the economic events with resources;
- preparation and interpretation of accounting information; and
- communication — reporting of accounting information to managers for decision making.

Time Dimensions of Management Accounting Information

The following exhibit presents the time dimension of management accounting information.

Time Focus	→	Focus on future course of action
Time Periods	→	Regular period basis (weekly, monthly, annually)
Time Value	→	Produced within a given period to maintain the value of information

Users of Management Accounting Information

The following exhibit depicts a clear picture on the users and management information required by them for decision-making.

Users		**Information**
Sales Manager	–	Sales trends, profitability, stock of finished products, turnover rates, performance, product line, etc.
Production Manager	–	Production rates, machine capacity, employee productivity, quality control, production expenses, etc.
HR Manager	–	Absenteeism rates, sickness, staff turnover rates, recruitment charts, training & development, appraisal, etc.
Office Manager	–	Office performance, budget, service, etc.
Procurement Manager	–	Materials, procurement orders, handling of materials, inventory control, etc.
Director	–	Aggregated, summarized information.

Financial Accounting Information System

Financial Accounting Information

Financial accounting information system provides the basic structure for collecting data. This system serves the interest of mostly external users. It follows the general accepted accounting principles. It presents historical information, annual reports covering entire organization.

Though the balance sheet and profit & loss account, to the external parties, particularly investors reveal the manner in which the resources entrusted by them to the firm have been utilized. Financial information system adopts twelve months period for reporting financial performance information to shareholders and investors, and other external parties. The statements are subject to the verification of statutory audit. Therefore financial accounting system stresses accuracy and precision of accounting data.

Information Requirements with Respect to Each Area

The managers need financial information to decide the things to be undertaken. The areas of information needs of the managers are: financial planning and budgeting, assets and liability management, profitability analysis, cash and funds flow management, evaluation of funds and investments, responsibility and profitability reporting.

Financial Planning and Budgeting: To have effective financial planning and budgeting the finance managers need information. The use of information technology by the information system has made it possible to develop real time flexible budgets and financial plans. Information regarding the activities in the enterprise can be subjected to perpetual investigation using intelligent agents software so that exceptions are reported automatically and without fail.

Assets and liability management: Information system can provide information to a finance manager for management of assets and liability, and monitoring their utilization on a regular basis.

Profitability analysis: Information system provides a finance manager with the information required for profitability analysis as well as modern tools of analysis of such information.

Cash and funds flow management: A large amount of information regarding activities in operating cycle is required for decision-making in respect of cash and funds flow management. The information system provides such information.

Evaluation of funds and investments: Investment decisions require information. The evaluation of funds and investments are done with the support of accounting information particularly the financial information provided by the system.

Responsibility and profitability reporting: It is a control technique which relies on financial information. Such information can be provided by the financial information system.

Tax Information System

Tax Information

Every business enterprise should maintain tax information records and abide by the rules and regulations of the government with regard to tax payment and submission of tax returns in time. They must file tax returns with the tax authorities. According to the norms fixed by the government the business organizations should pay sales tax, duties, entry tax, if they deal with import and export activities.

They must keep tax records for tax purposes. The tax information should be recorded in the relevant books and records. The AIS supports in gathering, analyzing and disseminating the tax information to the managers of the organization.

The sources of tax information for an organization are: the records maintained by the organization, the records maintained by the tax authorities concerned, and such other government offices which are dealing with tax returns. The process of tax information can be done with the help of records, books, registers maintained for the purpose by the tax accountants. The process of entering tax data, verification, and calculations are made by the person concerned. The output is the tax information which can be found in the tax records.

The above discussion reveals entire aspects on the broad categories of accounting information.

Summary

- AIS can be of: management accounting information system, financial accounting information system, cost accounting information system and tax accounting information system.

Self-Learning Activity

Try to answer the following questions on your own:

1. Write about management accounting information system.
2. Explain financial accounting information system.

CHAPTER 15 Accounting Information System Design and Development Process

Information System Design and Development

Before going to see about Accounting Information System (AIS) design and development process, we have to know about the information systems design and development process. Information system should not be allowed to grow as it grows. This will result in complete mess. IS may not provide what is needed and what is provided by it may not be needed for management, when the IS is allowed to grow irrelevant or unplanned manner. Information system serves as a nerve system for an organization. The hurdles in the flow of information may certainly disturb working system and demoralize the workforce. This calls for scientific approach in designing IS.

Approaches for IS Development

Organizations across the industry follow different approaches for developing IS. It is all based on their nature of business, levels in the organization, the level of importance and interest shown by the organization for IS development and above all the management ethics. Generally there are three basic approaches (see Table 15.1) followed across the industry viz.: (1) top down approach; (2) bottom up approach; and (3) integrated approach.

Table 15.1: IS Approaches

Process / Approach	Participation of Management Levels		
	Design	Implementation/Control	Operations
Top down	Top	Middle	All
Bottom up	Top	Middle	All
Hybrid	All	Middle	All

Table 15.1 clearly presents the participation of management levels in IS approach in different tasks of designing, implementation and control, and operations of IS in an organization. The approaches are discussed hereunder.

1. ***Top Down Approach***

   Top down approach is a form of bureaucratic approach. Here the top management decides the goals of the organization and determines the courses of action for achieving goals. An information system is developed to communicate the plan of top management to middle and lower management. This approach may be useful for organizations established to carryout a project during short span of time. The main deficiency of this approach is—it may loose the cooperation and coordination of the employees who actually involved in the work.

2. ***Bottom Up Approach***

   Here the top management restricts the role in deciding the company's wide objectives, policies and programmes. Keeping these in mind, the functional area-wise plans are set by middle management and lower management and finally the organizational design for MIS is drawn. The bottom up approach gives importance for reporting system, while top down approach insist on target and achievement. The merit of bottom up approach is the involvement of all the levels of management in deciding the design for IS. The demerit of this approach is—it is a time consuming process as the designing process involves the support of all the levels of management. By the time many changes may take place in the hardware and software requirements of the IS.

3. ***Integrated Approach***

   It is the fusion of the merits of top down and bottom up approaches. Here the top management gives importance to the opinions of the middle management and lower management in designing IS. On the basis of wide discussions only the required design is finalized. The merit of this approach is the involvement of the all the stakeholders of the IS within the organization.

AIS Design and Development Process

A number of accounting software packages are available offering a variety of features. They offer only the structure for AIS. At the most they reduce the programming effort. The development of AIS is much more than the software for ledger posting and reporting. It also involves procedures for capturing data and distribution, as well as analysis of accounting information. The modular approach can be fruitfully applied to the design and development of an accounting information system. The modular approach encompasses enterprise module, database module, interface module, application module, implementation module, and post-implementation module. The various stages of the modular approach to the system development are discussed hereunder.

Enterprise Module

The enterprise module of AIS development involves identification of basic entities, activity analysis, grouping of activities into subsystems, and setting priorities.

Identifying entities: Number of entities exist in a business and the list is as varied as the business activities are. Identifying broad entities, each contains a group of elementary entities. Kerner points out six basic entities in a business enterprise viz., customers, products, vendors, personnel, facilities and money. In AIS, there are three entities, namely, transactions, account and processing period. The interrelationships can be expressed using the E-R diagram as below:

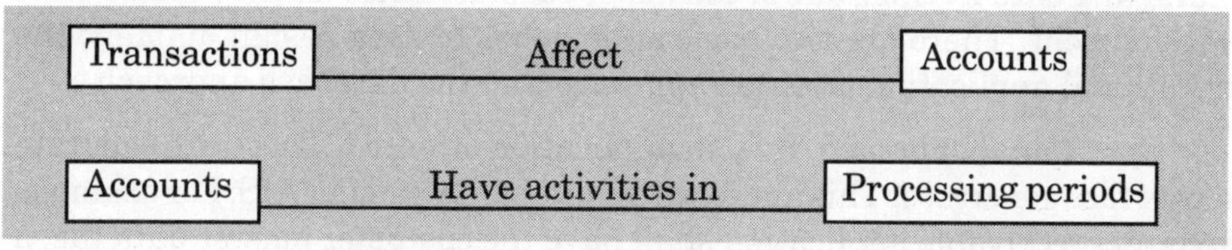

The entities are identified in the light of and with a view to defining the scope and focus of the AIS. The transactions shall be of different kinds, such as receipts, payments, sales, purchase, acquisition of assets or repayment of liabilities, etc., and each of them can be called a lower level entity. Similarly, accounts can be of different kinds, such as assets, liabilities, revenue, expense. Each of these heads can have lower level entities such as fixed assets and current assets. These entities can be further split into still lower entities like land and building, plant and machinery, etc. However, at this stage, the broad entities need to be identified. The details are worked out at the time of designing the databases.

Activity analysis: This stage is meant for identification of activities with the entities. It is essential to base the activity analysis on the basic entities identified. The next level of activity analysis involves identification of the life-cycle activities. As for transactions, there are four life-cycle activities: purchasing life-cycle, production life-cycle, revenue life-cycle, and investment life-cycle. Similarly, the processing period has two life-cycle activities, namely, planning and control life-cycle, and internal and external reporting life-cycle. At this level, the functions are to be defined, i.e., activity analysis on functions. It focuses only on those activities that create, update or use information in the database of the enterprise.

Grouping of activities into subsystems: After the activities are defined, they are regrouped to form subsystems. This can be done on the basis of organization structure with the help of structure charts and hierarchical diagrams, coordination of activities, and communication system. Finally, the subsystems are integrated with each other providing the building blocks for an accounting information system.

Setting Priorities: Once the subsystems are identified and integrated, the priorities need to be determined among the various subsystems and features in each system. It can be done on the basis of financial resources, implicit costs. It is essential to weigh the pros and cons of each subsystem on the basis of well-designed evaluation criteria defined in terms of the critical success factors and brainstorming sessions to determine priorities.

Database Module

Accounting information system processes large volume of data. Managing data is, thus, one of the major considerations in the process of its development. There are two basic approaches to data design, namely, the traditional application oriented approach and the database approach.

Traditional approach: It is an application oriented. There are separate sets of files generated. This approach is suitable for smaller AIS. For example, accounts receivable application shall have the customer master data file, a sales transaction file and a receipts from customers' transaction file. These are used only for accounts receivable application.

Database approach: It is a modern approach based on assumption that several applications require data sets. The common repository called database is managed by a management system known as database management system (DBMS). This approach takes care the problems of applications approach. A data dictionary is maintained and data can be called using the words specified in the data dictionary. It reduces the size and complexity of the application programmes. The data design process can be done by top-down approach and the E-R charts as drawn in enterprise module.

Interface Module

An interface module defines the data items and the formats of input, output and dialogue screens. It also defines the report formats and the screens for navigation from one part of information system to the other.

Input screens: The input screens are defined in the light of natural process of the business activity. Therefore, they depend primarily on the forms (such as invoice, purchase orders, sales order, expense voucher, etc.) that are used to record manually the data when they are first received by the enterprise. The factors like matching with forms (matching input screens with input forms), interactive (pointing out errors in data entry and permit corrections), consistency (in defining terms and location for certain common types of data items), simplicity, flexibility (amenable to modifications), and custom made for each category of user may be kept in mind while designing input screen.

Output screens: The reports may be prepared for further analysis by some other computer programme or by the user himself. The reports meant for users are normally kept in the form of text, tables, and graphs. Output screens are designed to display the reports/output accurately, timely and at low cost.

Dialogue screens: These are used for identifying and performing the tasks in the AIS. They define what can be done, how to navigate from task/procedure to another and how to perform various tasks that the AIS permits. The simplicity can be introduced by providing Graphical User Interface (GUI) and having limited number of menu items in one screen.

CASE tools for screen design: Computer Aided Software Engineering tools are used to design screens. The forms and screens designed using the CASE tools can easily be modified.

Application Module

This module extends the subsystems already identified in the enterprise module. For each subsystem identified, detailed processing procedures are defined in this module. The application module is primarily concerned with the processes involved in converting the input data into values that shall form part of the reports as defined in the interface module. It may be noted that only those processes are to be defined:

(a) that change the values in the databases, or

(b) that are not parts of the database but are required in the reports defined in the interface module.

Data flow diagrams are prepared to identify the basic processing procedures. DFDs describe the flow of data. The DFD basic symbols are used in this regard. They are entity (▭), data flow, (⟶) process (▭ or ○), and data store (⊏). After defining the processing procedure with the help of DFD symbols and diagrams, it is suggested that the DFD must be thoroughly tested before it is finalized. Future processing details may be chalked out and described in structured English (pseudo-codes). These pseudo-codes are later used for coding the applications.

Implementation Module

This module is primarily concerned with testing of the system, training the users and installation of the system.

Testing the system: The testing of various modules is done at various stages of development of AIS. Testing of system is the process of seeking answers to two basic questions:

1. Whether the AIS serves the information needs of the enterprise?
2. Does the AIS function correctly?

Unit tests: These tests are used at module level. These tests are performed to detect errors in interface, database, arithmetic operations, and control logic. *System test* is an integrated test should be conducted to check whether or not the units work correctly as a group. Fertuck suggests three strategies for testing the AIS. They are: *Clear box testing* in which tests are designed to establish whether the procedures followed for processing match the requirements of the application; *Black box testing* in which the system is tested for invalid data or that may cause error in the functioning of the system; and *Ticking box testing* assumes that it is never possible to deliver a totally error-free AIS.

Training the users: The users of AIS should be trained in a proper way to adopt themselves to the new designed AIS. The system analyst is the person who acts as agent to motivate, train and guide the users of AIS.

Installation: Installation is the process of replacing the old system with a new system. Broadly there are four approaches to installation. They are: *Parallel installation* where both old and new systems function; *Cold installation* is done when the old system is immediately discontinued and is replaced by a new system (it has not been found acceptable for AIS); *Pilot installation* may be installed in one of the units as pilot project and if it is feasible, the new system can be installed in other units of the business enterprise; and *Phase-in installation* may be done in stages. These stages are independent components of the AIS.

Post-Implementation Review

Each system must be reviewed after implementation is complete. Such review not only helps in identifying the weaknesses of the system but also prepares an agenda for modification for future. System audit can also be conducted to examine how successful the system is, in terms of cost, delivery schedule, completeness and quality.

As may be noted from the above, development of AIS requires involvement of manager at almost every stage. Manager's involvement has to be greater in the database module as it is he who understands data the best.

AIS Process (Input, Process, Output)

Sources of Data

The data and information which flow through an information system come from come from the following sources:

Business activities with individuals or organizations external to the business, such as sales, purchases, payments of cash, or receipts of cash.

Internal business activities, such as placing raw materials in to process, using direct labor, and transfers. or

The feedback resulting from output information and managerial decisions, such as the need to place orders for materials when the inventory reaches the order point, the need for or use of equipment, authorizations for overtime work, or the decision to write off an account receivable or obsolete inventory. Feedback resulting from the processing of data and information should inform management of the direction in which the business is moving. As a result of evaluating the information, management makes the necessary decisions to facilitate the accomplishment of its plans. These decisions have a stabilizing effect on the business and are designed to compensate when actual operations are off target.

Business is a continuing and complex activity. It is not static. Each managerial decision and business transaction affects operations and may be important to future activities. Feedback is the return of a portion of information output to input. Its function is to permit compensation for variations from the plan. The function of feedback can be compared to the function of a captain whose ship is off course, if a ship is off course, or if conditions warrant, the captain will note the situation and correct the course of the ship. By the same process, when operations vary from the plan, the condition is signaled, and through feedback, the system provides the information for management to make the necessary adjustments to maintain steady progress toward business goals.

Feedback also functions as a closed loop of control. The closed loop of control can be compared to a thermostat. If the water in a boiler is too cold, the thermostat will turn on the heating element. When the water is as hot as desired, the thermostat will turn the heating element off. In the information system, for example, an inventory control procedure may provide control information. Whenever the reorder point is reached for a specific item, the system will signal for a purchase. With the order and acquisition of an item, the total inventory available and on order will change. If sufficient quantities are on hand or on order when the item is again needed, no further order will be signaled. In a closed loop of control, information about the item being controlled can control the item further through feedback.

It can be noted that all data or information are channeled through management. Management at all levels — top, middle, and supervisory—is involved. Management must provide judgment and has full responsibility for perceiving the events that have occurred, for reviewing input into the system, and for completeness. Valid and complete input in to the system, and for completeness. Valid and complete input are essential for accurate, timely, and factual data and information processing and output. Adequate internal control must be established and maintained.

The flow of data and information in an information system is lofted through channels organically designed for accounting purposes alone. The three phases of data and information flow are input, processing, and output. They are universal to all systems as well as to each of the subsystems and procedures comprising the system. Each of the phases will be discussed in sequence.

Input Phase

Input in to the information system includes the operations of initial recording and classifying. Initial recording is the placing of data into the system for the first time, and doing this as early as possible is essential to effective data flow. Once in the system, data can be used, controls can be established, and the significance of the data can be determined. As financial data become available, they must be introduced into the system immediately or in a regular way.

The adequacy of the entire system is often related to the validity of data entered at the initial recording. At the point of initial recording, data are processed by the person entering the data, and data incorrectly recorded or omitted may result in misleading or inadequate information output. No system's output can be any better than its initial input data. Extra care at this point to ensure correct data entry will be more than justified.

Initial recording includes both the collecting of data and the making of record. Either the collecting or the recording of data can start the sequence of data and information flow into the system. They may be separated, or they may be accomplished at the same time. For example, collecting and recording are separate operations when a cash register collects data as to the different sources for which cash is received without a written notation. The data can then be recorded in a summary report at the end of each day or some other given period. Collecting and recording may also be accomplished simultaneously. For example, at the time a transaction, such as a credit sale, occurs, the data may be collected and recorded in writing on a sales ticket.

Data that are initially collected and recorded on a conventional document, such as a sales ticket, must be transferred later to some other media or special form of processing within the information system. In a manual system, the data from source documents are extracted and prepared for processing by summary in a journal enter. In many systems, the data are extracted from the source documents and entered in to a card, paper tape, or magnetic tape and, through these media, are ready for further machine or electronic processing into and within the system.

Substantial progress is being made in methods of collecting and recording data so that they will be ready for processing with fewer preliminary steps. Cards or magnetic tape can be created as a byproduct of an original transaction, such as writing up an order or ringing up a transaction on a cash register. The telephone can be used by salespeople out in the field to enter orders directly into the computer system. In such systems, the input for the system is completed at the time of writing up the original order or ringing up the transaction.

Before data are ready for processing within the system, they must be classified appropriately. The classifying of data relates to the identification scheme or coding that is required so that the data can be collected properly within the system and processed in accordance with a given plan.

The phases of data input include those necessary to bring data into the appropriate form to permit processing within the system. As a result information often becomes available to management through the steps of input. Data or information for many key daily reports are obtained during the input phase. Such data or information can be either a by-product of initial recording, collecting, making the record, or classifying by summarization of data extracted at points during input at which specific operations occur. Specific data proceeding operations and sometimes necessary as a part of input.

Processing Phase

The operations which transform business data into intelligible managerial information are what constitute processing. There are many variations to the sequence in which data may be processed within an information system. Data that have been introduced into the system in the proper form can sometimes be channeled through the system with little or no processing. In other instances, numb rough the system with little or no processing. In other instance, numerous processing steps are necessary. Processing includes:

1. Sorting or arranging
2. Summarizing

3. Calculating or comparing
4. Transcribing
5. Filing
6. Communicating
7. Reproducing

Sorting or arranging data relates to brining data together according to a specific grouping or sequence. In more complex and efficient information systems, data can be entered in random order and arranged in the desired grouping and sequence internal to the system. For example, order data could be entered into the system in the sequence that orders are received. Within the system, order data can be grouped according to types of product, information required, or other grouping. In simple systems sorting can be done manually to obtain grouping of similar data.

The information system enables *summarizing* the data into meaningful and useful information. Information systems can produce so much information that sheer volume alone may make evaluation of the information difficult. Good summary information is essential to eliminate unnecessary detail and to allow emphasis to be placed on interpretation.

Calculating is an important part of processing. When new data are entered in the system, they system, they are often added to or deducted from old information to obtain updated amounts as a normal part of the processing procedure. In addition, the more complex systems enable multiplication and division. For example, invoice amounts may be extended, straight-time hours multiplied by straight-time rates, payroll deductions subtracted, and so on.

Comparing is a form of calculation that is also an important part of an information system. It enables decisions, in which the factors can be identified in advance, to be accomplished automatically within the system. Only exceptions needing managerial action are brought to the attention of management through a system approach known as "management by exception". Managerial effort can thus be focused on the important items. For example, actual expenses can be compared to budgeted expenses, and the amounts over budget can be identified. If compared to a price list or a range of prices, and exceptions noted for acnes can be compared to ordering levels, and items that require reorder can be indicated.

The *transcribing*, *filing* or *communicating* of data within the system is basically a reproducing operation. It is common to maintain permanent files of data or information within a system which can be transferred from the file to a calculation or to output, or that can be duplicated whenever the processing system needs the facts involved to complete the processing of certain data or information.

It should be noted that the processing operations identified above may not relate exclusively to the data processing phase of data and information flow. These operations may also be a part of the input or output phases.

Output Phase

The output of the information system must be carefully planned to communicate to managemt the information necessary for planning and controlling the business. Such information, properly communicated, should justify the system. Unless the information is in such form that it is useful and understood, the system will not be fulfilling its function adequately.

With the great volume of information in the system, it is usually desirable to communicate only the information needed for a specific purpose in a given tabulation or report. Information that is in the system may be communicated many times without having to be withdrawn from the system. It is possible to use the same information for managerial report, for the annual report to stockholders, or for governmental reports such as income tax returns. The versatility of the information system output can be compared to a television programme in which several television cameras are focused on the same event from different positions. What is seen on the television screen can be selected by the director at the control. By the same token the information that is to become the output of the information system can be selected. The information that is selected may be from the point of view that best communicates to those for whom the information is intended. Unlike television, however, it is possible to extract information for government or for others, even though the information is reported in different sequences, degrees of completeness, and context for varying purposes.

Summary

- AIS design and development involves different stages as modules: enterprise module, database module, interface module, application module, implementation module and review. AIS process is based on systems concept.

Self-Learning Activity

Try to answer the following questions on your own:

1. What are the stages of accounting information system development?
2. Can you explain the AIS process?

CHAPTER 16

Accounting Information System and Decision-Making Process

Decision-Making

Decision-making is a very important phase of not only planning, but also for the whole management. After alternative courses are discussed, a decision is taken about the right course of action. Drucker says, "A decision is something that takes place prior to the actual performance of the action that has been decided upon. It is a conclusion that the manager has reached as to what he or others should do at some later time".

Definition

Terry defined decision-making as "selection of one behaviour alternative from two or more possible alternatives". According to William Glueck "decision-making is an act of choice by the managers from among two or more possible alternative courses in a given situation".

Decision-making in essence, is the important act of management. Decision-making permeates every part of management practice. Decision-making is an important round, which other management functions like organisation; directing and controlling are carried out. Drucker stresses the importance of decision-making as "whatever a manager does he does through making decisions. Those decisions may be made as a matter of routine. Indeed he may not even realize that he is making them. Or they may affect the future existence of the enterprise and require years of systematic analysis. But management is always a decision-making process".

Classification of Decisions

Decisions are classified into following categories:

1. Environmental decisions
2. Objective design decision

3. Output evaluation decision
4. Objective decisions
5. Subjective decisions
6. Programmed or routine decisions
7. Non-programmed decisions
8. Strategic decisions
9. Organizational decisions
10. Individual and group decisions
11. Emergency decisions.

Principles of Decision-making

According to Louis Allen the following basic principles provide a sound basis for management decisions.

Principle of Definition

A logical decision can be made if the real problem is first defined. Too often, time and effort are wasted because we do not think through what the problem or the objective is. We may not identify the real problem because we fall to take time to determine the basic factors that must be changed to arrive at a satisfactory solution.

Principle of Adequate Evidence

A logical decision must be valid in terms of the evidence on which it is based. A manager expert in decision-making can back his conclusions with facts or reasonable inferences drawn from facts. When the facts underlying a problem are assembled and understood, the decision will often be obvious.

Principle of Identify

Facts may seem to differ, depending on the point in time from which they are observed. From a different perspective, the same object will appear to be different to different people. A budget deficit means different things to the accountant, the salesmen, and the engineer. The relative importance of the same facts may differ from year to year.

To establish the validity of our facts, we must try to use the varying viewpoints involved and determine the significance of the time period during which the event happened.

Important Elements in Decision-making

The following are the important elements in decision-making:

Intuition

The element of intuition is useful in decision-making in view of time expediency and making purposeful use of decision-making ability. It is the outcome of the "inner feelings" of the decision maker.

Facts

Facts provide efficient and effective basis for making decisions. Before using facts, they are to be analyzed, classified and interpreted.

Authority

Authority means power to make decisions and to see that they are carried out. When a decision is acceptable to the organization, this lends authority to the decision maker.

Objectives of Decisions

The basic purpose of decision-making is to arrive at best possible solution for achieving desired results in the business. Hence, it has the following objectives:

1. One of the objectives of decisions is to help to reach the desired result by the management. Objectives are standard guideposts any management has to fulfill.
2. Decision-making has to make all functions of management to be performed effectively and efficiently.
3. Decision-making has to clear conflicts that may creep in at every stage of planning function.
4. Decision-making is a human process. It involves interaction with many people at lower and higher levels.

Types of Decisions

There are two categories of decisions.

1. ***Programmed decisions***

   These are generally routine, repetitive, and applicable to known problems. These decisions generally handle well-structured problems, which are familiar, complete and easily defined and analyzed.

2. ***Non-programmed decisions***

   These decisions are unique and become necessary due to certain unexpected and unprecedented situations. These decisions are not simple and are generally necessary when confronting ill-structured problems.

Group Decision-making

The manager may make a decision himself or he may assign the responsibility to a task force or a group to look at the problem objectively and come up with a recommendation. The group decision would become particularly appropriate for non-programmed decisions because these decisions are complex and few individuals have all the knowledge and skills necessary to make the best decision. However, there are some factors to be considered when determining which approach to take in the decision-making. These factors are proposed by Vroom and Yetton as follows:

1. The importance of the quality of the decision.
2. The extent to which the manager possesses the information and expertise to make a high-quality decision.
3. The extent to which the subordinates have the necessary information to generate a high-quality decision.
4. The extent to which the problem is structured.
5. The extent to which acceptance or commitment on the part of subordinates is critical to the effective implementation of the decision.
6. The probability that the subordinates will accept the manager's decision.
7. The extent to which the subordinates will be motivated to achieve the organizational goals. Depending upon these considerations, some considerations would necessitate the decision-making-process to be initiated by a team or a group for the participation of subordinates.

Essentials of Group Decision-making

To make the group decision-making more effective there are certain conditions essential. These essentials make the group to be objective and have a team spirit while making decisions. The essentials of group decision-making are:

1. Preliminary preparation needed to make the process more systematic and productive. Agenda setting becomes the focus of such planning.
2. The meeting atmosphere should be congenial and provide a backdrop for frank and free discussion. This is especially true for enhancing participation from among lower managerial levels.
3. Increased participation is a logical fallout from the foregoing and all participants should be motivated to contribute meaningfully during meetings.
4. Presentation of ideas should not attract criticism or division of any kind.
5. Objectivity includes the feeling among the participants that the ideas presented would be purely based on merit.
6. Organization and evaluation of ideas within a laid-down time frame is an imperative, which calls for strict observance of the specific agenda.

7. Prioritization of alternatives in decision - making is an important fact and should draw upon ideas from all participants.
8. Documentation and achieving of ideas presented, alternatives and decisions, assist in continuity and information access at a later date.

Advantages of Group Decision-making

Compared to individual decision-making group decisions are having certain advantages. They are as follows:

1. Since the group members have different specialties, they tend to provide more information and knowledge. Also, the information tends to be more comprehensive in nature and the group can generate a greater number of alternatives.
2. Implementation of the decision is more effective, since the people who are going to implement the decision also participate in the decision-making process. This also increases the commitment of the people to see the implementation to success.
3. The participative decision-making process builds up groundwork as a training group for subordinates, who develop the skills of objective analysis and deriving conclusions.
4. The group decision-making is more democratic in nature while the individual decision-making is more autocratic in nature. The democratic processes are more easily acceptable and are consistent with the democratic ideals of our society.
5. The number of effective participants is enhanced and provides an equal opportunity for participants.
6. Few meetings with an overall decrease in duration are required for problem solving.
7. Creates an "organization memory" of the proceedings of various meetings. Also external information can easily be accessed.
8. Provides a well-structured and controlled mechanism for meetings.
9. Anonymity of participants improves participation and encourages a more open presentation of ideas.
10. Participants remain focused during meetings and behaviour detrimental to the decision-making process is discouraged.
11. Permits participants to choose from a variety of structured and unstructured techniques and methods to perform the task.

Techniques of Group Decision-making

The prominent techniques of group decision-making are Brainstorming, Delphi technique and nominal technique.

Brainstorming

Brainstorming technique involves, a group of people usually between five and ten sitting around a table, generating ideas in the form of free association. This generated a variety of solutions that can be later analyzed and the unpractical solutions discarded. The idea is to have as many ideas generated as possible and no idea is criticized no matter how absurd it sounds and no evaluation of any idea is made until the end of the discussion. This encourages freewheeling, and one idea sometimes generates - another. This free association and unrestricted thinking may generate some novel idea and a unique solution, which was not thought of before.

Delphi technique

It is a modification of the brainstorming technique and involves obtaining the opinion of experts physically separated and unknown to each other. All these opinions are handled by a central coordinator, who consolidates the opinions and this information is sent back to the experts for further analysis and opinion refinement. The Delphi technique is characterized by the following sequential steps:

1. The problem is identified and sets of questions are built relating to the problem so that the answers to these questions would generate solutions to the problem. These questions are consolidated in the form of a questionnaire.
2. Experts in the problem area are identified and contacted. The questionnaire is sent to each member who anonymously and independently answers the questions and sends it back to the central coordinator.
3. The results of this questionnaire are compiled and analyzed and on the basis of the responses received, a second questionnaire is developed, which is mailed back to participating members.
4. The members are asked again to comment, suggest and answer the questions, possibly generating new ideas and solutions.
5. The responses to this second questionnaire are compled and analyzed and if a consensus has not been reached, then a third questionnaire is developed, pinpointing the issue and unresolved areas of concern.
6. The above process is repeated until a consensus is obtained. Then the final report is prepared.

One of the advantages of the Delphi technique is that the group members are totally independent and are not influenced by the opinion of other members. Also the members do not have to be present at one location, so that an expert who is geographically separated can also be asked for his opinion, so that the cost of bringing these experts together is avoided.

IS and Decision-making Process

The decision-making process involved several stages. In all the stages the significance and role of IS is admirable. IS feeds required information at all the stages right from identification of the problem upto the implementation of the decisions and even in reviewing and evaluating the decisions after implementing them.

1. ***Defining the Problem***

   Before a decision is taken the problem must be defined properly. It must be based upon experience rather than upon analysis. Drucker gives two steps in defining the problem namely 'finding the critical factor' and 'to determine the conditions for its solutions'. Critical factor means the crux of the problem, which must be found before defining a problem. This is the element (or elements) in the situation that has to be changed before anything else can be changed moved acted upon'.

The second step in defining the problem is to determine the conditions for its solution. To find solutions, the objectives for solution must be thought thoroughly. Drucker views that 'objectives should always reflect the objectives of the business, should always be focused ultimately on business performance and business results. They should always balance and harmonies the immediate and the long range future. They should always take into account both the business as a whole and the activities needed to run it'. Hence finding the right question, setting the objectives and determining the rules together constitute the first phase of decision-making. IS helps in this regard.

2. ***Analyzing the Problem***

   Analyzing the problem, according to Drucker, consists of classifying it and finding the facts. It is necessary to classify the problem in order to know who must make the decision, why must be consulted in making it and who must be informed. Without prior classification the effectiveness of the ultimate decision is seriously endangered; for classification alone can show who has to do what in order to convert the decision into effective action. Drucker further gives four principles of classification namely, the futurity of the decision (the time span for which it commits the decision can be reversed); the impact of the decision on other areas and functions; the number of qualitative considerations that enter into it; and the thickness of or periodicity of the decision. After the problem is defined and classified the facts are to be found. Facts are found by considering the relevant data and committing the irrelevant data with the support of IS.

3. ***Developing Alternative Solutions***

For every problem alternative solutions must be found. Only through alternative solutions we can distinguish a right decision from wrong decisions. Drucker says that 'alternative solutions are the only means of bringing out basic assumptions up to the conscious level, forcing ourselves to examine them and testing their validity. Alternative solutions are no guarantee of wisdom or of the right decision. But at least they prevent our making what we would have known to be the wrong decision had we but thought the problem through'. Information on the alternatives can be had from IS.

4. ***Finding the Best Solution***

Among the alternative solutions the best one must be chosen. Drucker laid down four criteria for picking the best from among the possible solutions:

(a) *The Risk*

The manager has to weigh the risks and gains of the course of action. 'What matters most is neither the expected gain nor the anticipated risk but the rates between them. Every alternative should therefore contain an appraisal of the odds it carries'.

(b) *Economy effort*

The line of action, which can give greatest results with least efforts, is chosen.

(c) *Timing*

If the solution is to put into action quickly the organization must be geared for that. On the other hand if the solution has long time for action, a slow start can be given.

(d) *Limitations of Resources*

As human resources are important among all resources, their limitations and competence must be properly assessed. If additional men are needed they can be added.

MIS supports the management to choose the best alternative by feeding proper information to decide the best alternative.

5. ***Making the Decision Effective (Action/Implementation)***

This implies the conversation of a solution into action. Motivation is needed to get things done. 'It required that any decision become "over decision" to the people who have to convert it into action. This in turn means that they have to participate responsibly in making it'.

Decision-making and Areas of Application — The Role of IS

According to the nature of problem different techniques can be used.

1. *Market analysis*

   Market analysis can be used for market strategy planning, preventive maintenances, programme planning, and manpower training programme design.

2. *Linear programming (LP)*

   For product mixes decisions, oil refinery operation, and capital structure planning, capital budgeting, advertising media assignment, Linear programming would be very useful.

3. *Assignment and transportation models*

   These models are useful for physical distribution planning, production planning, manpower assignment, and machine assignment and space allocation.

4. *Goal programming*

   Advertising decisions, economic predictions, investment analyses, etc., needs goal programming.

5. *Inventory models*

   This is specialized model for raw material inventory planning, retail sales and inventory planning.

6. *Network models*

   This model is useful for project scheduling, project budgeting, traffic control, pipeline routing, and commissioning communication networks.

7. *Dynamic programming*

   For complex systems analysis, sales distribution, planning production and inventory planning dynamic programming will be useful.

8. *Decision theory*

   Investment decisions, military strategy planning, medical decisions, gambling (football, basketball, betting), etc., needs decision theory.

9. *Game theory*

   Collective bargaining decisions, bidding strategy planning, and military strategy planning, needs game theory.

10. *Simulation*

    For complex systems analysis, stochastic systems analysis, shop scheduling and planning, and inventory policy planning, simulation techniques will be useful.

11. *Waiting line models (queues)*

    These models make the service facility planning, road and freeway design, and plant layout planning makes more effective.

IS and Management Decisions

Decision-making is a process of using formal procedure, tools and techniques to ensure that decisions are arrived in organization in an objective manner. Here MIS plays an important role. The role of MIS in managerial decision-making is decided by the levels at which decision are made as the nature of functions of levels are different but dependent on each other. Strategic planning finalizes the objectives of the organization and determines the courses of action needed to achieve these objectives. Hence, the information needs of this level is highly external and non programmable. Whereas the management control involves taking decision with regard to converting objectives set by strategic planning in to workable actions and set standards to measure the performance of operations level and providing exception report to strategic planning. Hence, the information requirements at this level are partly programmable and partly non programmable. In the case of operation management or transaction processing their information requirements are highly historical, routine, repetitive, short term in nature and fully internal.

Hence, the relevance of computer applications is high at lower level than at the higher level. This is attributed to the fact that the data/ information at the operational level are highly structured hence, can be easily programmed. At the higher level the information requirements are moving towards qualitative in nature and derived from external environment, therefore less programmable. Further at the higher-level information requirements are very complex as they are extremely depending on external environment and the involvement of too many variables. Therefore the nature of information requirements at different level for different purposes demands separate information support system for effective decision-making. This led to the emergence of Transaction Processing System (TPS), Decision Support System (DSS), Executive Information System (EIS), Geographical Information System (GIS), and Expert System. Except the TPS other systems are also called as Intelligent Support System.

Information through Information System

Decisions in management functions	
Management Function	*Typical decisions (managers)*
Planning	⇨ What are the organization's long term objectives
	⇨ What strategy will best achieve the objectives
	⇨ What should be the organization's short term objectives

(Contd...)

Organizing	⇨ How many subordinates should report directly to me ⇨ How much centralization should be there in the organization ⇨ How should jobs be designed ⇨ When should the organization implement their products
Leading	⇨ How do I handle employees ⇨ Who appear to be low in motivation ⇨ How will a specific change affects work productivity ⇨ When is the right time to stimulate conflict
Controlling	⇨ What activities in the organization need to be controlled ⇨ How should these activities should be controlled ⇨ What type of MIS should the organization have

What type of information is needed for decision-making?

Managers	*Required information for decision-making*
Accounting	⇨ What accounting firm should be used ⇨ Who should process our payroll ⇨ Should we give customer credit
Finance	⇨ What bank should be used ⇨ Should we sell bonds or stocks ⇨ Should be buy back some of our company stock
HRM	⇨ Where should we recruit our employee ⇨ Should we set-up a testing programme
Production	⇨ Which supplier should we use ⇨ Should we build the new plant ⇨ Should we buy the new machine
Sales	⇨ Which sales representative should we use in this district ⇨ Should we start the advertising campaign

Comparing programmed and non-programmed decisions

	Programmed decisions	*Non-programmed decisions*
Type of decision	Programmable/routine/generic	Non-programmable/unique
Nature of decision	Procedural/periodical/well defined information and decision criteria	Novel/unstructured incomplete channels

(Contd...)

Strategy for making decision	Reliance on rules and computation	Reliance on principles general problems-solving process
	Decision-making techniques	
Types of decision	*Programmed decisions*	*Non-programmed decisions*
General nature of the situation	Relatively unchanging	Rapidly changing
Decision-making techniques	Management science/ capital budgeting/ computerized solution	Judgment/Creativity

Accounting Information for Decision-making

Accounting information is required by the managers at all levels to make decisions of various kinds. Management has to make a number of short-term and long-term decisions. Short-term decision-making needs cost data, properly aggregated into fixed and variable components. Short-term decisions generally assume no change in the plant capacity and therefore, in fixed costs. Variable costing, identifying and classifying costs as fixed and variable, provides information for making such decisions. Fixed costs generally create problems in making decisions because of the difficulties involved in their allocations. Under variable costing, they are assumed to remain constant and therefore, are not considered relevant in decision-making. Variable costing simply treats them as period costs and thus, avoids the problem of allocation. Long-term decisions are taken by considering the accounting information of different nature. Long-term decisions are made by the top level executives for the future course of action.

Accounting information, whatever may be the type—cost information, management accounting information, financial information, tax information or any other accounting information—is useful and very important to make both short-term and long-term business decisions. The decisions made by the managers are: pricing special orders, dropping a product or a department, make or buy, sell or process further, shut down of a plant, inventory decisions, current liability decisions, long-term liability decisions, equity decisions, corporate income statement decisions, inter-corporate investments decisions, cash-related decisions, financing decisions, marketing decisions, production decisions, informed economic decisions, dividend decisions, and so on.

For the above decisions, the managers at various levels are in need of certain type of accounting information. The required accounting information regarding each type of decision will be provided by the accounting information system on time for timely decision-making. The AIS is responsible for providing such information for making decisions for the future course of action. The business decisions need quantitative information, which can be provided by the accounting information system.

The major areas of accounting information—management accounting information, financial information, cost accounting information and tax information can be had from the system. The managers so as to make proper, timely, cost-effective decisions to achieve the end results of the enterprise can use these major categories of information.

The above discussion has clearly given the role of accounting information in making business decisions.

Summary

- AIS provides all required accounting information to decision centres so as to make proper and timely business decisions. The information provision is on the major classification of AIS.

Self-Learning Activity

Try to answer the following questions on your own:

1. What are different types of decisions?
2. What is the role of AIS in making business decisions?

CHAPTER 17

Accounting Information System and Management Levels

MIS and Management Levels

Management Levels

Each organization is made up of several levels. These could be classified broadly into three categories: Top, Middle and Junior or operational levels. In most cases, the top management performs strategic planning and the other two levels provide support in the form of processed information. The middle management performs tactical planning and control, and needs information so as to discharge managerial functions in the organization. The junior or operational level management is involved in day-to-day operations and control, needs information for its daily working. The Exhibit 17.1 depicts a clear picture on the levels and functions, their tasks and location.

Exhibit 17.1

Management Levels, Tasks, Location and Functions

Task	Location	Management Functions	Level
Strategic planning	Management	Management	Top
Management control	Office	Planning and Control	Middle
Operational control	Factory and Field	Execution	Lower

The top management performs the strategic planning as a management function at the management level; the middle management performs the task of management control as planning and control function at the office level; and the lower management performs operational control as execution function at the floor level. The Figure 17.1 summarizes the interaction and role of these three levels of management in an organization.

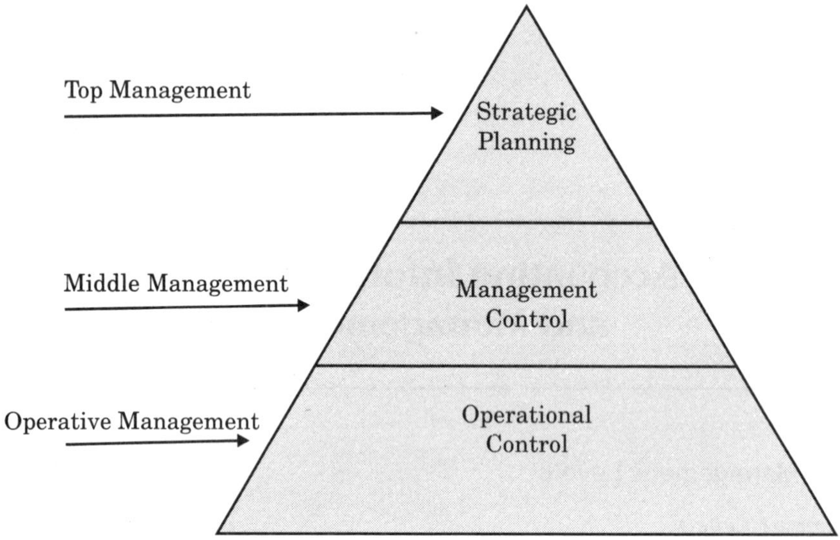

Fig. 17.1: **Management Pyramid**

The top management establishes the policies, plans and objectives of the organization as well as a budget framework under which various departments will operate. Middle management has the responsibility of implementing the policies and overall plans of the top management. Junior management has the responsibility of implementing the day-to-day operations and decisions of the middle management to produce goods and services to meet the revenue, profit, and other goals, which in turn will enable the organization to achieve its overall plans and objectives. The different levels of management are important for two reasons:

(a) information needs tend to be different levels of management; and

(b) amount of time required for any function varies considerably with each group.

IS and Management Levels

Information system provides selected decision-oriented information needed by management to plan, control, and evaluate the activities of the organization. It designed with a framework that emphasizes profit planning, performance planning, and control at all levels of management pyramid. It integrates all the business subsystems both financial and non-financial within the organization. An effective IS needs current and future information on all respects and areas for evaluating the corporate objectives, strategic or long-range planning, tactical or short-range planning, and operational planning for routine activities at the floor level.

IS is an integrating, continuing and future-oriented structure of all the resources of an organization i.e., six M's — Money, manpower, materials, machines, methods and management of information, designed to generate an orderly and integrated real time flow of information collected from internal and external sources, for use as the relevant bases for managerial decision-making in any functional area of business organization.

The Figure 17.2 presents the framework for IS in a typical organization, works for collection, process and dissemination of information to the needy persons at all levels of management.

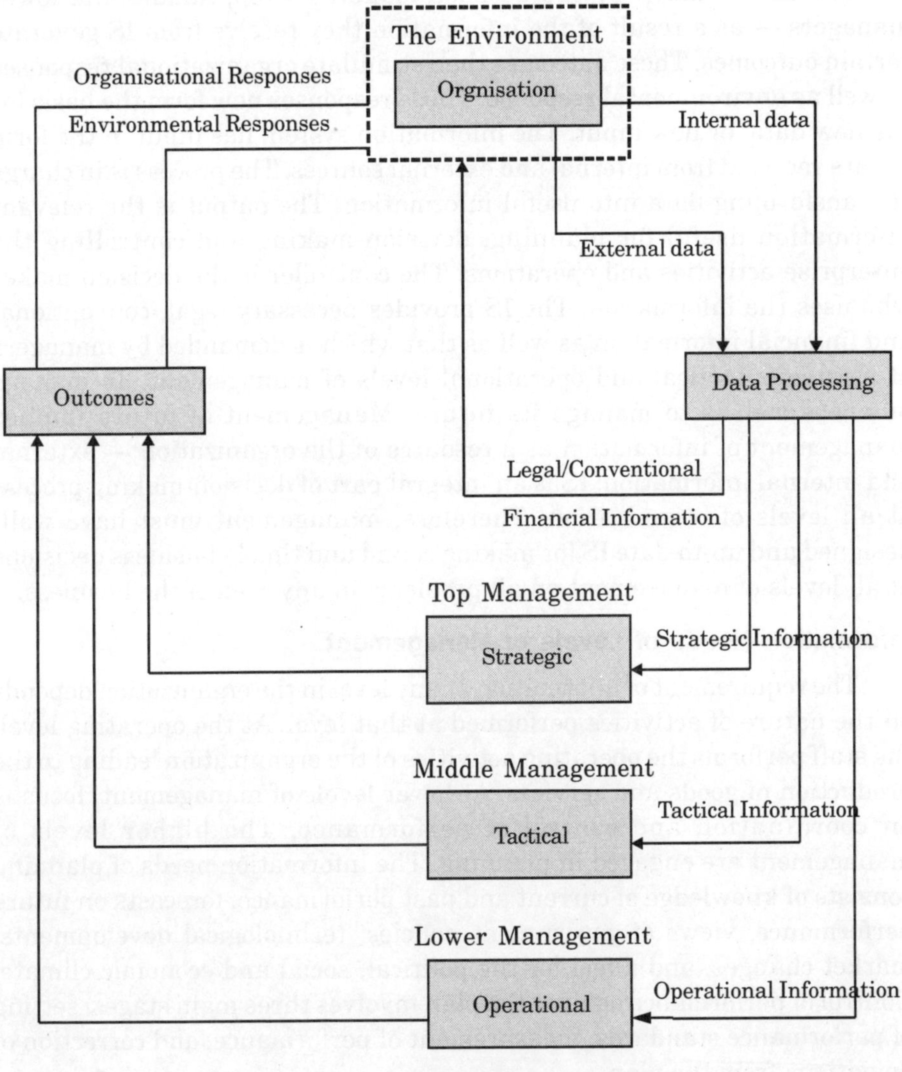

Fig. 17.2: **Information System Framework**

Data processing is the collection, transformation and retention of information. The organization and its environment generate data, which serves as the base (input) to data processing of internal and external data. Data processing ultimately provides strategic information to top level management for the strategic planning; tactical information to middle management for the management planning and control; and operational (technical) information to lower management for the operational planning and control. It also provides the legal, conventional and financial information to the external users in the environment as and when required by them.

The action taken by the decision-makers — top, middle and lower managers — as a result of the information they receive from IS generate certain outcomes. These outcomes then stimulate organizational responses as well as environmental response. These responses now form the basis for the new data, or new input. The information system has input in the form of data received from internal and external sources. The process is in charge of transforming data into useful information. The output is the relevant information useful for planning, decision-making and controlling the enterprise activities and operations. The controller is the decision-maker who uses the information. The IS provides necessary legal, conventional and financial information as well as that which is demanded by managers at strategic, tactical and operational levels of management. To manage business well is to manage its future. Management of future implies management of information as a resource of the organization — external and internal information. IS is an integral part of decision-making process at all levels of organization. Therefore, management must have well-designed and up-to-date IS for making sound and timely business decisions at all levels of management on all problems in any area of the business.

Information Needs of Levels of Management

The requirement of information at any level in the organization depends on the nature of activities performed at that level. At the operating level, the staff performs the operating activities of the organization leading to the production of goods and services. At lower levels of management, focus is on coordination and control of performance. The higher levels of management are engaged in planning. The information needs of planning consists of knowledge of current and past performance, forecasts on future performance, views of government policies, technological developments, market changes, and a feel for the political, social and economic climate. Control of performance against the plan involves three main stages: setting of performance standards, measurement of performance, and correction of deviations from the plan.

This requires detailed information on performance at the lowest level of the organization. Control may be exercised with the help of historical reports at the supervisory level or exception report at the middle level management. The historical report at worst, may be a complete printout of statistics going back over some period of time. Often it is produced by default, because the manager has been unable to define his real requirements. At best, it can be a comparison exercise; the period compared to the same period last year, classified on various parameters. In exception report, the computer sorts and selects only those items of information that the manager really needs. Obviously, rules have to be defined to establish what constitutes an exception. A significant deviation from the plan or standard may generally be considered as an exception.

The Figure 17.3 depicts about the information for various levels of management in an organization.

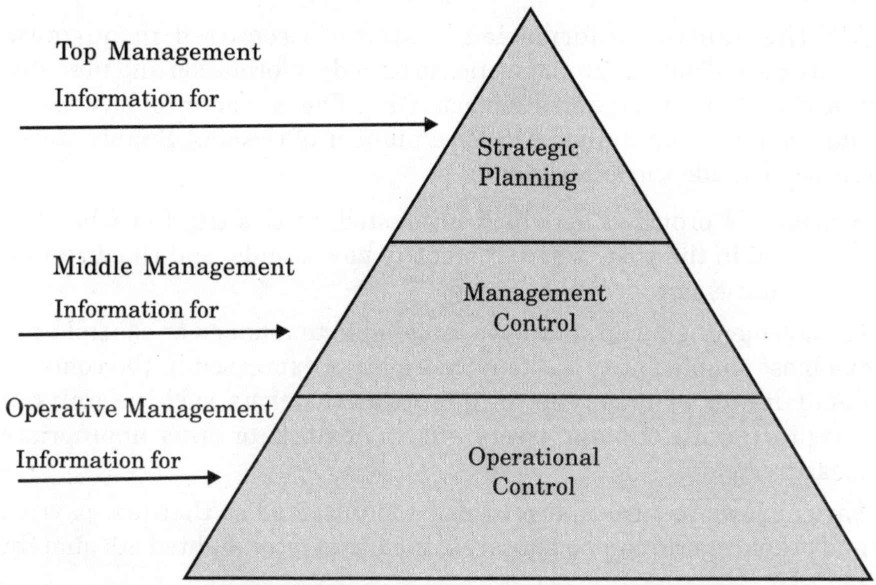

Fig. 17.3: **Information for Various Levels of Management**

The information needs of business organization at all levels of management are discussed below.

Operational information: At the operational level of the organization, staff handle operational transactions, such as orders, time-sheets, delivery notes, sickness notes, production work-sheets, inspection advices, stock records, etc. These documents are the working papers of the operational systems. The documents relating to business transactions are commonly referred to as "transaction documents". In fact, whenever a business transaction is executed, the parameters of the transaction are recorded in the form of a transaction document.

Tactical Information: At the middle level the managers are responsible for implementation and control. They are in need of tactical information to implement and have control over the activities done by their subordinates.

Strategic Information: At the top level the executives are concentrating on designing strategies to cope up with the changes in the environment so as to win the race by overriding the rivalries/competitors.

At the outset, the employees and managers at different levels of management pyramid need information to perform their tasks to achieve the organizational objectives. IS plays a vital role in feeding information to all levels of personnel in an organization.

AIS and information Needs of Management

AIS (Accounting Information System) is required in business organizations and not-for-profit entities to provide information and to enable effective control of the organization activities. The managers of businesses have adopted and maintained AIS for a number of reasons. Simply stated the reasons include the following:

- A means is provided by which interested parties can tell what has happened in the past, where the entity now stands, and the direction in which it is now or will be going.
- Management is facilitated. It is impossible to manage or control even the most simple entity without information expressed in the common denominator of money or in quantitative terms such as units of inventory, units of plant assets, shares of stock, or other appropriate measurements.
- Various laws require that records be maintained so that tax, payroll, and other reports can be prepared, filed, and later audited adequately.
- Routine activities such as billing, paying, receiving and shipping must be accomplished. Amounts owned by or to the entity must be recorded; otherwise, it would fail to collect what is due or fail to make timely payment of its debt.
- Those responsible for the custody of property would have no means of discharging their custodianship without knowing the value associated with the property, its quantity, and its location.

The accounting information system includes the records and processing structure by which the preceding and other objectives requiring quantitative information can be accomplished. The modern system must provide for many needs which extend far beyond the financial statements and the accounting department. The detailed and often statistical nature of the information needed by modern management is causing a re-examination of the role of information producing systems. In recent years, information systems have been designed to provide more and more quantitative information, including detailed facts about markets, production, and financial matters.

AIS should be justified by the contributions that it makes to enable management to manage effectively. The system should furnish timely information to management, thus setting the stage for good decision-making. Management has the right to expect that its information system will provide the information necessary to plan and control the operations of the business and accomplish the business goals and objectives. The system must provide information concerning historical costs and profitability. Periodic performance reports, covering all areas of management and supervisory responsibility must be available. Such reports provide identification of strengths and weaknesses in the current position and the magnitude and priorities of the future tasks.

The following discussion reveals the role of AIS in fulfilling the information requirements of managers at different levels in the organization.

AIS and Levels of Management

AIS is a combination of subsystems that function within the accounting system and within the organization to process data and to provide the information and internal control needed by management to carry out its responsibilities of stewardship over the assets, of control over operations, and to plan future enterprise activities. AIS is an aggregate that includes the subsystems within a business organization designed to provide the necessary managerial information and internal control.

Every business must have accounting information system to fulfill three specific needs. First, the system must provide for the internal informational needs of management. Second, the system must provide management with a means of controlling business activity. Lastly, the system must provide for the external informational needs of various individuals and organizations.

The following discussion will reveal the information requirements of each level of management in an enterprise.

Information requirements of the levels of management differ from one level to another based on the activities, responsibilities and duties of the personnel involved. The three specific needs that are to be fulfilled by an information system can be elaborated at three levels of management. The information requirements of the personnel at three levels of management can be of daily routine information, information for implementation and

Top Management

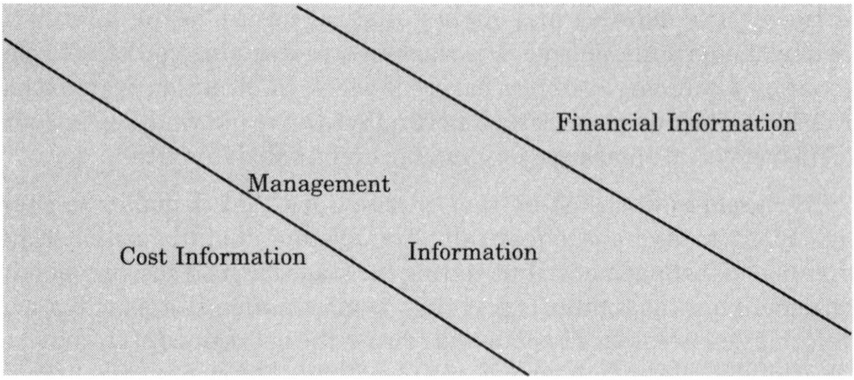

Lower Management Middle Management

Fig. 17.4: **Levels and Accounting Information Needs**

control activities, information for policy-making and decision-making. Mostly the operational level employees need the internal information as routine or daily information regarding the daily activities undertaken by them. The control information is required by the middle level managers in order to have control over the activities done in the enterprise. The top executives need external reporting information and information to make decisions and policies of the enterprise. The following discussion will reveal the information requirements of each level of management in an enterprise.

Information Requirements of Operational Level Management

Information should be available internally to disclose what has happened in the past. The need for historical information relates closely to the housekeeping need to record and process routine and daily business events. The operational level management must also be fully informed about the present. It is necessary to know who has responsibility for various assets, where each is located, how much should be on hand, and the vents that are in process. Current information may be especially meaningful when compared with information from other periods, budgets, or standards, enabling management to act when necessary. Information relative to the future should be available to enable management to pan effectively. Since the future is often similar to the past, the events of the past become the starting point in projecting the future.

Mostly needed information for the operational level management is operational information. The cost information about routine affairs of the enterprise is needed by this level of managers and employees. Operational or cost information should be fed with them to make routine decisions on daily activities undertaken in the business enterprise.

Information Requirements of Middle Level Management

One of the great challenges of the systems analyst is the design of an information system that will enable management to effectively control business. In a sense, the control need is a part of middle management's internal information need, yet it differs since control is dependent upon such factors as assignment of duties and organizational relationships. The timely and daily information that is necessary to operate the business effectively on a day-to-day and week-to-week basis must flow from the system. It does not flow from ledger balances exclusively, but is accumulated by many methods and at many points within the organization. A systems structure that enables management to control and also to measure and motivate performance has always been and will continue to be vital to managers. A reporting system called responsibility accounting helps the managers to control over the activities in a business enterprise.

The middle level managers need managerial accounting information to control over the affairs and for implementing the policies that have been framed by the top management. Mostly the managers at middle level in the management pyramid need the management accounting information.

Information Requirements of Top Level Management

The top management personnel need accounting information, which is useful to make business decisions, frame enterprise policies and strategies. The accounting information system provides such required information on time to them. The accounting information should flow from the bottom in the form of accounting reports for the purpose of making decisions. The top management is the responsible body to send reports to the external parties who are involved in the development of the business enterprise. The need to report information to those outside the organization is substantial in magnitude. Many of the external needs can be met with data that flows from the system to meet internal needs. The financial statements of different types will be prepared and published / sent to the external parties who are in need of such information.

It is understood from the above discussion that AIS plays a vital role in providing information and fulfilling the information requirements of the managers and employees at different levels of management in an enterprise.

Applications of Operational, Tactical and Strategic Information Systems to Business Functions

The operational, tactical and strategic information systems can be applied into different business functions. This section of the present chapter discusses the application of operational, tactical and strategic information systems to various business functions like accounting and finance, marketing, production and human resource. The Figure 17.5 presents a clear picture of these systems in a business organization.

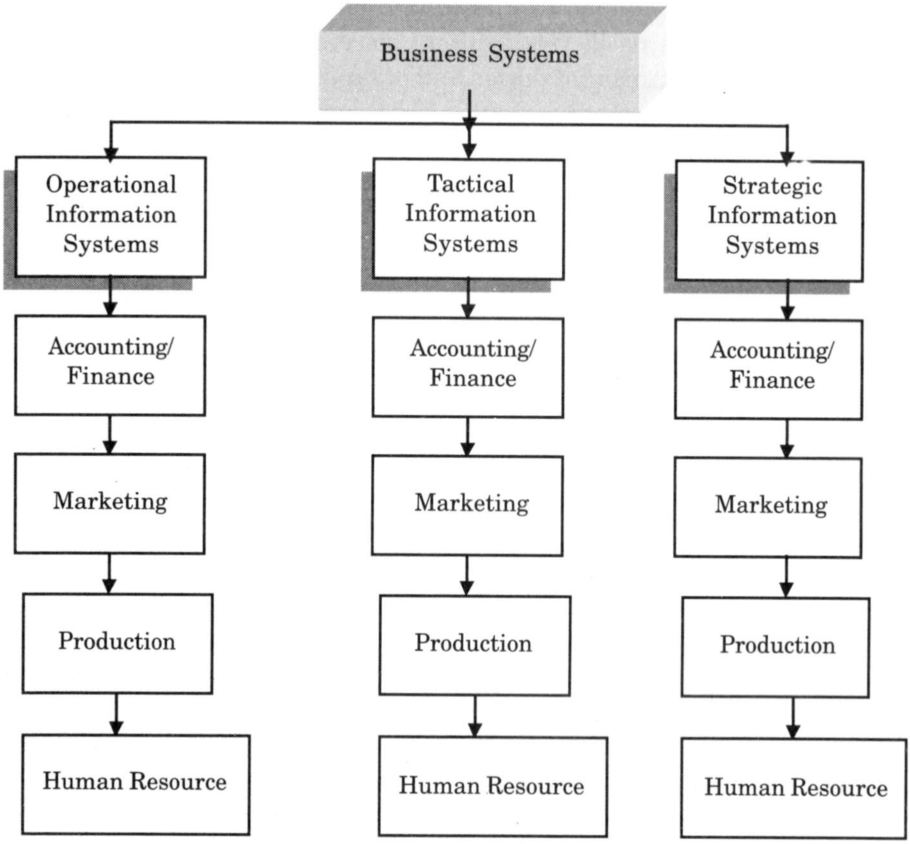

Fig. 17.5: **Application of Operational, Technical and Strategic Information Systems to Various Business Functions**

Applications of Operational Information Systems

The information systems that perform or support the completion of tasks such as calculation, printing, distribution of paycheques, verification, mailing of sales invoices, purchase orders, vendors cheques, customer identification, tasks regarding employees, manufacturing activities, etc., are often referred to as operational information systems. Operational information systems record, process, and report all routine and repetitive activities. The information they produce is usually detailed, highly structured, accurate, derived from internal sources, and produced regularly. The Exhibit 17.2 shows the details of operational information systems and activities that occur in all areas of business.

Exhibit 17.2

Activities – Operational Information Systems in Four Business Functions

Accounting/Finance	Marketing	Production	Human Resource
Fixed assets	Prospect leads	Purchasing	Position control
Sales order processing	Contact information	Receiving	Employee profile
Accounts receivable	Micromarketing and data warehousing	Quality control	Employee skills inventory
Accounts payable	Telemarketing	Shipping	Performance management
Inventory control	Direct mail	Automated materials handling	Government reporting
Purchase order processing	Point-of-sale	Computer aided design/manufacturing	Selection and recruitment
Payroll	Delivery tracking and routing	Image management	Training
Billing/invoicing	Electronic shopping	Material selection	
	Electronic advertising	Shop-floor scheduling	
		Mass customization	
		Shop-floor control	

Operational Financial Accounting Information Systems

Operational financial accounting information systems are typically task oriented. They focus on processing financial transactions to produce the routine, repetitive information outputs that every organization finds necessary. These outputs include paycheques, cheques to vendors, customer invoices, purchase orders, stock reports, and other regular forms and reports. The following are the financial accounting system modules:

- General ledger
- Fixed assets
- Sales order processing
- Accounts receivable
- Accounts payable
- Inventory control
- Purchase order processing
- Payroll, etc.

These financial accounting systems are integrated. Each system receives data from various sources and processes, and disseminates output in the form of information to other systems.

Applications of Tactical and Strategic Information Systems

Tactical information systems support management decision-making by providing managers with regular summary reports, regular exception reports, ad hoc reports and other relevant information helps them control their areas of responsibility and allocate their resources to pursue organization goals. In contrast, strategic information systems are goal-oriented. That is, they are designed to support organizational goals and direction setting. The Exhibit 17.3 presents about the activities of tactical and strategic information systems in four business functions.

Tactical Accounting and Financial Information Systems

The managers at tactical level make financial and accounting decisions with the support of tactical information systems. The tactical accounting and financial information systems are:

1. *Budgeting systems:* They permit managers to track actual revenues and expenses and compare these amounts to expected revenues and expenses. It also allows the managers to compare current budget amounts with previous fiscal periods budgets.
2. *Cash management systems:* The organization needs cash for two purposes: for working capital and for the acquisition of long-term assets. Cash management systems help managers to manage cash by providing sufficient information.

Exhibit 17.3

Activities — Tactical and Strategic Information Systems in Four business functions

Accounting/Finance	Marketing	Production	Human Resource
Tactical Information Systems			
Budgeting	Sales management	Materials requirement planning	Job analysis and design
Cash management	Advertising and promotion	Just in time	Recruiting
Capital Budgeting	Pricing	Capacity planning	Compensation and benefits
Investment management	Distribution channel	Production scheduling	Succession planning
	Competitive tracking	Product design and development	
		Manufacturing resource planning	
		Computer integrated manufacturing	
Strategic Information Systems			
Financial condition analysis	Sales forecasting	Site planning and selection	Workforce planning
Long-term forecasting	Market research	Technology planning and assessment	Labour negotiations
	Product planning and development	Process positioning	
		Plant design	

3. *Capital budgeting systems:* By using software managers can compute values and they can go for financial analysis and comparison.
4. *Investment management systems:* Managers by computer information systems manage stock and bonds portfolios. They can maintain online database for this purpose.

Strategic Accounting and Financial Information Systems

Strategic accounting and financial information systems typically include several types of systems for information flow:

1. *Financial condition analysis systems:* These systems support in reporting that automatically calculate and present the results of variety of analysis tools and ratios.
2. *Long-range forecasting systems:* Strategic planners demand forecasts on a variety of factors that will affect organization performance in the future. In this context, they use long-range forecasting systems.

Summary

- AIS plays a crucial role at all levels of management. There are subsystems with operational accounting information, tactical accounting information and strategic accounting information.

Self-Learning Activity

Try to answer the following questions on your own:

1. What do you understand about management levels and AIS?
2. Discuss about operational accounting information systems?

CHAPTER 18

Accounting Information Reporting System (AIRS)

Introduction

No planning and control procedure is complete without prompt and accurate feedback of operating results. Management must know how actual profit performance compares with the objective, and with past performance and to what extent variations from objective and past performance have been caused by various influencing factors. Therefore, the development of the system, or systems of reporting, is considered as part of accounting methods and systems, and is largely responsible for the change of outlook as well as approach to accounting systems. A modern business organization is welded into an efficient working unit by the link of communication between its different parts. This communication is through reports—oral, graphic, or written—designed to provide specific information. Reporting system has been introduced in quite small business and, naturally, the complexity of the reporting system has grown *pari passu* with the increase in the scale of business. Though it is fully recognized that a highly developed team spirit can reduce the need of wading through voluminous reports relating to the operation of the firm, the managers seem to feel that a regular system of reporting is a better guarantee of efficiency and cooperation than reliance on personal qualities.

Objects of Reporting

The primary object of reporting to management and external parties is to reach sound judgments on the basis of operating results. Another object, which is closely allied to this and is important in terms of efficiency, morale and motivation, is to secure understanding and acceptance of the judgment by the people engaged in various aspects of the work of the enterprise.

Reporting Needs of Different Management Levels

As the system of reporting has to meet the requirements of management at different levels, the approach to the reporting problem and statements would vary according to the reporting level. If the reports for top management have to be comprehensive and concise, so much the more have the reports to operating supervisors be specific and concise because the daily routines of production and selling demand that the supervisor be a man of action rather than an analyst. The reports to top management must show whether plans are sound, whether organization is properly established and whether delegated responsibility has been effectively used. Consequently, the reporting system must enable management to make comparison, to review organization and to appraise the efficiency and effectiveness of the subordinates. The reports directed to coordinating executives who are at middle level management should be such as to assist them in administering policies and in appraising the performances of operating supervisors. Specific and detailed reporting is required at the level of direct supervision. Operating supervisors should receive reports concerning the effectiveness of their operations showing planned performance, actual performance and variations from the plans. In order that operating supervisors may be able to use their reports for the control of future operations, it is necessary that the reports give specific information about the department reported on. Apart from these, foreman and superintendent are interested in daily report and may even like to know the position shift by shift.

The accounting reports prepared by the responsible persons can broadly be categorized into two categories: Internal reports and External reports.

Internal Reports

Internal management reports may be grouped under each of the categories like measure fulfillment of responsibility, provide information, and become the basis for action. Reports designed to measure fulfillment of responsibility are essential where authority is delegated. They provide a means of knowing the success or lack of success with which delegated authority is used, and the results obtained.

Information reports are intended to provide the information necessary for planning, determining policy, or for an overview of a given situation. Special study reports are of this nature. They tend to include trend comparisons over a specific period of time and are not designed to generate direct management action as in the case of control reports.

Reports that are the basis for action are intended to highlight areas in which corrective action is required. They are designed to emphasis variations from planned, budgeted, or standard performance and thus permit timely and effective control.

The report principle of AIS implies a design of internal reports to serve specific management needs. The form in which reports are prepared is determined to a large extent by the purpose of the report and the needs of those that are to use it for information control. The report presentation should be such that the user can comprehend it easily, and so it must be within the user's specific background of technical knowledge. Internal reporting must be flexible.

External Reports

Like internal reports, external reports should be prepared only for specific reasons. They are usually designed to keep persons outside of management informed about some phase of the business in which there is a special interest. With a properly designed system, most external reports can flow directly from information generated within the system for internal purposes. External reporting must often conform to third party specifications. In such instances, external reporting can be bothersome. For example, cost reports on government contracts, where classification and allocation are substantially different from the formation regularly generated by the system, will require extensive special handling.

Though accounting reports may be classified from various points of view, their classification according to the fineness of details embodied therein is appropriate from the standpoint of financial reporting. The various reports prepared and submitted, by keeping this, are enterprise report, control report, investigative report, and budget proposal report.

The *enterprise report* accumulates information about the enterprise as a whole and serves largely as a means of communication with the outsiders. It may be related to some specific activity or function of the enterprise, or its entire operation in the aggregate. Balance sheet, operating statements, income-tax returns, employment reports, etc., are some of the examples of this type of report.

The *control report* inter alia forms the subject matter of management accounting and is an important ingredient of control process. The information contained in the enterprise reports is elaborated in the control reports and is directed to a responsibility center. It is prepared on the basis of company-developed standards, couched in its own terminology, related to responsibility centers and subserves decisional needs.

Investigative report is the concomitant of control report inasmuch as, once an issue is highlighted through thė use of control reports, a special purpose study results in an investigative report. Meant for a particular purpose, it contains a special message and deals typically with the cause and remedies of specific problems. These reports are intermittent and are so devised as to serve the specific needs of situation under consideration.

An off-shoot of investigative report, *budget proposal report* only contains the proposals regarding the impact of facts revealed by investigative reports on production plan as well as profits and performance. It serves the correction phase of the managerial control cycle.

Modes of Reporting

Reports are prepared as statements, graphs and/or ratios and formulae. So far as the statements are concerned, they may deal with any one or more of the *statements:* actual against budgeted figures, comparative statements for a period of time, and statistical analysis of a particular type of expenditure over a period of time.

The information contained in the statements can also be presented by means of *graphs*, which give a better visual view of the data than the long array of figures given in the statements.

As regards the *ratios*, they may be part of a statement prepared for the other purposes or may form part of a separate statement for a specific purpose. Ratios are sometimes expressed as percentages also.

Sometimes, *formulae* are used to throw light on some aspects of the operations of business, especially the following: return on capital employed, break-even point, and profit-volume ratio.

Reports to the Board of Management, Top, Middle and Junior Management Levels

Various reports should be submitted to the board of management, top level managers, middle managers and to the junior level management.

Reports to the Board of Management: As the directors are not interested in the day-to-day management, their primary interest lies in the over-all working of the undertaking as highlighted by the profits. They are, therefore, interested in the profit and loss account as well as the balance sheet of the unit so much so that a monthly profit and loss account and balance sheet is usually given to the board. Over and above these, information statements on return on capital employed, trend in production and sales, and raw materials, general trend of costs, expenditure on development and research, report on the anticipated future results, etc.

Reports to the Top Management: Top executives are interested more in the operational side of the undertaking than in the purely financial side. They live up to this role by receiving reports of variances from the budgeted figures and these are very carefully studied and analysed.

Reports to the Middle/Divisional Management: The middle management is interested in operational reports such as, report on sales, reports on purchases, report on production, report on costs, and reports on financial and office management.

Report to the Junior Level Management: The day-to-day working reports are needed by the junior level managers. Since they, at the floor level, they are interested to know the daily operations in the organization. Such daily reports regarding the activities undertaken at the floor level must be submitted to the junior level management.

AIRS in an Enterprise

The following figure depicts a clear picture on the accounting information reporting system in a typical enterprise. The accounting reports are received from various departments (subsystems) by the accounting information system. The AIS in turn will process those information particulars and send reports in the prescribed formats to the appropriate authorities on time and as and when the personnel at various levels of management require them.

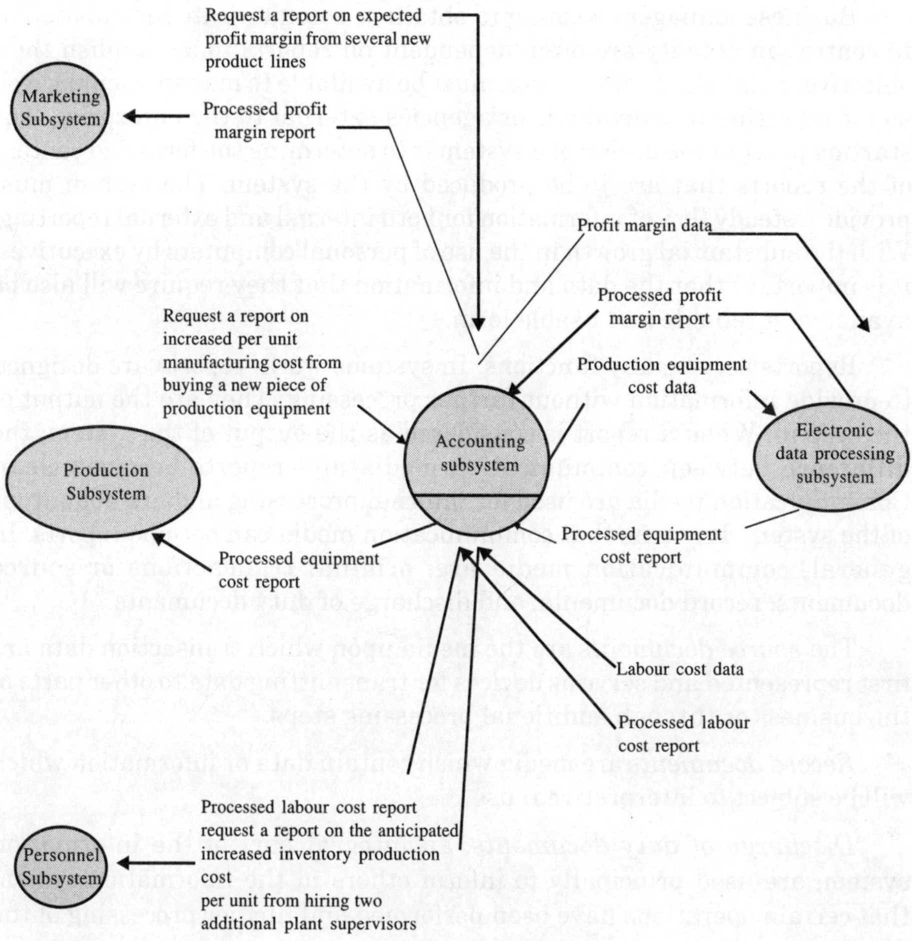

Fig. 18.1: **AIRS & Subsystems**

Reporting System Design

The system should be designed to permit effective reporting, both internally and externally, since reports are a primary systems product. A major objective of every system is to provide information. Therefore it follows that every system should be designed for effective reporting to enable the communication of information. Attempts to design a system that will provide internal reports only or external reports only would not be realistic except in unusual or extraordinary situations. Information used in both internal and external reports should normally flow from the same system. Much of the information that was the basis for internal management reports will eventually appear in external reports. The design of a system so that the flow of reported information will be used for internal planning and control as well as external use is an important implication of the report principle in accounting information system.

Business managers wishing to obtain or communicate information or to control an activity are often dependent on reports to accomplish their objective. Significant information must be available to management as well as for reporting to individuals or agencies external to the enterprise. The starting point in the design of a system is to determine the form and content of the reports that are to be produced by the system. The system must provide a steady flow of information for both internal and external reporting. With the substantial growth in the use of personal computers by executives, it is important that the data and information that they require will also be available in reliable and usable form.

Reports serve many functions. In systems work, reports are designed to provide information without further processing. They are the output of the system. When a report is considered as the output of the system, the difference between communication media and reports becomes clear. Communication media are used for internal processing and are not output of the system. It is true that communication media can become reports. In general, communication media are: original transactions or source documents, record documents, and discharge of duty documents.

The *source documents* are the media upon which transaction data are first represented and serve as devices for transmitting data to other parts of the business or through additional processing steps.

Record documents are media which contain data or information which will be subject to interpretive reuse.

Discharge of duty documents, an integral part of the information system, are used principally to inform others in the information system that certain operations have been performed and further processing of the data can continue.

The basic requirements of good media design are: favourable mental attitude, ease of entering data, ease of using data, reduce tendency to error, and paper and printing economy.

Consideration is also given to the problem of media control while designing the reporting system. The centralized media control unit is responsible for: new or revised form approval, the technical aspects of form design, form inventory control, form identification and form review.

Reporting System Implementation

After completion of all the stages involved in the reporting system design process, it is the responsibility of the management to implement the reporting system. The managers have to collect certain information before implementing the reporting system for effective implementation of the reporting system in the organization. Reporting system implementation consists of instructing the personnel to prepare the reports in the prescribed formats, training of users, and modifications. The reports are prepared in the given formats by the personnel in the organization. The formats are to be designed at the stage of the system design (AIS). We already had discussed the AIS design process. At the reports screen development stage, the different formats should be designed for the purpose. Proper training should be given to the employees who engaged in the reporting process. They have to be trained for effective reporting. The new formats, new reporting system principle and practice should be explained to the users in the reporting system department. If the users find any difficulty in using the system, the analyst should verify and clear the doubts of the users. They have to go for modifications and alterations based on the queries and difficulties of the users. Then only the implementation process will be a successful one.

Reporting System Evaluation

The reports are prepared by the personnel at different departments and at various levels in the organization. The reports are to be submitted both to the internal management and the external parties who involved themselves directly or indirectly in the organisation's activities. The reports are evaluated by the authorities after submission. They are evaluated on the basis of the criteria like the information needs, reporting formats that are used, reporting period, and so on. Reporting system evaluation leads to effective reporting system in the organization. The auditors, management, government, and appropriate authorities evaluate the financial reports, as the case may be.

Summary

- AIS provides all required accounting information through reports to the needy persons in the management based on their requirements. There are different kinds of reports: enterprise, control, investigation and budget reports.

Self-Learning Activity

Try to answer the following questions on your own:

1. What is an AIRS?
2. How can you design an AIRS?

CHAPTER 19 Computerized Accounting Information Systems

In this chapter, the differences between manual and computerized accounting information systems and the benefits of using computerized accounting systems to produce output for decision-making are discussed. The variety of output that can be produced by a computerized information system and the importance of integration and compatibility of all the components of a computerized accounting system, and of the need to ranked great care when switching from a manual system to a computerized one are also discussed.

Most business, except the very smallest, now uses computers to handle their accounting data. When businesses switch to computerized accounting, they soon discover that bookkeeping and accounting skills are more important than computing ones. This is bécause users of many computerized accounting systems have very little to learn in order to use them. In Window-based software, user can see from the entry screen of the Sage Instant Accounting 2000 accounting package, the interfaces look fairly familiar — the file menu is usually in the top left, for example, and many of the icons are the same and have the same meanings across a whole range of software produced by different companies.

The methods adopted in computer-based accounting adhere to the fundamental principles of accounting covered in this and other accounting textbooks. No matter how sophisticated and easy to use a computerized accounting system is, it will not overcome the need for bookkeeping and accounting knowledge by those in control. Imagine, for example, how anyone who does not know how to prepare journal entries could correct an error in an original entry correctly from an accounting point of view and, just as importantly, understand why it is important not to erase the original entry.

Apart from a need for knowledge of accounting principles in order to best convert a business from manual to computer-based accounting, some accounting knowledge is required to help understand the significance of many of the outputs from a computerized accounting system, just as it is required in respect of output from a manual accounting system.

Thus, computerized accounting systems to not remove the need for some accounting knowledge among those responsible for key accounting tasks or from those who use the output from the accounting systems. In fact, some accountants working in practice would tell you that they believe there is an even greater need for accounting knowledge among those who record the transactions in a computerized accounting system than in a manual one.

Benefits of using a Computerized Accounting System

There are many benefits from using a computerized accounting system. Overall, probably the greatest benefit comes from the fact that a computerized accounting system can do the same things as a manual system, but does them better. Thus all the features in a manual system, such as the one shown in the Exhibit 19.1, can be replicated in a computerized accounting system which not only does them quicker, more accurately, and 100 per cent consistently, but can also do them more frequently and do other things as well.

Exhibit 19.1

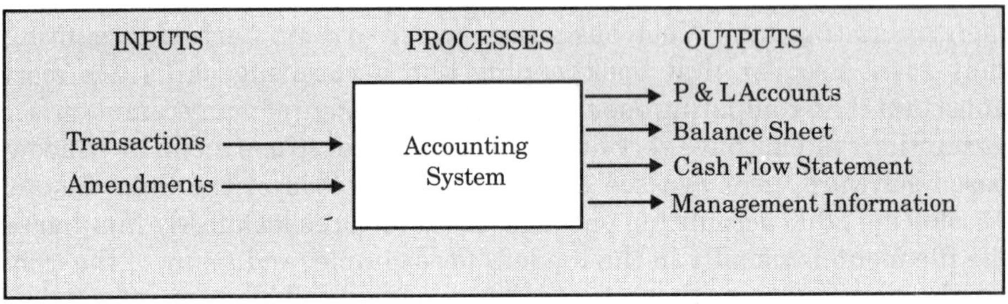

Speed and Accuracy

The main aim of computerizing an accounting system is to perform the processing stage electronically, much more quickly, consistently and accurately than if it were done manually. However, transactions and amendment details have to be input into the process:

1. in the correct from;
2. in the correct order; and
3. in a timely manner.

Although there is scope to use electronic methods of entering some of this information (e.g. EPOS systems and document scanning), it requires a good deal of initiative and an organized way of doing things in order to do so. Nevertheless, improved accuracy is one of the more obvious benefits of any kind of computerized accounting system.

Further time saving can be achieved by immediate output of reports, such as customer statements, purchase analysis, cash and bank statements, and details about whether the business is meeting sales targets. Such reports and statements can be produced both on request and, automatically, by the computer searching through information generated and saved within the accounting system and then producing whatever report is required.

Error Detection

Effective reporting is often required in order to improve the decision-making process. For example, a computerized accounting system should be capable of detecting when a customer appears to be running up excessive debts with the business, so offering the chance for the credit controller to take remedial action.

Another area is the need to remain within budgets. Many business expenses can get out of hand if they are not checked at regular intervals. A computerized accounting system should be capable of an activity called exception reporting, a process of issuing a warning message to decision-makers when something unexpected is happening: for example, when expenditure against a budget is higher than it should be. In a manual accounting system, the situation can occur that errors or unwanted transactions to unnoticed until too late when the repercussions have already incurred unnecessary costs to the business.

Enhanced Reporting

For many businesses, the task of producing reports on a regular basis, such as VAT returns, payroll processing, cash flow analysis, and financial statements, can be time-consuming, tedious and unrewarding. The use of a computerized accounting system speeds up the process to the point, in some cases, where it is done automatically without any need for human intervention, thus reducing the monotony of producing lengthy reports requiring extensive preparatory analysis of data. In many cases, such as VAT returns and pay slips, businesses find that they can use computer printouts or electronic output, e.g., on computer disks, instead of having to manually complete official or standard forms.

Computerized Accounting Books

Many businesses now make good use of accounting packages which are readily available and have been well tested. Such packages are commonly modularized with, typically, the sales ledger, purchase ledger, general ledger, stock control, sales invoicing, sales order processing, purchases order processing, fixed assets, payroll, bill of materials, and job costing—all being offered as separate modules in their own right. When a business decides to computerize its accounting system, it acquires only those modules it needs rather than a complete range of modules. For example, sole trader would have no use for a payroll module.

The various ledgers and accounts maintained in a computerized accounting system mimic those kept in a manual system. The General Ledger, for example, will adhere to the basic rules of double entry bookkeeping in that each debit entry has a corresponding credit entry — if a customer is issued with an invoice, the transaction giving precise details of the invoice will be stored in the credit sales records to form part of the customer history and then the double entry is made by crediting sales accounts and debiting a debtor's account.

The difference lies in the method of entry—each transaction is entered only once (accountants refer to this as a 'single entry' system) and the software automatically completes the double entry. This has a down side, however, in that some computerized accounting packages will post various amounts into suspense accounts when it is unclear as to where postings are to be made. These require manual intervention and journal entries to remove the items from the suspense account and complete the original double entry.

Flexibility

The information stored is available instantly and can be used to produce statements, ledger account details, analysis of how long debts have been outstanding, etc. immediately it is requested. For example, the computerized Sales Leger will hold all details about customers. The starting point would be to enter the details concerning the customer (name, address, etc.) along with the balance brought forward from the manual system (if such a transfer is occurring; otherwise, if it is a new customer, an opening zero balance will be created automatically by the software). All transactions that correspond to customer, such as the issue of an invoice or receipt of payment, are entered into the system and automatically posted to the customer's account. Customers can, at any time, be issued with a statement of their account, and the business can always obtain an up-to-date and complete history of trading with any particular customer. The purchase ledger will operate exactly the same way in that supplier details are held and, once entered through the purchases module, all transactions relating to individual purchasers will automatically be posted to the appropriate creditor account.

Bank payments and receipts are a central feature of computerized accounting systems. Someone with virtually no bookkeeping knowledge can operate the modules. For example, if an electricity bill is paid, the system will prompt for the details required in order to process and record the double entry.

Account Codes

In order to use a computerized accounting system efficiently and effectively, someone with both accounting skills and a good knowledge of the business will be required to organize the accounts and ledgers in the first instance. Some of these packages are written for no specific business and need to be 'tailored' to the one that is going to use it. Most require businesses to define what accounts they are to have in their general ledger and how such accounts are to be grouped. For example, fixed asset accounts may have account references commencing with 'F', while expense accounts commence with 'E'; the package will probably have its own default set of account codes (the computerized equivalent of the folio in a manual system), and it may be necessary to override the defaults in the accounting package in order to use the business's own account code list. In addition, part of the setting up of a computer system will require the tailoring of the package for certain reports such as the profit and loss account and balance sheet.

Knowledge of Double Entry

Most packages are capable of allowing businesses to set up their preferred methods for dealing with depreciation of fixed assets and regular payments of, for example, rent and rates. However, as you saw with the need to correct entries to a suspense account arising from the computer not knowing how to complete a double entry, such packages to require a good 'knowledge' of double entry so that adjustments can be made through their journal entries. For example, the computer will not overcome some errors and omissions such as the operator misreading an amount on an invoice or crediting a payment to a wrong customer account. Anyone correcting these errors will require a full knowledge of the relevant part of the accounting system as well as bookkeeping and accounting principles.

Computerized Stock Control and Modular Integration

Automation of much of the data processing can be taken further when integrating other modules. Stock control offers the benefit of keeping very close tabs on stock levels. If an invoicing package is also in use, then an invoice can be generated in such a way that an operator can collect the details of the business or person to invoice from the sales ledger and details of all stock to be invoiced from the stock files. Once the invoice has been raised, the recorded stock levels fall accordingly, the sales ledger is updated and crediting sales and debiting debtors' control make the nominal entries.

Sales Order Processing

Sales order processing allows an order to be placed into the system and can then be used at a later stage to generate an invoice. Sales order processing is important to many businesses as it gives them an indication about what stock levels are required. Having sales orders on computer also offers the advantage of being able to avoid any orders being left overdue and late. Computers can produce outstanding order reports and such things as 'picking lists' (a list of items to be taken out of storage and given or shipped to customers) very quickly.

Purchase Order Processing

Purchase order processing allows an operator to print an order to send off to a supplier or, in some more advanced systems, it may be transmitted over a direct link into the supplier's accounting system where it will be recorded and converted into an issue from stock. The computerized purchase order system also serves the useful purpose of allowing instant access to information about what is on order. By entering stock in order against various stock records, it reduces the likelihood of issuing multiple orders for stock unnecessarily.

Modular Integration

The full use of all modules in this integrated manner allows a business to access stock details and gets a complete profile on its status in terms of what it left in stock, what is on order, what has been ordered by customers. Furthermore, most packages keep a history of stock movements so helping the business to analyze specific stock turnovers.

Computerized Accounting Information Systems

An accounting information system (AIS) is the total suite of components that, together, comprise all the inputs, storage, and transaction processing, collating, and reporting of financial transaction data. It is, in effect, the infrastructure that supports the production and delivery of accounting information.

The objective of an accounting information system is to collect and store data about accounting transactions in order to generate meaningful output for decision-making. The shoebox containing receipts for all purchases and a chequebook kept by the corner shopkeeper is, in itself, an accounting system, as is the set of day books and ledgers kept by the local department store and the integrated computerized accounting system of a company such as Ford, BT, or British Airways.

There is no need for an AIS to be computerized in order to be described in this way. Computerization may only have been introduced on some of the accounting tasks, such as the accounting books, the payroll system, or the stock control system. When the entire suite of accounting tasks and records is computerized, the benefits are clearly greater than when only parts of the AIS are computerized. Most people assume you are talking about a fully computerized accounting system when you refer to an AIS and this is how we shall use the term in the rest of this chapter. However, much of what follows, apart from the benefits of full integration, is also applicable to partially computerized AISs.

Along with the improvements in the technology, information systems have been computerized. Improvements in this technology have replaced manual bookkeeping systems with computerized ones. The revolution in the information systems, which started in the early 1950s when the first business computers became available, is still in progress. Large mainframe computers have been replaced by small and fast personal computers at lower costs. As a result, accounting information systems that were previously performed manually are now performed by computers in most companies. Companies can now capture, process, store, and transmit data with the help of computers. Whereas data collections and processing were performed manually in historical systems, on-line collection and processing of data are performed by computerized systems.

In manual accounting information systems, processing of data is slow and subject to error. Fortunately, improvements in the technology have enabled companies to collect, process, and retrieve data quickly. In addition, there is less likelihood for error when data are processed with computers. In this case, functions of manual AIS that were explained in the preceding section, can be explained for computerized AIS as follows:

Data Input Function

In manual AIS, the data are captured with the source documents and directly processed in journals and transferred to ledger accounts. On the other hand, in computerized AIS, after data are captured, they should be converted into machine-readable form. In most computerized AIS, source data automation devices that capture data at the time and place of their origins are used. For example, bar code scanners used in retail stores can record the sale transaction just as scanning devices read the codes located on the products.

In addition to the data scanned into the computer, there do exist data bases that contain stored data for future processing. A database includes information about entities. An entity is something about which information is stored. For example, information about existing customers is stored in databases. In this case, customers represent entities. Information about customers such as account number, credit limit, and current balance of the customer can be stored in the database. Master files are used to store data about entities in databases in an computerized AIS. Master files have replaced the subsidiary ledgers that are used in manual systems. For example, records in accounts receivable master file include customer name, customer account number, address, and balance due. Master files are frequently updated as transactions are taking place. For example, as sales are made or receivables are collected, accounts receivable master files are changed.

In addition to the accounts receivable master file, master files are kept for all other balance sheet and income statement items such as accounts payable, fixed assets and expenses. In computerized AIS, relational tables can be used to establish master files. Another concept in accounting is relational tables, which are the tables that include detailed information for every entity.

Data Processing

After the data are collected and entered into computers, they are processed. The most common data processing activity is data maintenance. Data maintenance is the processing of transactions to update stored data. For example, when sales transaction takes place, data are entered into the computer. In turn, computer immediately updates sales and accounts receivable files. In computerized systems, records are updated by using primary keys that uniquely identifies each record. For example, when a sales transaction takes place, related customer file should be updated. In order to find related customer master file, customer account number can be used as the primary key because every customer has unique customer account number. In other words, it is not possible that two or more customers have common customer account number

Information Output

After the data are entered into the computer and processed, information output is produced to meet the needs of the users. Information is presented in three forms: a document, a report, or a response to a query. Documents are records of transactions or company data such as invoices. These documents can be printed out using printers. In addition, they can be stored as electronic images in the computer databases. Reports are prepared for internal and external users. For example, to meet the needs of external users such as creditors, financial statements should be prepared. In addition, computers can be programmed to display financial information automatically in a required form such as spreadsheets. Today, electronic communication systems enable companies to transmit financial reports to the users electronically. This, of course, eliminates paper work and reduces costs. In addition to the reports produced for the needs of external users, reports can also be produced to meet the needs of the internal users such as managers.

Sometimes, documents and periodic reports may not be enough to meet the needs of the users. If unexpected problems arise, managers can enter the system and query the information they need. A user enters a request into the computer to get the information, and the computer performs necessary tasks to solicit the required information. Once found, the information is retrieved and analyzed by the user. In a manual AIS, transactions are first recorded in journals and then they are posted to ledger accounts. At the end of each accounting period, financial statements are prepared by using the ending balances of ledger accounts. On the other hand in a computerized AIS, all the information is gathered in relational tables. In this case, financial statements can be prepared at any time by entering necessary commands into the computer.

Software Tools in the Accounting Process

This section includes the most-frequently used software tools and their most appropriate use. Accountants must be familiar with the software tools because they help the users perform the accounting functions more effectively and efficiently.

Accounting Software

This software contains the basic accounting functions such as input, processing and output. There are two classifications of accounting software as low-end and high-end. Low-end is all-in-one software, which means all of the functions of accounting system are performed within one software. Therefore, low-end software is used for small companies. On the other hand, in high-end software, each accounting function comes in a separate module. Each module checks data for correctness, processes it, and updates all relevant accounts, and finally, produces outputs such as documents and reports. Personal computer (PC)-based accounting software allows companies to computerize their manual systems and to provide better and timely information. In addition, PCs have been connected to another PCs via networks. This allows companies to process indefinite number of transactions occurring at different locations simultaneously within several minutes.

Income Tax

Because tax laws are frequently changing, it is becoming exceedingly difficult to deal with them. Therefore, manual tax preparation is becoming more and more difficult and time consuming. Fortunately, tax preparation software is currently available for companies. Therefore, instead of processing tax manually, companies can use computer software to perform the same functions. As a result, even complex calculations can be performed via computers in a short period of time.

Audit

Information technology has also computerized the auditing profession. If auditors perform auditing functions manually, it takes time. However, audit software packages are currently available for auditors. For example, trial balance software enables auditors to input the working trial balance, handle all types of adjusting entries, and automatically compute the adjusted trial balance. In addition, software package can access customer's files, select a statistical sample of the accounts, and print a working paper sheet. Auditors have used personal computers to reduce their costs significantly.

Word Processing

Word processing is computer-assisted creation, editing, correcting, manipulation, storage, and printing of textual data. Accountants use word processing software to prepare reports, billings, memos, and financial statements.

Graphics Software

Graphics can be prepared using graphics software. Graphics can be printed on paper or displayed on slides, transparencies, and photos. Many auditors and managerial accountants use the graphics software to graph the data in financial statements and reports.

Image Processing

Creating, storing, and updating paper forms of documents take time. In addition, it is very costly to process and store documents. Fortunately, these costs can be eliminated with the help of document imaging systems. Image processing captures electronic image of data so that it can be stored and shared. With the help of document imaging, accountants can scan paper documents into the computer and process all of the files electronically. Companies that use document imaging are moving toward paperless offices.

Electronic Data Interchange (EDI)

Electronic data interchange enables companies to communicate with each other electronically. Therefore, EDI enables companies to exchange documents electronically with each other. For example, computerized network enables purchaser and the supplier to exchange purchase orders and invoices electronically in the form of images.

Electronic Funds Transfer (EFT)

Companies can now connect to banks through EFT. This system enables companies to make payment and collection electronically. In this case, when company wants to pay for accounts payable to a supplier, it can do it via EFT. Furthermore, whenever company makes sales, transactions are immediately charged to consumer's bank account and simultaneously credited to company's account. In addition, all relevant accounts such as accounts receivable and cash are updated immediately by the computerized system.

The use of the computerized systems mentioned above has led to the automation of accounting information system. Accounting information systems equipped with these kinds of technologically advanced tools can now perform accounting functions more effectively and reduce costs.

Full Integration and Compatibility

For an AIS to be fully effective, all the components need to be integrated with each other, otherwise information gets lost, mis-entered from one record to another, or duplicated (often incorrectly as each version of it is updated at different times). Major errors may ultimately arise if integration is not 100 per cent. In a computerized AIS, there is the added problem that some of the components or modules may be written for use in a different operating system and may not be immediately compatible with the other modules with which data is to be exchanged, retrieved, or transferred. This was a major problem until the late 1980s, since when much of the difficulty of operating system incompatibility has been eradicated.

However, with software the problem still remains — even documents prepared on one version of word processing software may not transfer with 100 per cent accuracy to an earlier or later version of the same software, never mind to other word processing packages. The same holds for spreadsheets and database files. Therefore, at the planning stage, it is important to ensure that all hardware and software that is to be used is 100 per cent compatible and that, where it is not, steps are taken to ensure that a workable alternative way of communicating data and information between modules is found.

Outputs

An AIS, computerized or manual, can, of course, produce whatever reports you wish, so long as the relevant data is stored within or accessible to the AIS. Where a fully computerized AIS is clearly superior is in the range of reports it can produce virtually instantly and in the way it can be programmed to produce periodic reports precisely when they are scheduled to be available. No longer is there any need for decision-makers to wait two weeks for the summary of the previous month's business activities. It is now available as soon as business closes at the end of the last day of the month.

Some of the other reports produced by most manual AISs can also take a very long time to produce. Some, however, only take an hour or two to prepare manually. However, a computerized AIS can produce these reports in second, and as often as the decision-makers wish. These include aged debtors reports (a list of debtors showing how much they each owe, and for how long the amounts have been outstanding); price lists; stock levels and reordering stock quantities; lists of invoices and credit notes; and audit trail information to enable errors to be traced and corrected (whereby the route a transaction took through the accounting records to the financial statements is revealed). The savings in personnel and time and, therefore, costs that can result from fully computerizing the AIS cannot be understated, even for smaller businesses who wish to maximize their efficiency. In the early days of computerized AISs, the output was all on paper. Now, much of it is electronic.

Electronic Dissemination

One of the major benefits of computerized AIS is that output generated from it need not be in hard copy. It can be visual on a computer screen, or distributed electronically on CD or floppy disk, or by direct file transfer to another computer over a LAN, WAN, Intranet, Extranet or the Internet.

While many organization still require that information be passed to them on their own forms, the IT revolution of the last few years has led to many organizations being willing to accept printout generated from a computer, or even floppy disks containing the document, instead of having their own forms completed and returned. For example, fairly standard and repetitive information generation, such as VAT receipts and payments, are common to most businesses, and Customs and Excise will accept computer-generated VAT returns. The Inland Revenue will accept computer-generated payroll data.

There is also an increasing use of email to transmit documents and the governments now accept personal income tax forms in this way. In fact, the governments currently accepts all the following documents electronically:

- starter/leaver details
- daily coding
- annual ands budget code number updates
- pension and works number updates

- end of year returns
- expenses and benefits
- construction industry vouchers

Benefits of Electronic Submission of Documents

Among the recognized benefits of electronic submission of documents and hence, potentially, of a computerized AIS are:

- speed
- improved accuracy in that what is sent is what was intended to be sent
- improved accuracy in that what is sent is received, and in the form intended
- lower administration costs
- greater security
- less use of paper
- immediate acknowledgement of receipt

Benefits of Electronic Transmission of Funds

Of course, if electronic submission of documents is a recent phenomenon, electronic transmission of funds has been around a good deal longer. Among the benefits attributed to it and again, potentially, to a computerized AIS are:

- certainty of payment on a specific date
- certainty that exactly the amount due to be paid is paid
- immediate acknowledgement of receipt
- lower administration costs
- lower bank charges
- greater security

Benefits of Linking AISs

Another significant recent change brought about by computerization of AISs is the growth in electronic data exchange between supplier and customer. Some very large companies now insist that their suppliers link their stock systems to the customer's AIS. The customer can then interrogate the stock records of the supplier to see if items are available and place orders directly into the supplier's AIS without any need for physical transmission of an order document. This has helped the growth of just-in-time stock keeping by customers who, rather than holding their own stock, simply order it from their suppliers when required. Among the benefits attributed to it again, potentially, to a computerized AIS are:

- speed
- lower administration costs
- greater awareness of the current position
- improved control of related risks
- greater security of a continuing relationship between the parties

Issues to consider when introducing a fully computerized AIS

When you computerize an accounting system, you have some decisions to make. These include:

1. Deciding whether to mimic what you have been doing manually or start from search and redesign everything. For example, you may only have been using one ledger in the manual system, but may choose to use three or four in the computerized system. You may have had a two-column cash book in the manual system but decide to have a columnar cashbook in the computerized system.
2. Deciding whether to buy a general accounting package 'off-the-shelf' or create one from search. Depending on the size of the business, creating one from scratch may be done using a spreadsheet and a database package or it may involve having computer programmers writing the entire system.
3. If you decide to buy one off-the-shelf, you need to decide how much to customize it, if at all.
4. If you decide not to customize it, or aren't able to customize parts of it, you may need to change the terminology you use when referring to parts of the accounting system. For example, you may need to refer to the Nominal Ledger rather than the General Ledger and to the Purchases Journal rather than the Purchases Day Book. For example, Sage uses the term 'Customers Module' rather than Sales Ledger and 'Suppliers Module' instead of a Purchases Ledger.
5. You need to decide who is going to be responsible for overseeing the project.
6. You need to decide how long you are going to allow for the new system to be developed and make plans to introduce it accordingly.
7. You need to decide who is to be trained in using it and when.
8. You need to decide how long you will run the new system in parallel with the existing manual system before you stop using the manual system.
9. You need to identify the hardware you will need and ensure that it is in place at the appropriate time.

10. You need to identify who is going to test the new system and what data is to be used to do so.
11. You need to weigh up the costs and benefits of computerizing the accounting system and decide whether it is actually worth doing it.

These are just some of the issues you need to deal with. Many more will appear as each of these questions is answered and many more will materialize as the project proceeds. The most popular software used by small and medium-sized businesses in the UK is Sage. However, you should look at a range of available alternatives, such as Pegasus, QuickBooks, and Microsoft Great Plains, before proceeding to purchase the package you intend using. Factors to consider obviously include price, but they also include capacity, hardware requirements, ease of use reliability, appropriateness of the way data is entered, stored and secured, and the range and style of reports that can be produced. You also need to consider compatibility of package with any other systems or packages you might wish to link to if that is, in fact, a possibility in the first place. Accountants are not normally the must knowledgeable people to answer these technical questions and guidance from an IT specialist is often advisable. Once the package is installed and fully operational, you need to monitor its effectiveness and reliability and need to have contingency plans in place should it ultimately prove to have been a mistake. (In other words, you need to ensure you can revert to the previous system if necessary.) When you come to review your hardware or operating system with a view to upgrading it, you need to ensure the package will continue to run without any problems when you upgrade. You also need to consider carefully before committing to an upgrade of the accounting package, in case things that used to work no longer function or need to be done in very different ways. You also need to ensure that the data stored in the system is backed up regularly and that password or other security devices are in place in order to prevent unauthorized access to it. Overall, you need to think the whole thing out very carefully before committing to the switch and you need to ensure you have all the controls over the system in place before it starts to be used. Nevertheless, although great care and a lot of effort must be expended when converting to a computerized accounting system, there is no doubt that the benefits of having an appropriate one will vastly improve the quality and reliability of the accounting data and information.

Summary

- The variety of output that can be produced by a computerized information system and the importance of integration and compatibility of all the components of a computerized accounting system, and of the need to ranked great care when switching from a manual system to a computerized one are also discussed.

- Apart from a need for knowledge of accounting principles in order to best convert a business from manual to computer-based accounting, some accounting knowledge is required to help understand the significance of many of the outputs from a computerized accounting system, just as it is required in respect of output from a manual accounting system.
- There are benefits such as speed, accuracy, volume, etc., with computerized accounting systems.

Self-Learning Activity

Try to answer the following questions on your own:

1. What are the benefits of computerized AIS?
2. Can you state the issues to consider when introducing a fully computerized AIS?

CHAPTER 20

Cooperative Accounting Information System

Cooperative Accounting Information System

Accounting is the mirror replicating the business activities of a firm. Cooperatives have adopted the traditional system of account keeping. A cooperative enterprise had to maintain a day book as the only book of prime entry with columns for receipts and payments. Transactions were recorded in the book in a serial order. There was hardly any credit transaction. It was therefore simple and easy to close the cash balance.

In cooperative account-keeping system transactions involve either receipt of money or payment of money. Even credit transactions involve in effect though not actually, receipt of money and payment of money. Thus, it involves one receipt and another corresponding payment. These receipt and payment aspects of transactions form the basis for the traditional system of account keeping. Cooperative account-keeping systems may better be described as 'Receipts and Payment System for Account keeping'. (See Figure 20.1)

CAIS is an economic transaction based information system (see figure 20.2). Most of these economic transactions take place in the course of day-to-day operations of the cooperative enterprises. The focus of CAIS has more on generation of information for using managerial decision-making process.

CAIS is designed to achieve the objective:

1. to meet the statutory reporting needs of the cooperatives; and
2. to provide reliable information on accounts to top, middle and operation level of management.

CAIS deals with transactions which are of financial nature and can be expressed in terms of money. It caters to the information needs of both

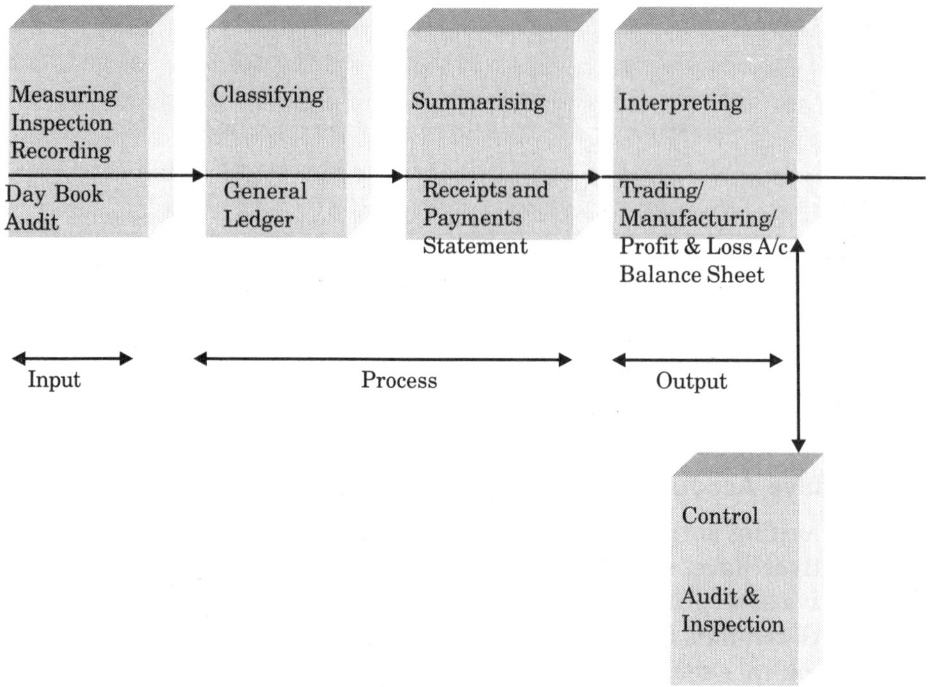

Fig. 20.1: **Cooperative Accounting Process**

internal and external users. This is quite simple and well-structured information system. The information contained in the accounting record is recognised by the cooperative law and as such these records are treated as evidence in the Court of Law, in case of dispute. The source of data is mainly internal to the cooperative and thus, database is well defined, integrated and controlled. CAIS, as any other system, encompasses four sub-systems viz., input, process, output and control.

At the input stage, the cooperative accountants collect various accounting information needed for recording based on the principles of cooperative accounting system. They record transaction based on the principle of treating a transaction as either receipt of payment of money in Day book, the book of original entry.

At the second stage processing of accounting information recorded the transactions recorded in the Day book are posted to General Ledgers and Special Ledgers. Receipts and Payments Statement, a summary of transactions made, is also prepared on the basis of totals of the balances arrived in General and Special Ledgers.

The third stage is the output stage where the final account statements (trading/manufacturing account and profit & loss account), balance sheet and accounting reports like enterprise reports account documents, investigative reports and budget proposal report are prepared for the purpose of submitting to various levels of management, the financing bank, federations, administrative authorities publish the same for the public.

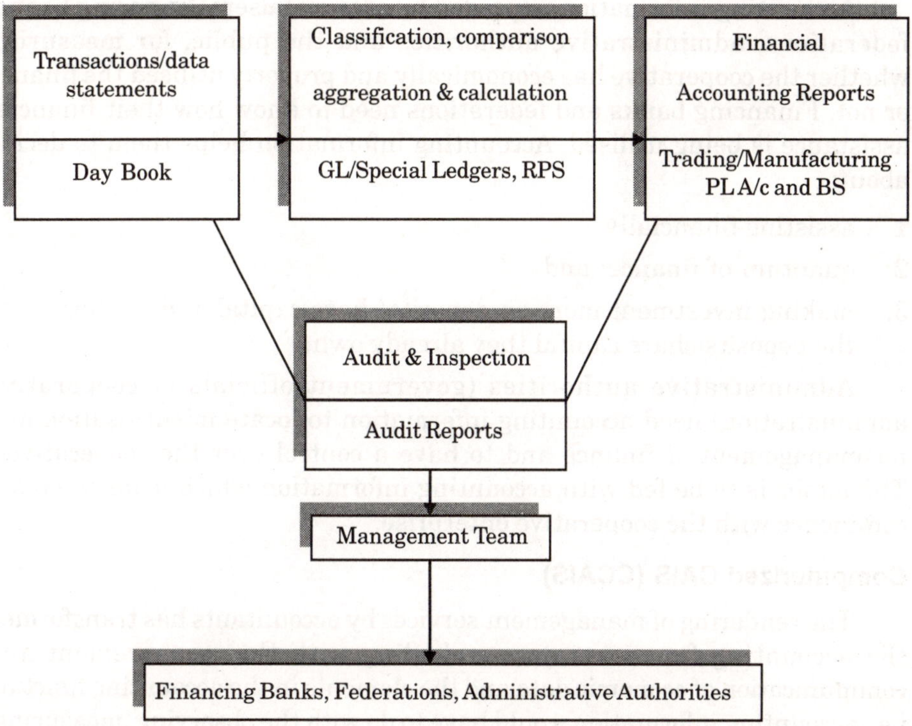

***Fig. 20.2:* Cooperative Accounting Information System**

The auditors (both internal and external) are responsible for reviewing and checking the account statements at the control stage of CAIS. Audit and inspection is to be done in line with the cooperative law principles and values. After the verification they issue Audit information reports.

To Whom Accounting Information

Accounting information is needed by two categories of people, who use accounting information to measure a cooperative's performance against established standards and goals—internal external.

Internal users are those who are associated with management of the cooperative enterprise for which information is sought to be retrieved and processed. The management team consists of General Body, Board of Directors and employees. General body and Board of Directors require accounting information in the form of accounting statements to judge a cooperative enterprise's management by reference to these statements. The employees of the cooperative enterprise are interested in the accounting information because both, their present and future are tied up with the enterprise's fortunes.

Accounting information is needed by external users, financing banks, federations, administrative authorities and the public, for measuring whether the cooperative has economically and properly utilised the finance or not. Financing banks and federations need to know how their financial assistance is being utilised. Accounting information helps them to decide about:

1. assisting financially;
2. quantum of finance; and
3. making investment more on deposits/share capital and holding on to the deposits/share capital they already own.

Administrative authorities (government officials of cooperative administration) need accounting information to locate misutilisation and mismanagement of finance and to have a control over the cooperatives. The public is to be fed with accounting information which leads to create confidence with the cooperative enterprise.

Computerized CAIS (CCAIS)

The rendering of management services by accountants has transformed the accounting function into one dealing with the measurement and communication of economic data and the elements in the accounting function i.e., accounting information would have to do with the observing, measuring, recording, classifying summarizing, interpreting and inspection of economic data. Thus, the management has to carve out a place in its organisation chart for a responsibility which has to do with the entire process of quantitative information gathering, inclusive of accounting function but definitely not limited to it. The purpose is to organise the entire figure-gathering process into a sophisticated management information system which would supply to all levels of management with the information they need to run the business.

CCAIS is, the computerised information system with the flow of accounting information through the system, management may be appraised on a timely and effective basis of the need for decisions. Cooperative Accounting System can be said to have been computerised only when most of the more important accounting operations, i.e., recording, posting, tabulating etc., are completed through mechanical devices, that mechanization may be said to have been introduced in accounting system of the cooperative enterprises.

The principal factors responsible for the growth of mechanized computerized accounting in cooperatives are:

1. increase in the size of cooperative units leading to an enormous increase in the accounting data to be collected and recorded in a limited time;
2. the need of the modern management to have a detailed analysis of accounting and statistical data promptly in order to run the cooperative business efficiently; and
3. a number of accounting statements and returns etc., have to be submitted to financing banks, federations, administrative authorities and various levels of management. It requires speedy collection and preparation of statements of accounting data.

Advantages of CCAIS

Staff of the Accounting Department

(a) Monotony of electrical labour will be greatly reduced;
(b) Saving time;
(c) Affords and opportunity to the best from the present staff for promotions; and
(d) Results in improved conditions of service.

Members

(a) Accurate and prompt information;
(b) Cost of book-keeping will be considerably reduced;
(c) Business prestige is enhanced;
(d) Scope of control machinery is widened; and
(e) Accounting records are always kept up-to-date.

Public

Creates confidence in the minds of public with the cooperatives.

There may be chance for retrenchment of accounting staff, errors in pickingup and wrong keying, and data loss. It is thus, obvious that there should be proper planning of the equipment to be installed staff should be trained.

Development of CCAIS

Development of CCAIS consists of six steps.

1. *Cooperative Enterprise Module*
   - Identifying entities
   - Activity analysis
   - Grouping activities in sub-systems

2. *Database Module*
   - Traditional
   - Database approach
3. *Interface Module*
   - Input screens
   - Report screens
   - Dialogue screens
   - CASE tool
4. *Applications Module*
   - Data Flow Diagram (DFD)
5. *Implementation Module*
   - Testing
   - Installation
6. *Post-Implementation Review*
   - Review of accounting system installed.

To sum up, all forms of Cooperatives should have an accounting information system. The exact way in which accounts are kept and present will depend on the nature of the society's business. Many National Cooperative Federations publish book-keeping manuals and model account books for the use of member cooperatives carrying on different form of business. Accounting information system would help the cooperatives to keep accounts systematically and submission of same as accounting reports to federations, financing banks, administrative authorities and different levels of management so that the performance can be appraised.

Accounting Information Reporting System in Cooperative Banks

As for accounting information reporting system, the cooperative banks are submitting external reports to the government, federal cooperative agency, regional cooperative promotion bureau, NGOs and other promoting agencies, other cooperatives, which have transactions with the cooperative banks, and to the member customers and the public. To the government, federal cooperative agency, regional cooperative promotion bureau, NGOs and other promoting agencies the cooperative banks have to submit periodical reports on the financial position and business activities. The cooperative banks send reports regularly to other cooperatives and members about the transactions i.e., credit availed, repayments made, balance to be paid, defaults, etc., with the bank (See Figure 20.3).

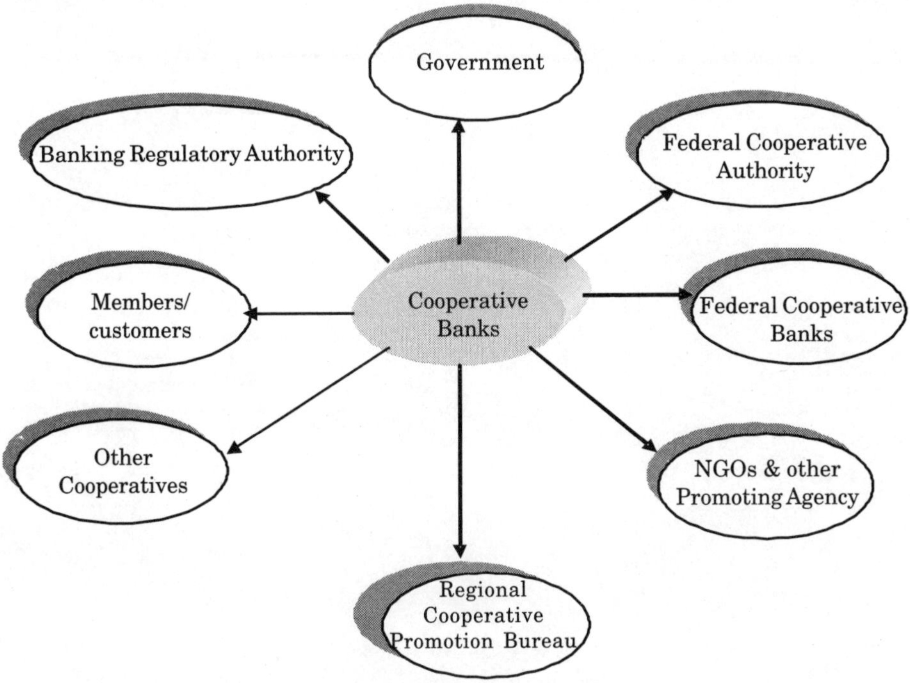

Fig. 20.3: **Accounting Information Reporting System in Cooperative Banks**

Summary

- The application of AIS into cooperatives is known as cooperative accounting information systems. Its work based on the cooperative accounting process.
- The development of cooperative accounting information system is like the AIS design and development process. We find accounting information reporting systems in cooperatives.

Self-Learning Activity

Try to answer the following questions on your own:

1. What does mean by cooperative accounting information system?
2. Discuss about accounting reporting systems in cooperatives.

References

Atkinson, Anthony A., Banker, Rajiv D., Kaplan, Robert S., Atrill, Peter, McLaney. *Management Accounting for Non-Specialists*, 3rd Edition, Prentice Hall, 2002.

Bailes, Jack C., Kleinsorge, Ilene K., "Cutting Waste With JIT". *Management Accounting*, 1992, pp. 28-32.

Borthick, A. Faye. "Helping Accountants Learn to get the Information Managers Want: The Role of the Accounting Information Systems", *Journal of Information Systems*, 1996, pp.75-86.

Burrower, Ashley W, *Core Concepts of AIS, Issues in Accounting Education*, May 2005, Vol. 20, issue: 2.

DeLuzio, M.C. "The Tools of JIT", *Journal of Cost Management*, Summer, 1993, pp.13-20.

Frank Wood and Alan Sangster. *Business Accounting — Financial Times*, 9th Edition, Prentice Hall, 2002.

Grabski, Severin V., Marsh, Robert J. "Integrating Accounting and Manufacturing Information Systems: An ABC and REA-Based Approach", *Journal of Information Systems*, 1994, pp. 61-81.

Hayes, R.H. "Why Japanese Factories Work", *Harvard Business Review*.

Henri Fayol (1949). *General and Industrial Management*, New York: Pitman Publishing, pp. 107-109.

Hilton, Ronald W., Maher, Michael W., Selto, Frank H., *Cost Management*, International Edition, McGraw Hill, 2000.

Homgren, Harrison and Robinson. *Accounting*, 3rd Edition, Prentice Hall, New Jersey, 1995.

Horngren, Charles T., Bhimani, Alnoor, Datar, Srikant M., Foster, George. *Management and Cost Accounting*, 2nd edition,

Horngren, Charles T., Bhimani, Alnoor, Foster, George, Datar, Srikant M. *Management and Cost Accounting*, Prentice Hall, 1999.

Horngren, Charles T., Sundem, Gary L., Stratton, William O.

Hutchison, Paul D, White, Craigh and Daigle, Ronald J. Advances in AIS and International Journal of AIS, First Ten Volumes (1992-2003), *IJAIS*, October 2004, Vol. 5, Issue: 3.

I.M. Pandey. *Management Accounting*—A Planning and Control Approach, Vikas Publishing House Pvt Ltd, New Delhi, India, 1983.

International Cooperative Alliance (1991), *Compendium*, New Delhi.

Introduction to Management Accounting, 12th Edition, Prentice Hall, 2002. July-August, 1981, pp. 57-66.

Lin Fengyi. "A United Accounting Information Framework to Modelling Bank Accounting Systems", *Journal of Applied Business Research*, February 2004,Vol.20, Issue: 4.

Karthikeyan, M., *Cooperative Accounting Information System*, *Management Accountant*, ICWAI, Culcutta. 2004.

Man Mohan & S.N.Goyal, *Principles of Management Accounting*, Sahitya Bhavan, Agra, India.

McBride, Maranda, Harrison, Sheilah, Clark, Brian. "Dock-To-Shop Is Just-In-Time", *IIE Solutions*, 2000, pp. 34-41.

Niall Lothian, *Measuring Corporate Performance*, Chartered Institute of Management Accountants, ISBN 0 948036 35 4.

Michael E. Porter and Victor E. Miller (1995), "How Accounting Information Gives Competitive Advantages", *Harvard Business Review*.

Miller, Pam Anders, Kelle, Peter. "Quantitative Support for Buyer-Supplier Negotiation in Just-In-Time Purchasing", *International Journal of Purchasing and Materials Management*, 1998, pp. 25-30.

Milligan, Brian. *Just-in-time: What's It Going to Take to Make It Work*, *Purchasing*, 1999, pp. 40-45.

Murthy, Uday S., Wiggins Jr., Casper E. "Object-Oriented Modeling Approaches for Designing Accounting Information System", *Journal of Information Systems*, 1993, pp. 97-112.

Nash, John F. *Accounting Information Systems*, Second Edition, PWS.

O'Brien, John, Sivaramakrishnan, K. "Coording Order Processing And Production Scheduling in Order Initiated Production Environments", *Journal of Management Accounting*, 1996, pp.151-171.

Office of the Chief Information Officer (OCIO) Enterprise Architecture Programme (2007). *Treasury IT Performance Measures Guide.* U.S. Department of the Treasury.

Lin Fitzgerald, Robert Johnston, Stan Brignall, Rhian Silvestro and Christopher Voss, *Performance Measurement in Service Businesses*, Chartered Institute of Management Accountants, ISBN 0 948036 78 8.

Philip E. Fess and Carl S. Warren. *Accounting Principles*, South Western Publishing Co., 1987.

Robert N. Anthony, et.al, (2003), *Accounting — Text and Cases*, Tata McGraw-Hill, New Delhi, India.

Romney, Marshall B., Steinbart, Paul John, Cushing, Barry E. *Accounting Information System*, Seventh Edition, Addison-Wesley, 1997.

Schwartz, Beth M., McGovern, J. Michael. *Time Versus Money: Who's Calling the Shots*?, Transportation & Distribution, 1998, pp. 33-36.

Stephen A. Moscove and Mark G. Simkin (1991), *Accounting Information Systems*, New York.

Sutton, Steve G. The Role of AIS Research in Guiding Practice, *International Journal of AIS*, March 2005, Vol. 6, Issue: 1.

Terry and Franklin, *Principles of Management*, Eighth Edition.

Trunk, Christopher. "Manufacturing Systems Software: Briding the Information Gap", *Material Handling Management*, 2000, pp. 57-61.

Van de Walle, Steven and Roberts, Alasdair, "Publishing Performance Information: An Illusion of Control?" *Performance Information in the Public Sector: How it is Used*, Van Dooren, W., Van de Walle, S., eds., Houndmills: Palgrave.

Young S. Mark. *Management Accounting*, 3rd Edition, Prentice Hall, 2001.

Website: http://ipspr.sc.edu/scip/publications

Index